Listeners Guide

to musical understanding

Listeners Guide

to musical understanding

LEON DALLIN
Professor of Music
Long Beach State College

WM. C. BROWN COMPANY PUBLISHERS
Dubuque, Iowa

MUSIC SERIES

Consulting Editor
    FREDERICK W. WESTPHAL
    Sacramento State College

Fourth Printing 1969

Printed in U. S. A.

TO LYNN—
   Who did much more than "only stand and wait."

preface to the
second edition

The second edition of LISTENERS GUIDE TO MUSICAL UNDERSTANDING, like the first, is designed as a textbook for general students at the college level, but it is appropriate for everyone interested in increasing his knowledge and enjoyment of music. Its purpose is to teach the art of intelligent and perceptive music listening. No prior training or experience in music is assumed. Technical terminology is kept to a minimum while a working vocabulary of common and essential terms is developed. The book deals with music itself, not with such peripheral matters as biographical anecdotes or pictorial allusions.

A survey conducted on representative campuses revealed that a high percentage of students enrolled in introductory music classes did not read music and that even those who could play an instrument did not really comprehend abstract examples of printed music. Teachers who used the first edition confirmed these findings. Music notation, therefore, is not used in the body of the text, and no reference is made to the Appendix of Musical Examples printed at the back of the book for the benefit of teachers and any students who may find it helpful. The ability to read music is not prerequisite to the pleasures of music listening.

The listening material suggested for each unit of study is described objectively. In the selection of recorded examples, four criteria were considered: (a) musical quality, (b) appeal, (c) suitability, and (d) availability. The specified examples or equivalents can be found in most institutional record libraries. The composers and works, except as noted, are listed in the current *Schwann Long Playing Record Catalog* and are readily available. The amount of listening can be varied, either abridging or supplementing that suggested, to suit individual requirements. Performance times are given as an aid in planning classroom listening and outside assignments. The timings (in minutes:seconds), while accurate for a specific recording, are only approximate for other performances. Elapsed time is also used as an aid in the perception of musical form.

Studying in turn the materials, forms, and the periods and styles of music makes it possible to begin with music which is immediately pleasing and to postpone consideration of those idioms which are less familiar and generally less appealing to the uninitiated. Modern music, which sometimes receives short shrift, is abundantly represented in the recommended listening throughout the book and is the subject of a special chapter, as are folk music and jazz.

The information presented in the text combined with the recommended listening stimulates the formation of broad and discriminating musical tastes. With its emphasis on general principles which can be remembered and listening experiences which can be relished, the LISTENERS GUIDE launches readers on a program of enduring pleasure and personal enrichment.

table of contents

illustrations

tables

introduction

Music has been an integral part of man's culture since the dawn of civilization. Human beings have used rhythms and pitches for expressive purposes throughout recorded history and for thousands of years before. There is speculation that primitive music even antedates speech. Through the ages, music has figured prominently in a wide range of human activities—in man's rituals, religions, ceremonies, and amusements.

There is no completely satisfactory explanation for the universality of music. It is not essential for life, yet life without it is unimaginable. It does not provide basic requirements or satisfy obvious instincts, but it has flourished with all peoples in all times and places.

Now, developing an appreciation of music and the arts is more important than ever before. Modern efficiency is making more leisure time available. If it is to be utilized for more abundant living, worthwhile and enduring sources of pleasure must be cultivated. One of the most rewarding is music, and unlike many recreational activities, it is accessible throughout one's lifetime.

As a starting point, everyone likes some kind of music. The purposes of systematic listening and study are to increase the enjoyment of music a person already likes by adding to his knowledge and understanding and to broaden his tastes so that he finds pleasure in additional types and styles of music. This book pursues both objectives, the relative emphasis depending upon one's perspective and previous exposure to music. Reading the book should prove of value in achieving the twin goals of greater understanding and broader taste, but reading alone assures but little progress. The reading must be followed by listening. A perusal of a travel folder is no substitute for

1

a trip, and reading about music is no substitute for hearing it. Music must be given an opportunity to speak for itself.

For practical reasons, most of the listening will be done by means of recordings. Modern recording and playback equipment has reached an unprecedented degree of perfection. Still, there is an elusive quality in a live performance that a microphone cannot capture. More important, the empathy between performers and audiences is possible only in the concert hall. Recordings are a wonderful convenience and provide repeated hearings on demand, but only in live performance situations is the full impact of the listening experience achieved. Record listening should be supplemented by concert attendance whenever possible. The performances do not have to be by professionals. Living presence compensates for the technical limitations of students and amateurs.

The electronic age has revolutionized the listening habits of the world's peoples. Gone is the time when music was available only to the privileged and on special occasions. Gone is the time when audiences were limited to the capacity of a concert hall and when sound could be preserved only as long as an instrument continued to vibrate. The treasures of music now await the entire population at the turn of a dial or the push of a button. With the inventions which make this possible so much a part of 20th-century life, it is difficult to realize that they have come into general use within the memory of senior citizens.

Sound recording has not been enlisted exclusively in the cause of art. It also serves the purposes of commerce and industry. Our ears are bombarded with sounds from loud-speakers while we shop, eat, work, and travel. Neither music nor advertising has been quite the same since the advent of the singing commercial, and now that music's efficacy in increasing production has been recognized, it competes regularly with the din of factories. When we seek diversion, music is generally in the background, if not in the foreground. We are engulfed in sound during our waking hours. In this situation a distinction must be made between *hearing* and *listening*.

A person hears a juke box playing in the background but listens to the person with whom he is speaking. A person hears a room full of people talking but listens to one conversation. The ears and mind are capable of concentrating on one sound source to the exclusion of others. This is attentive listening, the first requirement if one is to appreciate music. Persons whose exposure to music is limited to random encounters in the course of other activities are bypassing opportunities for enjoyment every day.

In the chain of musical expression there are three mutually dependent links—the composer, the performer, and the listener. Composers and performers are among the most ardent listeners, and it is not uncommon for musicians to be active in all three roles. Most people, however, are content to be listeners most of the time. Just to learn the craft of the composer or to acquire the technical proficiency of an artist performer requires years of arduous study and hours of daily practice, not to mention talent. Fortunately, the pathway to becoming a perceptive listener is considerably less demanding. Only the inclination and a modest amount of conditioning, which consists of listening to worthwhile music, are required. Appreciation inevitably follows sufficient acquaintance with good music. The process is hastened perhaps by acquiring knowledge about music, but most important is a judicious selection of listening experiences.

Music which has only transient appeal, which is already assimilated in our culture, or which functions primarily on a subconscious level will receive only passing notice in this study. The field is thus limited to music of enduring value which has achieved or which merits wide recognition and which sustains interest under scrutiny. Musical works which qualify are legion. The problem is not one of finding worthy examples but of making choices from the infinite possibilities. Limitations of time and space suggest a search for prototypes in various forms and styles and for various mediums which will serve as touchstones to the vast treasury of music.

To open the doors to this treasury, it is not necessary to study the rudiments of music or to play an instrument. These activities provide a source of pleasure and accomplishment for some, but for others they are sheer drudgery. If a person has outgrown his youthful enthusiasm for such things and has reached maturity without coping with them, chances are he never will. Fortunately, this is no barrier to the joy of music listening. If one has a particular interest in music fundamentals or in learning to play an instrument, that is another matter, but it is going the long way if the objective is to become an informed listener. There are more direct and pleasant routes.

One such course is charted here. It consists mostly of listening—listening to sounds of inherent beauty organized with consumate skill and brought to life by incomparable artists. Lest the impression be created that there is nothing to do but to bathe in sound, it must be understood that concentration and attentive listening are required. Specific features of the music must be sought out, learned, remembered, and recognized. Music, even a familiar piece, becomes more understandable and more meaningful in the process. There may be no obvious logic for liking music, but there is high correlation between preferences and the amount and sort of listening. It follows naturally that the person with the broadest and most extensive listening experience possesses the greatest potential for enjoyment. It is never too late, or too early, to begin acquiring this experience.

PART I

The Materials of Music

characteristics of sound

Objects which vibrate when energy is applied to them set the surrounding air in motion. The air transmits the vibrations, and human ears perceive as sound vibrating frequencies between approximately 20 and 20,000 per second, the limits varying somewhat with individuals and circumstances.

Three conditions are necessary for sound: (1) a *source*, (2) a *medium of transmission*, and (3) a *receiver*. Any object capable of causing the air molecules to vibrate in the appropriate frequency range can serve as a source of sound. The medium of transmission between the sound source and the receiver is normally the air, but water and solids also transmit sound vibrations. The ear serves as the receiver, responding to the vibrations and sending impulses to the brain which are interpreted as sound. Microphones and recording devices are receivers only in the sense that they detect and store vibrations for subsequent reproduction.

The characteristics of sound are *pitch, loudness, color*, and *duration*.

Pitch

The first characteristic of sound is *pitch*. Pitch is directly related to the vibrating frequency of the sound source: the faster the rate of vibration, the higher the pitch; the slower the rate of vibration, the lower the pitch.

To experience the perception of pitch differences, listen to several notes played at random on the piano starting toward the left end of the keyboard and progressing toward the right end. Differences in pitch will be apparent to all who have normal hearing. The keys of the piano produce notes of graduated frequency and pitch from slow and low on the left to fast and high on the right.

When tuned to standard U.S. pitch (A = 440), the lowest note on the piano has a frequency of 27½ vibrations per second. The white key third from the right end of the piano keyboard produces a note with a frequency 128 times greater, 3520 vibrations per second. The frequency of the highest note on the piano is over 4000. Even so, the perceived pitches of the piano and all musical instruments fall in the middle and lower portions of the audible range. If the rate of vibration of the lowest note on the piano were halved, it would be below the audible range, but the frequency of the highest note could be doubled twice and still be heard by a young person. The ability to hear high pitches declines with age.

Now listen to the sounds produced alternately by two adjacent keys on the piano, from a white key to a black or vice versa if they are next to each other. Adjacent keys on the piano produce the smallest pitch difference used in music (except in the Orient and in a few contemporary experiments). Nearly everyone can hear the difference and can tell whether the second tone was higher or lower in pitch than the first. Pitch perception this acute is essential for the complete comprehension of music. Actually, most people can distinguish between pitches with much less difference, especially in the middle register. Recognizing small differences in pitch is easiest in the middle registers, somewhat more difficult in the high and low registers.

Faulty pitch discrimination can often be improved with a few minutes of drill. It is not that the ability to hear pitches actually improves so much as that one learns what to listen for and how to interpret what he hears. The results of such drill can be measured and general pitch acuity determined by playing pairs of notes, one after the other, in different registers of the piano and with varying distances between them. Students indicate whether the second note is higher or lower than the first. With a few minutes of practice, the percentage of individuals who cannot make a perfect score will be relatively small.

A distinguishing characteristic between tones and noises is the presence or absence of pitch. Musical sounds are produced by regular vibrations at a constant rate and have a definite pitch. Noises are produced by erratic vibrations with variable frequencies and have no precise pitch, though they can be classified generally as high or low. Some sounds combine elements of tone and noise.

Loudness

The second characteristic of sound is *loudness*. The perception of loudness is the subjective reaction to intensity. The intensity or energy of a sound is related to the area and the amount of displacement in the vibrating body producing it. Other factors being equal, a large vibrating surface produces a louder sound than a small one, and wide fluctuations produce louder sounds than narrow ones. The perceived sound, however, is also affected by the medium of transmission and the distance from the source. Since air is the normal medium of transmission, it may be regarded as constant. Loudness is roughly inversely proportional to the square of the distance from the source of the sound.

Musical instruments are designed to take advantage of the physical properties of sound in the matter of loudness. A string of the length and diameter used on a violin vibrating by itself would be barely audible. The body of the instrument increases the area of vibrating surface and amplifies the tone. A sound board in pianos serves the same purpose. Also, the amount of displacement in the vibrating surface of most instruments can be regulated by performers by striking, blowing, bowing, or plucking with more or less force, providing a wide range of dynamic levels.

The human ear has amazing adaptability to variations in loudness. It can detect the faintest whisper or rustle of leaves and yet is capable of withstanding the shock of thunder and cannons. Composers take full advantage of this ability and explore dynamic ranges approaching both extremes. A unit of sound representing the smallest change the ear can discern is called a decibel. The sound produced by an orchestra playing full force is approximately 100 decibels. In other words, the ear can detect 100 graduations of loudness between the threshold of sound and the volume of the full orchestra.

Tone Color

Musicians use a word of French origin, *timbre*, for the third characteristic of sound, but *tone color* and *tone quality* convey the same meaning and are easier to remember and pronounce. Color is the tonal characteristic which enables one to distinguish the sounds of the various instruments. The tones produced by each instrument contain, in addition to the fundamental frequency heard as the pitch, a distinctive pattern of higher frequencies. These higher frequencies, present in most sounds and all musical tones, are *overtones*. Overtones are the coloring components in sounds which make it possible to identify their sources. Though overtones under normal conditions are too weak in relation to the fundamental to be heard as pitches, a simple experiment will make some of the more prominent ones in a piano tone audible.

Select any white key in the lower part of the piano. Starting with the selected key, count up eight white keys. Those familiar with music will recognize this as an octave. Depress the second key without playing it, and hold it down. Now strike the first key sharply, and release it immediately. The pitch of the second key will sound faintly but audibly. The pitch of the second key can be verified by playing it. This experiment will work under favorable conditions (in a quiet room with a well-tuned piano) with the twelfth, fifteenth, and seventeenth white keys above the selected key. Attentive listeners may be able to hear the pitches of these keys depressed singly or in combinations concurrently with the pitch of the first key if it is held down until its tone begins to fade. In this way the overtones are amplified but are heard in conjunction with the predominant fundamental tone, as they are normally.

The effect of overtones on tone quality can be demonstrated by comparing the sound of a modern high fidelity record player with that of an old or inexpensive model or the sound of a new LP record with that of an old 78 r.p.m. record. Similar effects can be obtained by reducing the high frequencies with the treble control or a filter. In each instance the difference in the perceived sound is due primarily to the relative presence or absence of the high frequencies of the overtones. High fidelity sound reproduction is possible now that the complex problems of reproducing the frequencies of the entire audible range have been solved, and recorded sound at its best recreates to a remarkable degree the vivid color and beauty of live sound.

Instruments and voices produce several overtones of varying intensity extending into the upper limits of the audible range. In distinguishing the sounds of the various instruments and individual voices, the ear detects minute differences in sound waves, including those differences caused by overtones. To duplicate this feat in the laboratory requires an array of complicated equipment. The aural capabilities are utilized to the fullest, but not taxed, in detecting the subtle differences by which the sources of sound are identified.

Still finer shadings of quality distinguish the tone of a concert artist from a beginner and the tone of a Stradivarius violin from a factory production model. Musicians readily differentiate between the tone of a valuable instrument and a cheap one and between the tone of a professional player and a young student. Discrimination of this sort requires experience and an adequate basis for comparison but no special ability.

Composers consciously exploit the myriad tone qualities at their disposal, and no small part of the music listeners' delight derives from the exquisite coloring of musical sounds.

Duration

The fourth attribute of sound is *duration*. Sounds may be long or short, lasting from a small fraction of a second to many seconds. All instruments can play short notes, but there are practical limitations on the duration of tones. Wind instruments and voices can sustain tones only for the duration of one breath; string instruments for the length of one bow. A piano can sustain a tone only as long as the string continues to vibrate from the initial impetus imparted to it by the hammer. The piano tone is loudest at the moment of impact, and from that instant it diminishes constantly to the vanishing point. Tones in the lower register of the piano with a loud start can be heard for several seconds. Those in the upper register are audible for a much shorter period. Of all the instruments, only organs can sustain tones indefnitely.

Musicians develop skills in breathing, blowing, bowing, and fingering which enable them to create the illusion of almost continuous sound. At least listeners are rarely aware of the physical limitations imposed on duration.

Other attributes of sound are sometimes listed, but only these four—*pitch, loudness, color,* and *duration*—are accounted for in musical notation.

Notation

A reasonably precise system of notation has evolved through the ages for the characteristics of sound. It serves as a means of communication between composers and performers and as a method of preserving the music of previous generations. Modern notation dates back to about 1600, and musicologists can read and transcribe the music manuscripts of much earlier periods.

Composers can designate any pitch or combination of pitches by means of note symbols placed in relation to an arrangement of five lines enclosing four spaces following a sign. These devices tell the performer which note or notes to play on his instrument, and since each note has by agreement a certain frequency, the specified pitches can be realized with absolute precision.

The notation of loudness is less exact. A set of signs, really abbreviations of Italian terms, indicate relative degrees of loudness from very loud to very soft, or in extreme cases from very, very loud to very, very soft. Appropriate signs indicating the degree of loudness or softness plus certain additional signs indicating gradual or sudden changes from one to the other are given at strategic places in written music. Performers must exercise judgment in the interpretation of these signs since they are only relative.

When composers specify a particular instrument, they are designating tone color. They hope, of course, for a gifted performer playing an adequate instrument. In addition, composers may include in the notation special instructions regarding the type of tone or style of playing desired. They may also indicate the use of devices which affect the tone color, such as mutes.

Modifications in the shape of note symbols are used to show relative duration. The same symbols denote duration by their shape and pitch by their location. Though only relative values are established by the shapes of the symbols, this may be supplemented by an indication of how many units of a specified type will occur in a minute. This gives the notation of duration an absolute value which otherwise is lacking.

Being able to read and write music or the lack of this ability has very little to do with the listening process for either musicians or nonmusicians. Often nonmusicians think they are missing something when they hear a concert or a recording because they cannot read music. They may suspect that the ability to read music makes sounds more meaningful. Such is not the case. If musicians get more out of hearing music than others, it is because they have learned to listen better, not because they read music. They do not sit in a concert visualizing the symbols for the music they are hearing. They couldn't if they tried, and even to attempt it would reduce rather than enhance their pleasure. One who reads language but not music has only to compare his reaction while watching a play or movie to recognize the validity of this statement.

You will not need to read music or even program notes to appreciate the voluptuous beauty of the following example. Listen for the broad sweep and infinite variety of its musical sounds from soft to loud, low to high, transparent to full, and somber to brilliant.

MAURICE RAVEL: *Ballet, Daphnis and Chloé* (1912)
    (1875–1937)   Suite No. 2
                    1. Daybreak   5:25
                    2. Pantomime   6:00
                    3. General Dance   4:35

> The great Russian impresario, Diaghilev, commissioned Ravel to compose music for a ballet. *Daphnis and Chloé*, from which this suite is taken, was the result. For sheer beauty of musical sound this work is without peer. It exploits the full dynamic range of the orchestra from the soft rustle of the opening to the thundering climax of the end. It uses the full pitch range of the orchestra from the top register of the high-pitched instruments to the bottom register of the low-pitched instruments.

Supplementary Material

SCIENCE IN THE ORCHESTRA, 3 sound films, British Information Services

    1. Hearing the Orchestra   13:00
> The nature of sound and its transmission. The structure and mechanism of the ear.

    2. Exploring the Instruments   14:00
> How different pitches are produced and the range of various instruments.

3. Looking at Sounds   12:00

> Demonstration of harmonic components (overtones) by means of an audiospectrometer.

THE SCIENCE OF MUSICAL SOUNDS, Sound film, Academy Films   11:00

> Explores the basic principles of sound production using three types of musical instruments: harp, flute, and xylophone.

THE SCIENCE OF SOUND, 2–12″ LP's, Folkways 6007 (Abridged version 6136)

> Recordings produced by the Bell Telephone Laboratories describing and demonstrating the phenomena of sound, including how we hear, frequency, pitch, intensity, loudness, fundamentals and overtones, and quality.

THE SOUNDS OF MUSIC, Sound film, Coronet   11:00

> Characteristics of musical sound and principles of amplitude and frequency. Illustrations using string, wind, and percussion instruments.

CHAPTER 3

sources of musical sound

The first source of musical sound was the human body. It possessed an ideal sound source in the vocal chords, and the body could also produce sounds by stamping, clapping, and slapping. In prehistoric times these innate sources were augmented by external devices, and the development of instruments began.

Instruments expand the dimensions of sound. They can produce sounds which are louder and both higher and lower than those possible with the body unassisted. They add to the available tone colors and make possible the playing of combined pitches by a single performer. Some instruments contribute agility and others sustaining power to the sound resources.

The sounds of music are produced by the voice and by bowing, blowing, striking, and plucking an assortment of instruments. Keyboard instruments couple one of these basic sound producing processes with a keyboard mechanism. The functions of instruments are to provide a responsive source of sound, a means of amplifying that sound, and ways of controlling its pitch, duration, and loudness. Modern instruments in the hands of adroit performers attain these objectives to a high degree, but for warmth, intimacy and immediacy of appeal the human voice remains supreme. The sound sources of concert music are described and pictured in the following pages, and the suggested listening provides an introduction to the great music created for each voice and instrument.

Voices

Voices are classified according to range, sex, and somewhat according to quality. From high to low the basic classifications are: *soprano, alto, tenor,* and *bass*. Soprano and alto designate respectively high and low female and unchanged male voices. Tenor and bass designate high and low changed male voices. Observe that the range of a high, mature male voice still is lower than that of a low female or unchanged voice. The compass of any one voice is limited, but the span from the top of the highest soprano voice to the bottom of the lowest bass voice is about four octaves (compared with a piano range of a little over seven octaves).

The terms *soprano*, *alto*, *tenor*, and *bass* are applied not only to voices and singers but to the parts they sing in ensembles and to corresponding parts in instrumental music.

The most ordinary range for a woman's voice lies between that of a true soprano or alto. This intermediate voice is called *mezzo-soprano*. The parallel male voice with a range between that of tenor and bass is known as *baritone*. These, together with the four previously named, constitute the six usual voice types. Further distinctions are made, primarily in operatic music, on the basis of style and quality.

SOPRANO voices are subdivided into *coloratura, lyric, dramatic,* and *mezzo*. Coloratura sopranos have unusually high voices and specialize in performing music *colored* by ornamentation, runs, and rapid passages requiring great agility. In operas, the heroine's role often calls for a coloratura soprano. Lyric sopranos concentrate on beauty of sound rather than extreme range or power. Their literature demands a light vocal quality and a melodious, flowing style. A lyric soprano voice is ideal for many art songs and for leading parts in light operas and musical comedies. Arias in grand operas, too, may require lyric soprano style and quality. Dramatic soprano is the appelation for sopranos with powerful voices and pronounced histrionic ability. Operatic roles portraying intense emotions are assigned to dramatic sopranos, and only sopranos of this type can cope with the heavy orchestral accompaniments and emotional demands of Wagnerian music drama. Mezzo-soprano voices lack both the brilliance of the higher soprano voices and the richness of the lower alto voices. Since more women's voices fall in this category than any other, supreme vocal quality and musicianship are essential for mezzo-sopranos who make a career of singing. *Carmen* is one of the few operas with the leading role assigned to a mezzo-soprano, but many supporting parts in operas are sung by mezzo-sopranos.

Various types of soprano voices are illustrated in the following selections.

LEO DELIBES: *Opera, Lakmé* (1883)
(1836–1891)   Act II. Bell Song   5:10
    Lakmé, the beautiful daughter of a Hindu priest, sings this coloratura aria at a religious festival attended by British soldiers, including her lover, Gerald.

GIUSEPPE VERDI: *Opera, La Traviata* (1853)
   (1813–1901)   Act I. Sempre libera (Always Free)   3:50

> *La Traviata* is based on Dumas' *Camille*. The coloratura heroine sings of a life of freedom and pleasure in this brilliant aria.

HEITOR VILLA-LOBOS: *Bachianas Brasileiras No. 5* (1938)
   (1887–1959)   1. Cantilena   6:50

> Composed "in memory of Bach," this song for lyric soprano and eight cellos evokes the nocturnal beauties of nature.

GEORGES BIZET: *Opera, Carmen* (1875)
   (1838–1875)   Act III. Micaela's Air   4:25

> In this lyric aria Micaela brings Don José news of his mother and pleads with him to leave the gypsy, Carmen, and return home.

RICHARD WAGNER: *Opera, Tristan and Isolde* (1865)
   (1813–1883)   Act III. Liebestod (Love Death)   7:20

> This dramatic lament is Isolde's last utterance before she is reunited with Tristan in death.

GIACOMO PUCCINI: *Opera, Tosca* (1900)
   (1858–1924)   Act II. Vissi d'arte (I lived only for art)   3:00

> Tosca, in this dramatic aria, sings of her life unselfishly devoted to art and love.

GEORGES BIZET: *Opera, Carmen* (1875)
   (1838–1875)   Act I. Habanera   4:00
                        Act I. Seguidilla   3:50
                        Act II. Gypsy Song   3:45

> Carmen, a mezzo-soprano in the title role, sings the taunting *Habanera* as she begins her flirtation with Don José, a soldier. She tempts him with the prospect of a rendezvous in the seductive *Seguidilla*. The *Gypsy Song* is sung by Carmen for the entertainment of her merrymaking friends at the inn of Lillas Pastia.

    Voice classifications beyond the basic types are determined more by the particular selection being sung than by the voice. The literatures are not mutually exclusive, and the repertoire of most singers includes songs of various types. Singers for obvious reasons choose numbers which show their voices to advantage, but many are equally at home in two or more styles.

    ALTO and CONTRALTO are used synonymously, though contralto sometimes seems to carry the connotation of a particularly deep alto voice. There is no distinction between them in the literature. It exploits the low tones of the female voice. The quality, typically and in the following examples, is rich, resonant, dark, and "throaty."

G. F. HANDEL: *Oratorio, The Messiah* (1742)
(1685–1759)   9. O thou that tellest good tidings   5:30
>   This, *He shall feed his flock,* and *He was despised* are the three arias for alto (or contralto) in Handel's immortal *Messiah*.

GUSTAV MAHLER: *Das Lied von der Erde (Song of the Earth)* (1908)
(1860–1911)   4. Von der Schoenheit (Of Beauty)   6:40
>   *The Song of the Earth* is really a symphony for orchestra with two solo voices, alto and tenor, which alternate in its six movements. The texts are free translations of Chinese poems contemplating aspects of earthly existence.

TENOR voices, like soprano voices, sometimes are classified according to type. *Robusto* (robust), *lyric, dramatic,* and *heroic* are adjectives commonly attached to tenors. *Tenor robusto* is the type with tremendous power in the upper register featured in Italian opera. This is the type of voice to which most young tenors aspire. *Lyric* tenors, also referred to as "Irish" tenors, are the counterpart of lyric sopranos. Their voices possess the same qualities, and they sing the same type of music, ofttimes the same songs. *Dramatic* and *heroic* tenors have much in common with robust tenors, but the terms are associated with German opera. These tenors often begin their careers as high baritones and through training and practice add to their natural range the high tones necessary to sing tenor roles. The following examples, without specific designations, illustrate various types of tenor voices.

RUGGIERO LEONCAVALLO: *Opera, I Pagliacci (Punchinello)* (1892)
(1858–1919)   Act I. Vesti la giubba   2:30
                                (On with the play)
>   Having learned of his wife's infidelity, the tenor Canio sings this anguished aria as he prepares for the performance of a comedy.

GIUSEPPE VERDI: *Opera, Rigoletto* (1851)
(1813–1901)   Act I. Questa o quella   1:40
                                (One is as fair as another)
                        Act IV. La donna è mobile   1:50
                                (Woman is fickle)
>   The Duke, portrayed by a tenor, sings of women but reveals his own fickleness in these rollicking arias.

GEORGES BIZET: *Opera, Carmen* (1875)
   (1838–1875)   Act II. Flower Song   3:15
> Don José discloses a flower preserved from his first meeting with
> Carmen and sings of his devotion in this tenor aria.

W. A. MOZART: *Opera, Don Giovanni (Don Juan)* (1787)
   (1756–1791)   Act I. Dalla sua pace   3:50
                              (On her all joy dependeth)
                       Act II. Il mio tesoro (To my beloved)   4:10
> In the second of these arias, the tenor executes florid passages similar
> to those associated with coloratura sopranos. It was replaced by the
> first when the tenor engaged for the Vienna performance found the
> original too difficult. Both love songs are included in modern scores
> and performances.

RICHARD WAGNER: *Opera, Die Meistersinger (The Mastersingers)* (1868)
   (1813–1883)   Act III. Prize Song   5:45
> The *Prize Song* with which Walther wins the song contest and the
> hand of Eva figures prominently in the *Prelude* to the opera and is
> also heard in Act II.

BARITONES, like mezzo-sopranos, are in competition with the most
prevalent voice type of their sex. They cannot hope to impress audiences
with extremes of range or feats of brilliance. They compensate with solid
production and skillful interpretation. The designation is not customary in
choral music, but operatic parts are entrusted to baritone voices.

GEORGES BIZET: *Opera, Carmen* (1875)
   (1838–1875)   Act II. Toreador Song   4:25
> This rousing song about the glory of the bull ring is sung by the
> baritone, Escamillo, to an entranced group, including the impres-
> sionable Carmen.

RUGGIERO LEONCAVALLO: *Opera, I Pagliacci (Punchinello)* (1892)
   (1858–1919)   Prologue   7:45
> Tonio, a baritone playing the role of a clown, slips through the
> closed curtain and explains in song that the play to be presented is
> based upon life and that the players are real people, not mere actors
> on a stage.

BASS is the general term for all low male voices. Subdivisions, as with
other voices, are predicated more upon the role or selection being sung than

upon the characteristics of the voice. A bass singer especially proud of his low notes may advertise himself as a *basso profondo*. One who claims a range encompassing that of bass and baritone combined (or who lacks extremes of either) may adopt the title of *bass-baritone*. A bass specializing in a lyric style will be known as a *basso cantante*, and one associated with comic roles will be known as a *basso buffo*.

W. A. MOZART: *Opera, The Magic Flute* (1791)
 (1756–1791)   Act II. In diesen heiligen Hallen 4:15
             (Within these sacred halls)

> In this aria the bass, High Priest Sarastro, consoles the despairing Pamina and assures her that Prince Tamino will soon be free to marry her.

MODEST MUSSORGSKY: *Opera, Boris Godunov* (1874)
 (1839–1881)   Act I. Prayer of Boris   3:00
           Act IV. Monologue   5:00

> Immediately following his coronation as Tsar of Russia, Boris, a bass, prays for mercy and guidance in his reign. In the *Monologue* the dying Boris bids his son farewell and gives him advice as successor to the throne.

W. A. MOZART: *Opera, Don Giovanni (Don Juan)* (1787)
 (1756–1791)   Act I. Madamina (Catalog Aria) 5:00

> In this humorous bass aria, Leporello, Don Giovanni's manservant, recites a catalog of his master's conquests—640 in Italy, 231 in Germany, 100 in France, 91 in Turkey, and in Spain 1003!

The practice of publishers, for reasons more pecuniary than artistic, to issue songs with piano accompaniments in high, medium, and low versions fosters the interchange of literature between voice types and between male and female voices. Because of this, all of the foregoing examples were drawn from extended works with orchestral accompaniments, mainly operas. The singers in operatic roles must perform the parts as they are written to be in agreement with the orchestra and the other singers. Furthermore, the full potential of any given voice type will be exploited in the part of a leading character. Singers are selected for operatic roles on the basis of having a voice that fits the part, and they concentrate their efforts on a limited number of roles for which their voices are best suited. Successful composers of opera are aware of the special abilities and problems of singers and as a rule provide them with ample opportunities for vocal display and, after strenuous scenes, a chance to recuperate.

The human voice as a musical medium has one exclusive attribute. It is the only source of musical sound that can convey a message or tell a story.

Instruments Played by Bowing

One method of producing a tone is to draw coarse hair dusted with rosin across a taut string. The hair is fastened at each end to a stick originally curved in the manner of an archer's bow but now bent in the opposite direction. The name, however, is retained. The hair is obtained from horses' manes and tails, and most of it comes from Russia. The sticks are made of Brazil-wood, and the best comes from the state of Pernambuco in Brazil. Fittings are attached to the stick to hold the hair smooth and straight and to make the tension on the hair adjustable. The act of drawing the bow over the strings is *bowing*, and instruments played by bowing are *string instruments*.

Modern bowed string instruments are the product of a long period of evolution which culminated with the perfection of the violin family around 1600. They all have four strings with one end tied firmly to a tailpiece and the other wrapped around a peg that is turned to adjust the tuning. Near the fixed end the strings pass over a bridge which transmits the vibration of the strings to the body of the instrument. The body serves as a resonating chamber and amplifies the sound of the vibrating strings to useful levels. Its distinctive shape results partially from experiments leading to the perfection of its resonating characteristics, but the indentation at the middle of each side is a practical concession which permits the bow to function on the outside strings. Protruding from the body of the instrument is a narrow neck which accommodates the left hand of the player and allows his fingers easy access to the strings. Length, tension, and diameter determine the pitch of the open strings. Pitch changes are made by depressing the strings against the finger-board with the fingers. Variations in loudness, tone quality, and style are made by applying the bow to the strings in different ways. Slight variations in tone quality also can be made by a motion of the hand stopping the strings known as *vibrato*. Vibrato affects the pitch slightly but not audibly. It appears as a shaking motion of the hand. Another tone modification is obtained by inhibiting the vibration of the bridge with a small device of wood, metal, or rubber called a *mute*.

The four bowed string instruments arranged from the highest pitched and smallest to the lowest pitched and largest are: *violin, viola, cello* (also called *violoncello*), and *bass* (also called *string bass, contrabass,* and *double bass*). The strings are the most versatile instruments. Together they have a pitch range almost as wide as that of the piano. They are equally at home in rapid pyrotechnics and slow, sustained melodies. They are capable of great expressiveness and brittle wit. It is small wonder that they are both the

FIGURE 1. *Violin and Viola*

prima donnas and the work horses of every instrumental ensemble from which they are not excluded.

The VIOLIN is the most brilliant and agile of the string family. This is partially because its relatively short, thin strings respond instantaneously to the slightest pressure of the bow, and partially because its small size allows a very efficient technique of stopping the strings with the fingers of the left hand. The instrument is held in a horizontal position under the chin, and the bow is drawn at right angles to the string by the right hand and arm. Violins are the sopranos of the string section and more often than not play the melody, but they are just as effective in a variety of supporting roles. Cataloging their capabilities is impossible, but the suggested listening gives an impression of their versatility.

NICCOLO PAGANINI: *Caprices, Op. 1*
  (1782–1840)   24. Theme and Variations (Theme p. 312)   4:50

Paganini was the greatest violinist of his age. With him the tradition of the virtuoso performer began. His 24 *Caprices* for unaccompanied violin exploit every facet of violin technique, including some features he originated. Publication of most of his compositions was withheld during his lifetime to preserve his secrets.

EDOUARD LALO: *Symphonie Espagnole, Op. 21* (1875)
  (1823–1892)   1. Allegro non troppo   7:30

> The title notwithstanding, this is a concerto for violin and orchestra. It is a brilliant display vehicle in the Spanish idiom with strikingly varied writing for the solo instrument.

The VIOLA is the alto member of the string family. Violas are slightly larger than violins, but not enough to be immediately apparent to the casual observer except by comparison. They are played in the same manner as violins. Their range is lower, more so than the difference in size would indicate. The ideal ratio of string length to pitch is compromised somewhat to keep the instrument within practical dimensions for under-the-chin playing. Heavier strings less tightly strung compensate for the reduced length in producing the desired pitch. These adjustments contribute to the distinctive tone quality of the viola which tends to be more somber than the violin and a bit nasal. Listening is suggested which provides direct comparison with the violin, with which the viola is most easily confused.

BELA BARTOK: *Concerto for Viola* (1945)
  (1881–1945)   2. Adagio religioso   5:15
                3. Allegro vivace   4:20

> The *Adagio* with its typically somber viola style and quality is followed without interruption by the *Allegro* demonstrating the agility of which the instrument is capable. The high register of the viola, used at times in this and other solo works, is less common in orchestral writing.

W. A. MOZART: *Duo No. 2 in B-flat,*[1] *K.424*[2] (1783)
  (1756–1791)   3. Andante con variazioni   7:45

> This duo for violin and viola provides an ideal means of comparing the tone quality of the two instruments, especially when a theme stated by one instrument is imitated immediately by the other.

The CELLO has the same basic shape as the violin and the viola, but it is much larger. It is held between the player's knees and is supported by an

---

[1] Keys unless otherwise indicated are major.
[2] The works of Mozart are identified by K. numbers. These numbers relate to the order of the works in a chronological catalog of Mozart's compositions compiled by Dr. Ludwig Koechel in 1862.

FIGURE 2. *Cello and Bass*

end pin resting on the floor. This playing position, which is upside down in comparison with the violin and viola, and the cello's greater size necessitate different fingering and bowing techniques. The highest open string on the cello is tuned just one step higher than the lowest open string on the violin, but a cellist can play many notes in the violin range. Violins and cellos have essentially the same ratio of size to pitch, so a cello in its high register can be mistaken for a violin. The low register is rich, sonorous, and distinctive. The cello is the tenor of the string family, but in ensembles two parts are often taken by violins, and the cellos are moved down to the bass.

J. S. BACH: *Suite No. 4 in E-flat for Cello, S.1010*[3]
   (1685–1750)   2. Allemande   2:55

> This suite for cello unaccompanied is one of six Bach wrote in the years 1717–1723. The characteristic middle and low registers of the cello are heard in the *Allemande*.

JOSEPH HAYDN: *Concerto in D for Cello, Op. 101* (1783)
   (1732–1809)   2. Adagio   5:30
                 3. Rondo: Allegro   5:00

> These two movements of the concerto, in contrasting tempos and styles, demonstrate the extreme registers of the cello and some of the intricate figurations playable on string instruments.

The DOUBLE BASS, STRING BASS, CONTRABASS, or simply the BASS is the largest of the string family. It is so large the player stands or perches on a high stool beside it, and the full weight of the instrument is borne by an end pin resting on the floor. The lowest bass string is as heavy as a small rope, and its pitch is almost as low as the lowest note on a piano. The other strings are only slightly smaller, and considerable energy must be imparted by the bow to set them in motion. Strong fingers are essential to stop them for the different pitches. Notes higher than the lowest violin pitch are possible but rare on the bass. The normal bass range overlaps the lower cello range and reaches into that of the viola. The tone of a single bass tends to be fuzzy and lacking in focus. This effect is reduced with a group of basses, but even so they seldom are used in a solo capacity or unsupported by other instruments.

CAMILLE SAINT-SAENS: *Carnival of the Animals* (1886)
   (1835–1921)   5. The Elephant   1:35

> This is one of the few instances in which the orchestral string basses play the principal melody unassisted.

Instruments Played by Blowing

A number of instruments with quite different shapes, sounds, and mechanisms are played by blowing. Instruments played by blowing are *wind instruments,* and their sound is produced by a vibrating column of air. At

---

[3] The identifying numbers for Bach works are from the thematic catalog compiled by Wolfgang Schmieder.

one time wind instruments could be divided conveniently on the basis of the material from which they were made—wood and brass. The terms *wood-wind* and *brass*, derived from this division, are still used to classify instruments, though metal is now substituted for wood in the manufacture of some "woodwind" instruments.

The sound of all wind instruments stems from a vibrating column of air, but the means of setting the air in motion varies. In playing brass instruments the lips, activated by the breath, become vibrating membranes, and in contact with mouthpieces of assorted sizes and shapes they energize the air inside the instruments. The lips, breath, and mouth function rather differently in producing sound in woodwind instruments. A stream of air issuing from the lips strikes the edge of a hole in flutes and piccolos and produces the sound in the same way sound is produced blowing over the top of a small bottle. With clarinets and saxophones a thin, finely shaped piece of cane called a *reed* is the primary source of vibration. The reed is firmly attached to the mouthpiece at one end. The other, parallel with the tip of the mouthpiece, is inserted between the lips. Air passing between the reed and the mouthpiece causes the reed to vibrate. The reeds of oboes and bassoons consist of two pieces of cane bound together as double reeds with just enough space between them at the center for the passage of air. The free end of the double reed is inserted between the lips, and both halves vibrate when air is forced between them.

A distinction also can be made between woodwinds and brasses on the basis of their mechanisms. The woodwinds have several holes located along the instrument which are opened and closed by the fingers or by keys and pads activated by the fingers. The pattern of open and closed holes in conjunction with the manner of blowing determines the pitch. There are alternate fingerings for some notes, but most patterns produce only one pitch.

The mechanism of the brass instruments is most clearly illustrated by the trombone. The trombone has a slide which can be extended or shortened to change the length of the tubing through which the air passes. The principle is the same for the other brass instruments, but changes in tube length are accomplished by valves. Each valve is connected to a different length of tubing through which the air passes when the valve is depressed. Otherwise this tubing is bypassed. The air takes the longest route through the horn when the valves are all down and the shortest way when they are all up. Various combinations of three valves suffice for all the pitches on the instrument. The fourth valve with which some brass instruments are equipped serves either to improve the intonation or to change the key of the instrument. Several pitches are obtained with each valve combination by altering the manner of blowing and the formation of the lips. *Embouchure* is the term used to describe the formation of the lips and the placement of the tongue in relation to the mouthpiece of wind instruments.

The tone of brass instruments, like that of strings (but not woodwinds) can be modified by mutes. Mutes for brass instruments made of various materials and in assorted shapes and sizes are inserted in the bell, that is, in the flared open end of the instrument. All have the effect of reducing and muffling the tone, the exact quality depending upon the construction and material. Unlike the other brass instruments, French horns are shaped so the player can insert his hand in the bell of the instrument. French horns are muted or *stopped* with the hand rather than with a mechanical device. *Stopped* notes on the horn sound delicate and far away when they are soft, brassy when they are loud and accented.

In Table 1 instruments listed in the first column are most common and widely used. Those in the second column are essentially a larger or smaller version of a basic instrument on the same line in the first column. Instruments in the third column are either further modifications of basic instruments or special purpose instruments used mostly in bands and/or popular music.

TABLE 1

WIND INSTRUMENTS

	Basic Orchestra	Large Orchestra	Band and/or Popular
WOODWIND			
APERTURE:	Flute	Piccolo	Alto flute
SINGLE REED:	Clarinet	Bass clarinet	E-flat clarinet Alto clarinet Contra bass clarinet
			Saxophones Alto Tenor Baritone
DOUBLE REED:	Oboe: Bassoon	English horn Contrabassoon	
BRASS			
VALVE:	Trumpet French horn Tuba		Cornet Sousaphone Baritone (Euphonium)
SLIDE:	Trombone	Bass trombone	

Instruments on the same line in Table 1 generally are constructed and their music written in a manner which enables a player to transfer technique

FIGURE 3. *Flute and Piccolo*

from one to another with minimum difficulty. For example, a flute player with a modest amount of practice can play a piccolo or an alto flute. Likewise, a person who plays any one of the clarinets readily can adapt his technique to the others. The same relationship exists between all the saxophones, between oboe and English horn, and so on.

The FLUTE is the soprano of the woodwind family. It is held parallel to the floor extending to the player's right in a position permitting him to blow over an opening near the left end of the instrument. Ancestors of the flute were made of wood, but now flutes are made of silver alloy with an occasional specimen of gold or platinum. The flute is very agile and often serves to spin a delicate filigree in the orchestral fabric. The tone is breathy and sensuous in the lower register, clear and bright in the upper register.

KENT KENNAN: *Night Soliloquy for Flute & Strings* (1936)   3:35
   (1913–   )

> Kent Kennan is best known to music students as the author of textbooks on orchestration and counterpoint, but this work is evidence of his talent for melody and instrumental color.

EDGARD VARESE: *Density 21.5* (1935)   3:55
   (1885–1965)

> *Density 21.5* was written for Georges Barrère who owned a custom-made platinum flute. The density of platinum is 21.5. The writing for the flute is not typical, but the extreme registers are well displayed.

The PICCOLO is a miniature flute about half the size of its counterpart. It is the highest pitched orchestral instrument, reaching within one step of the highest note of the piano. Its low register is thin and of limited usefulness. Its special purpose is to double at a higher level lines appearing in other instruments, particularly the flute. In its upper register the piccolo has a a sparkling tone which becomes shrill and piercing when it is played loudly.

JOHN PHILIP SOUSA: *Stars and Stripes Forever* (1897)   3:25
   (1854–1932)

> The piccolo is featured on a high, decorative melodic line in the second half of this march.

P. I. TCHAIKOVSKY: *Nutcracker Suite, Op. 71a* (1882)
   (1840–1893)   6. Chinese Dance   1:00

> In this dance the piccolo is employed in the most usual way, playing the same melody as the flute an octave higher.

FIGURE 4. *Clarinet and Bass Clarinet*

The CLARINET has a wide practical compass with distinctive colorings in its low, middle, and high registers. The low register is rich and mellow. The middle register has a neutral quality which blends well with other instruments and lends itself to accompanying parts and filling in harmonies, though it is also used for solos. The higher register becomes progressively more penetrating and, except with expert players, pinched at the top.

C. M. VON WEBER: *Concertino for Clarinet, Op. 26* (1805)   8:15
(1786–1826)

> Weber exploits the clarinet in all of the traditional ways in this "small concerto" for solo clarinet and orchestra.

IGOR STRAVINSKY: *Three Pieces for Clarinet* (1918)

1882–)	1. M.M. = 52	2:00
	2. M.M. = 168	2:40
	3. M.M. = 160	1:35

> The contrasting qualities of the different registers of the clarinet are evident in these unaccompanied pieces for the instrument. The "M.M." numbers indicate the rate of speed at which each piece is to be played.

The BASS CLARINET extends the clarinet sound into the bass range. A comparative newcomer in the musical world, it has found favor for its velvety low register. It is often added to the bass line, occasionally appears in brief solo passages.

The SAXOPHONES are too familiar both by sight and sound to require detailed discussion. They are hybrids fusing a single reed (like a clarinet) with a metal body (like the brasses) in a conical shape (like an oboe). The saxophones are the only widely used instruments which can be attributed to one individual. They were developed by Adolphe Sax of Brussels about 1840. The *alto, tenor,* and *baritone* saxophones are the most familiar because of their use in dance bands, but a complete family of saxophones is manufactured. Any recording of a large dance band will demonstrate the sound of a saxophone section. Saxophones are responsible for much of the fullness in dance, marching, and concert bands. The suggested listening is drawn from the less abundant literature for saxophone as a solo instrument.

JACQUES IBERT: *Concertino da Camera for Saxophone* (1935)

(1890–1962)	2. Larghetto	3:50
	3. Animato molto	4:00

ALEXANDER GLAZOUNOV: *Concerto for Saxophone* (1934)   12:30
(1865–1936)

> Both of these works are for alto saxophone. The style of playing and
> the tone quality of the instrument in recordings of these solo com-
> positions is rather different from that ordinarily heard in popular
> music and jazz.

The OBOE, with its double reed, has a more "reedy" sound and plaintive
quality than the flute, clarinet, or saxophone, and it is less dexterous. The
oboe is associated with simple, pastoral melodies, but it is only slightly less
versatile than the other members of the woodwind family. Its lowest note is
about the same as that of a flute, but a flute can play higher. In ensembles
the oboes customarily play between the flutes and the clarinets, which exceed the oboe range both top and bottom.

W. A. MOZART: *Quartet in F for Oboe & Strings, K.370* (1781)
(1756–1791)   2. Adagio   3:45

> This quartet for oboe, violin, viola, and cello treats the oboe as a solo
> instrument accompanied by the three strings. The writing for oboe
> in this slow movement is fairly typical, unlike the preceding and fol-
> lowing fast movements which make extreme technical demands on
> the oboist.

G. P. TELEMANN: *Sonata in C minor for Oboe & Harpsichord*
(1681–1767)   5. Grave   1:00
                       6. Allegro cantabile   1:20

> These movements of Telemann's sonata—one slow and sustained,
> the other fast and sprightly—show the oboe in contrasting moods.

ENGLISH HORN is a misnomer if there ever was one. The instrument is
neither English nor a horn. The origin of the name is shrouded in mystery.
There are many theories but few facts. The English horn is an oversized
and lower-pitched oboe which emphasizes the "reedy" and plaintive qualities of that instrument. Except in its lowest register the English horn is difficult to distinguish from an oboe.

JEAN SIBELIUS: *The Swan of Tuonela* (1893)   6:50
(1865–1957)

> Tuonela, the land of death in Finnish mythology, is surrounded by
> a broad, black river upon which floats a swan. The quality of the
> English horn is admirably suited for this somber tone painting.

FIGURE 5. *Alto Saxophone, Tenor Saxophone, and Baritone Saxophone*

FIGURE 6. *Oboe and English Horn*

FIGURE 7. *Bassoon and Contrabassoon*

The BASSOON plays in the same pitch range as the cello, and they frequently are used together on the bass line in orchestral music. The bassoonist in an orchestra or band is much busier than is generally suspected, because his part is so often hidden in the background. When the bassoon is used prominently, it often is cast in the role of comedian because of the dry, raucous tone of which it is capable. It is equally at home in lyric melodies and is more flexible than its awkward size and shape would suggest.

BURRILL PHILLIPS: *Concert Piece for Bassoon & Strings* (1938)   3:40
(1907–   )

> This piece, one of a comparatively small number featuring the bassoon, provides an ideal introduction to the characteristics of the instrument. The piece is not entirely comic in nature, but it is not to be taken too seriously, either. The work is found on Columbia record ML–4629.

W. A. MOZART: *Concerto in B-flat for Bassoon, K.191* (1774)
(1756–1791)   2. Andante ma adagio   4:50

> Mozart wrote many concertos, probably more than any other great composer, so it is not surprising to find one for bassoon among them. This movement is essentially lyric, a style in which the bassoon is equally effective.

The CONTRABASSOON, with a range extending almost as low as a piano, supplies the very bottom notes to the woodwind section. Its lugubrious sound is rarely heard alone except for special effects. Its usual function is to play the bass line with the string basses and/or tuba and to double the bassoon part an octave lower. Listeners are seldom conscious of the contrabassoon, but it would be missed if it were not there.

MAURICE RAVEL: *Ma Mere l'Oye Suite (Mother Goose)* (1912)
(1875–1937)   4. Conversations of Beauty and the Beast   4:15

> This movement depicts the fairy tale *Beauty and the Beast* with the beast aptly portrayed by the contrabassoon, first heard about one minute after the beginning.

The TRUMPET is the highest and most brilliant of the brass instruments. Formerly restricted in all but their highest register to fanfare-like figures and inclined to overpower the modest forces of the other sections of the orchestra, the trumpets were reserved (with a few notable exceptions) for rhythmic figures, sustained tones, and climaxes. Mechanical improvements and orchestral resources more in balance with their power now enable

FIGURE 8. *Trumpet and Cornet*

trumpets to display the versatility of which they are capable and to utilize their full range of dynamics and pitches.

JOSEPH HAYDN: *Concerto in E-flat for Trumpet* (1796)
(1732–1809)   3. Spiritoso   4:45

> Haydn's *Trumpet Concerto* was written for a then newly invented keyed trumpet rather than for a modern valve trumpet, but the key mechanism allowed Haydn to write for the trumpet in the modern manner. This early trumpet masterpiece nowadays is played on the standard instrument and is learned by every serious trumpet student.

The CORNET is similar to the trumpet in size, shape, range, and sound. Its tone is less incisive due primarily to differences in the internal shape of its mouthpiece. Trumpets are the rule in orchestras and dance bands. Cornets are used, often in conjunction with trumpets, in concert and marching bands. Stravinsky includes a cornet in some of his best known works. The original version of *Petrouchka* (1911) has a solo for the cornet in Scene Three (the music for the ballerina's entrance and waltz). In the revised version (1947), this solo is given to a trumpet, demonstrating the interchangeability of the two instruments. Cornet is specified in the score of the *Soldier's Tale.*

IGOR STRAVINSKY: *Histoire du Soldat (Soldier's Tale)* (1918)
(1882–   )   Part 2. Royal March   2:45

> The cornet is used prominently and typically in this march. Do not confuse it with the trombone, clarinet, or bassoon which also have solo passages.

The FRENCH HORN, more often called simply the HORN, is a noble instrument with enough power to dominate an orchestra and enough control to blend with a delicate string passage. The horn has by far the widest range of the brass instruments, going almost as high as a trumpet and lower than a trombone. It is an important member of the brass section and an adjunct to the woodwind section, frequently serving as a link between the two. It is a magnificent solo instrument and an admirable accompanying instrument. Because of the horn's versatility, composers and arrangers are tempted to overwork it.

BENJAMIN BRITTEN: *Serenade for Tenor, Horn, & Strings, Op. 31* (1943)
(1913–   )   1. Prologue   1:20
                               5. Hymn   2:00

The *Prologue*, which returns as the *Epilogue*, is played without using the valves on the horn. The pitches thus produced are those of the natural overtone series and do not always correspond with conventional tunings. The extremes of the French horn range, from its highest note to its lowest, are heard in the course of the *Hymn*.

FIGURE 9. *French Horn*

RICHARD STRAUSS: *Concerto No. 1 in E-flat for Horn, Op. 11* (1884)
(1864–1949)   3. Rondo: Allegro   4:50

Richard Strauss' father was a horn player, so Richard had ample opportunity to hear the instrument. He obviously was well acquainted with its capabilities when he wrote this concerto at the age of twenty. The solo part was so difficult, however, his father declined to play the première.

The TUBA provides the foundation for the brass section and indeed for the whole orchestra. Its normal function is to reinforce the bass line in loud passages. In the standard orchestra and band literature the tuba practically never has a solo, or even an exposed part. This situation is dramatized in Kleinsinger's whimsical *Tubby the Tuba*. The work is intended for children, but adults are not immune to its charm. Besides, it is one of the very few works featuring the tuba and the only one, it appears, readily available on recordings.

FIGURE 10. *Tuba and Sousaphone*

FIGURE 11. *Trombone and Bass Trombone*

GEORGE KLEINSINGER: *Tubby the Tuba* (1945)   11:45
   (1914–   )

> The narrator describes the plight of *Tubby the Tuba*, and typical
> sounds of the tuba and several other instruments are illustrated
> before Tubby finds a melody he can play. Victor Jory is the narrator
> on Columbia record CL 671.

SOUSAPHONES are portable, bass, brass instruments named for John
Philip Sousa, the March King. Designed for ease of carrying, they take the
place of the tubas in marching bands and sometimes in concert bands. The
circular shape and forward-facing bell are familiar sights in football half-
time shows.

BARITONE horns are closely related to trombones in range and sound
but are shaped like a small tuba and have valves. EUPHONIUMS are similar
instruments. Baritones and euphoniums are band instruments exclusively.

TROMBONES and BASS TROMBONES are the only instruments with
slides. The two types of trombones can play the same music for the most
part, and in their middle registers their tones are indistinguishable. The
ordinary trombone plays with greater ease in the high register. The bass
trombone tone has a little more body, and the instrument is equipped
with an attachment activated by a valve which extends the range down four
tones.

PAUL HINDEMITH: *Sonata for Trombone* (1941)   10:15
   (1895–1963)

> This sonata is in one movement but four distinct sections, any one of
> which effectively demonstrates the tone quality and characteristics
> of the trombone.

L. VAN BEETHOVEN: *Three Equali for Four Trombones* (1812)
   (1770–1827)   1. Andante   2:40
                                  2. Poco adagio   2:10
                                  3. Poco sostenuto   1:15

> The sounds produced by the four trombones in the *Three Equali*
> (Renaissance record X 31) and those produced by the three trom-
> bones and one tuba in a symphony orchestra are very similar.

Instruments Played by Striking

Instruments played by striking are *percussion* instruments. There are
two types of percussion instruments—those producing definite pitches and
those producing indefinite pitches.

TABLE 2

PERCUSSION INSTRUMENTS

DEFINITE PITCH

Frequently used:	*Infrequently used:*
Timpani (Kettledrums)	Glockenspiel (Orchestra bells)
	Xylophone
	Tubular bells (Chimes)
	Vibraphone

INDEFINITE PITCH

Frequently used:	*Infrequently used:*
Snare drum (Side drum)	Tenor drum
Bass drum	Tambourine
Cymbals	Gong (Tam-tam)
Triangle	Castanets
	Wood block
	Temple blocks
	Claves
	Maracas
	Whip (Slap-stick)
	Ratchet
	Tom-tom
	etc.

The TIMPANI, also called KETTLEDRUMS (but not by musicians), are the most useful and used of the percussion instruments. They consist of a kettle-shaped, metal body over which a head is stretched. The heads formerly were made of calfskin, but in recent years plastic heads have been introduced. At least two timpani are used. The most common sizes are 25 inches and 28 inches in diameter. Large orchestras also have available a smaller one 23 inches in diameter and a larger one 30 inches in diameter. Several pitches can be played on each one. The range is determined by the size and the precise pitch by the tension on the head. The tension is adjusted by hand screws around the rim and by a pedal mechanism. Timpani are played by two felt-headed sticks, one held in either hand. Notes can be sustained by a rapid alternate striking by the sticks, called a *roll*. Timpani are capable of a wide dynamic range by varying the force with which they are struck and of some change of quality by varying the hardness of the stick heads and the location of the striking. A special effect possible only with pedal-equipped timpani is gliding from one pitch to another while the tone is sounding.

A GLOCKENSPIEL is a set of metal bars of different sizes each one of which produces a specific pitch when struck with a hard mallet. The pitch

FIGURE 12. *Percussion Instruments*

is very high, the quality clear and metallic. A portable version of the glocken-spiel with a lyre-shaped frame called a BELL-LYRA, is used in bands.

A XYLOPHONE is similar to a glockenspiel except that its bars are made of wood, it is larger, and its pitch is lower.

TUBULAR BELLS, also called CHIMES, are long, metal tubes open on one end and closed on the other. They are made in complete sets, but each tube is individually suspended on a rack. Bell parts often have but few pitches, and sometimes only the tubes actually required are hung on the rack. When struck with a wooden mallet on the corner of the closed end, the tubular bells produce a sound similar to that of real bells.

The DRUMS are round, wooden frames of various depths and diameters covered on both ends by skin or plastic heads. Tension on the heads is adjust-able within limits, but no precise pitches result. DRUMS are struck with assorted sticks and beaters. The SNARE DRUM is the smallest. Its name stems from the metal bands or *snares* stretched across the bottom head which create a rattling sound. When the snares are released, a snare drum sounds more like a tom-tom. SIDE DRUM is another name for snare drum. The BASS DRUM is the largest drum. The TENOR DRUM is a less frequently used, medium-sized drum. Similar medium-sized drums used in military and march-ing bands are sometimes given specialized names.

CYMBALS are large, plate-shaped instruments of finely wrought brass. They are played in two ways. Holding one in each hand, the player strikes them together in a *crash*, or one cymbal is *suspended* and struck with beaters.

A TRIANGLE is made from a metal rod bent into a triangular shape. It is struck with a smaller metal rod to produce a light, bell-like sound. A ring-

ing effect is produced by rapid strokes with the beater alternately hitting one
side of the triangle and then another near the corner.

The infrequently used percussion instruments are employed for special
and exotic effects. In addition to those listed in Table 2, any object which
emits a sound when struck can be used as a percussion instrument. Some
idea of the possibilities can be had from the instrumentation listed for the
first suggested listening example, *Ionization*.

EDGARD VARESE: *Ionization* (1931)   5:25
  (1885–1965)

> The score of this work calls for 13 performers and 35 different in-
> struments, not all strictly speaking percussion, including: crash
> cymbal, bass drum, tam-tams, gongs, side drum, triangle, wire
> brush (used as a striker), slap-stick, military drum, high and low
> siren, string drum, lion's roar, Chinese (temple) blocks, claves,
> snare drum, suspended cymbal, sleigh bells, tubular chimes (bells),
> castanets, celesta, tambourine, anvils, piano, and chains. Both
> snare and side drums are specified, also gongs and tam-tams,
> though the terms usually are synonymous.

BELA BARTOK: *Sonata for Two Pianos & Percussion* (1937)
  (1881–1945)   3. Allegro non troppo   6:45

> Bartok creates distinctive effects by imaginative use of conven-
> tional percussion instruments in this sonata. The instruments in
> order of their appearance are: pianos, xylophone, timpani, cymbal
> crash (very soft), triangle, side (snare) drum without snares, bass
> drum, side drum with snares, and suspended cymbal with soft-
> headed stick.

These are concentrated examples of percussion. In normal instrumental
ensembles the percussion element is used more sparingly owing to the limited
and highly specialized nature of the percussion sound.

Instruments Played by Plucking

Many string instruments such as guitars, ukuleles, banjos, and Auto-
harps are played by plucking, but the HARP is the only orchestral instrument
played exclusively in that manner. The harp strings, one for each note, are
strung in a straight line in an elaborately beautiful frame. The pitch of each
string can be changed with a system of pedals to produce raised and lowered
inflections of notes. Glissando, in which the fingers are drawn rapidly from
the low strings to the high and/or back playing all the intervening strings, is a
characteristic harp effect.

FIGURE 13. *Harp*

45

MAURICE RAVEL: *Introduction and Allegro* (1906)   10:35
   (1875–1937)
> This work for harp accompanied by 2 violins, viola, cello, flute, and
> clarinet includes brilliant virtuoso writing for the harp.

P. I. TCHAIKOVSKY: *Nutcracker Suite, Op. 71a* (1892)
   (1840–1893)   8. Waltz of the Flowers   6:25
> The introduction to this waltz contains one of the most famous harp
> passages.

Though the usual way of producing the tone on violins, violas, cellos,
and basses is by bowing, tones can also be produced on these instruments
by plucking the strings or *pizzicato*, as it is called. The string instruments
are played pizzicato exclusively in the following symphonic movement.

P. I. TCHAIKOVSKY: *Symphony No. 4 in F minor, Op. 36* (1878)
   (1840–1893)   3. Scherzo: Allegro   4:55
> The entire string section of the orchestra is heard playing pizzicato
> in the first part of this movement and again after the middle part
> played by the wind instruments.

Keyboard Instruments

The coupling of a keyboard with a sound-producing medium is of
ancient origin dating back to the Greeks, but the keyboard itself neither
vibrates nor directly causes vibration. It serves indirectly to activate the
sound-producing force and is used because it facilitates the striking, blowing,
or plucking which actually generates the sound.

A long evolutionary period was required to bring the keyboard to its
definitive form, and several predecessors of the modern instruments became obsolete in the process. Of the various prototypes, only three basic
keyboard instruments survive: the piano (more correctly the pianoforte),
the organ, and the celesta. To these perhaps should be added the harpsichord,
an instrument which flourished 1600–1800 and is now enjoying a revival,
and the electric and reed organs which are significantly different from conventional (pipe) organs.

Striking a piano key activates a felt hammer which in turn strikes a
string or strings to produce the sound. The celesta action is essentially the
same except that a hard hammer strikes a metal bar. Depressing a pipe organ
key opens a valve allowing air to blow through a tone-producing pipe. With
a reed organ or harmonium the air blows over a metal tongue which is set in
motion to produce the sound. Harpsichord keys are connected with a
mechanism which plucks the string in response to a downward motion of

the key. Of the keyboard instruments only electronic organs produce sounds in a way not found in other instruments.

The PIANO is used in more combinations and in more different ways than any other instrument. It is a stellar solo instrument; it is used to accompany solo voices and choruses, solo instruments and ensembles; it is combined with other instruments in sonatas and chamber music; it is included in symphony orchestras and dance bands; it serves as a teaching aid in public schools; it is found in homes, churches, club rooms, and bars. Because it is so fundamental to the study of music, all serious music students learn to play it.

The hammers in the piano mechanism fall back instantly after striking the strings, leaving them free to vibrate until arrested by dampers. Dampers drop on the strings stopping the vibration when the keys are released unless restrained by the action of a pedal. Depressing the right pedal lifts all of the dampers allowing the strings to vibrate after the keys are released. The left pedal reduces the amount of tone. Grand pianos have an extra pedal in the center which sustains the sound only of keys which are down at the time the pedal is applied.

Ordinary piano sounds are too well known to require illustration, but recent composers, Ravel among them, have evoked new effects from this familiar source.

MAURICE RAVEL: *Gaspard de la Nuit (Gaspard of the Night)* (1908)
(1875–1937)   3. Scarbo   8:45

> The inspiration for these "Poems for Piano" was Aloysius Bertrand's book of prose poems of the same title. The two preceding pieces of the set contain different but no less exciting new piano sounds.

The PIPE ORGAN is the most imposing of instruments. The largest models have four keyboards or *manuals*, each similar in appearance to that of a piano. They have, in addition, a pedalboard with a size and location which permits playing with the toes and heels. All the keys are connected mechanically, pneumatically, or electrically to thousands of pipes of various shapes and materials ranging in size from smaller than a pencil to larger than a stovepipe. Each type has a distinctive sound. The player selects the desired tone quality and to an extent the pitch by means of *stops* located above the keyboards. Air under pressure formerly coming from manually operated bellows but now usually from electric blowers is supplied to all the pipes. Depressing a key activates a valve allowing air to flow into the pipes selected by the stops and causing the pipe to sound its note. The organ has a tremendous range both in volume and pitch.

Large organs are not mass produced, and hardly any two are identical. Smaller organs are more inclined toward standardization, having only two manuals and lesser numbers of pipes and stops, but they are completely adequate to play most of the organ literature. For those acquainted with the organ only in the restrained atmosphere of a religious service, the resources of the full organ may come as a revelation.

J. S. BACH: *Toccata and Fugue in D minor, S. 565* (1717)   9:15
(1685–1750)

> Bach was equally at home playing and writing for the organ. This work is equally familiar in the original organ version and in the transcription for orchestra.

Electronic organs attempt with varying degrees of success to simulate the sounds of pipe organs. Electrical circuits and speakers replace blowers and pipes. They do not match the magnitude and scope of large pipe organs, but they have the advantage of economy and compactness.

A reed organ is actually a sort of large, keyed harmonica. Air supplied by a foot-operated bellows or electric fan activates metal-tongued reeds when the keys are depressed. The keyboard is like that of a piano but shorter. *Harmonium* is another name for small reed organs.

The CELESTA is most easily described as a keyboard glockenspiel. A cabinet supports a small piano-like keyboard and encloses a series of metal bars which sound when struck by hammers connected to the keys. Because of the keyboard, greater dexterity is possible and multiple notes are easier on a celesta than on a glockenspiel. The celesta is a regular member of symphony orchestras where it is grouped with the percussion instruments.

P. I. TCHAIKOVSKY: *Nutcracker Suite, Op. 71a* (1892)
(1840–1893)   4. Dance of the Sugarplum Fairy   1:45

> This is the first orchestral composition to include the celesta. The tinkling of the celesta solo is placed in sharp relief by the velvety low tones of the bass clarinet.

The HARPSICHORD, supplanted by the piano, all but disappeared from the musical scene though much of the keyboard music written prior to 1800 was intended for it. Musicologists interested in the authentic reproduction of early music sparked a move to take harpsichords out of museums and into recording studios and concert halls. This movement led not only to a re-evaluation of the music but of the instrument itself. Contemporary composers have been stimulated to write for harpsichord, and it has even made a tentative debut in popular music.

In appearance the harpsichord is like a small, angular, grand piano. The keyboard is shorter, and traditionally the black and white color of the keys is reversed in relation to the piano. The harpsichord tone is produced by an intricate mechanism which plucks a string when a key is struck. Unlike a piano, hitting a key harder or softer does not influence the tone. This is done by modifying the bite of the plucking device with a pedal. The old instruments are very fragile, but modern ones are relatively sturdy and durable. In some, nylon is used in place of leather or crow quills for the plectra, and steel frames are used in place of wood.

DOMENICO SCARLATTI: *Sonata in A minor for Harpsichord, L.429*[4]   3.30
  (1685–1757)

> Scarlatti sonatas, unlike those of later periods, are in one concise movement. This one is typical of the more than 500 sonatas Scarlatti composed for harpsichord.

MANUEL DE FALLA: *Concerto for Harpsichord* (1926)
  (1876–1946)   1. Allegro   3:10

> Though this work is called a concerto, it requires only five players (violin, oboe, flute, clarinet, and cello) other than the harpsichord soloist. It utilizes the antique instrument in a thoroughly contemporary idiom.

Each of the foregoing suggested listening examples features the specified voice or instrument with normal background in a complete work or movement. The suggested listening, therefore, introduces not only the various voices and instruments but some of the masterpieces of music created for them. If a more concise introduction to the instruments is desired, the following recordings and the one film are designed expressly for that purpose.[5]

BENJAMIN BRITTEN: *Young Person's Guide to the Orchestra, Op. 34* (1946)
  (1913–   )   (Variations and Fugue on a Theme of Purcell)   16:40

THE COMPLETE ORCHESTRA, Music Education Record Corporation,
  Box 445, Englewood, New Jersey.

INSTRUMENTS OF THE ORCHESTRA, Capital HBZ–21002

INSTRUMENTS OF THE ORCHESTRA, RCA Victor LE–6000/LES–6000

INSTRUMENTS OF THE ORCHESTRA, Vanguard VRS–1017/8

---

[4] Scarlatti harpsichord works are identified by numbers from the complete edition of Allesandro Longo.

[5] Full-color wall charts of the instruments of the orchestra are available from J. W. Pepper & Son, Inc., 231 North Third Street, Philadelphia, Pennsylvania 19106.

TABLE 3

RANGES OF VOICES AND INSTRUMENTS

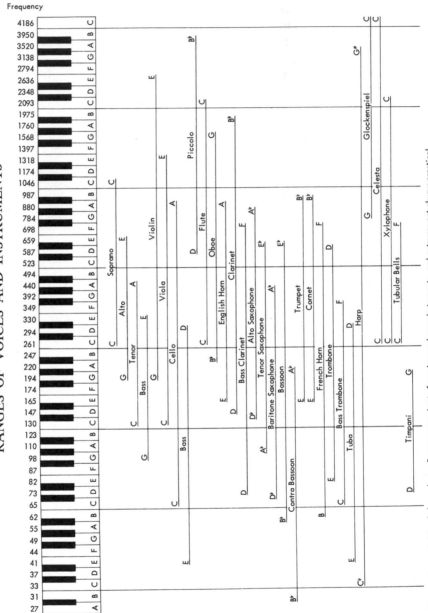

Frequencies rounded to whole numbers. Ranges approximate for voices and some instruments, and extremes not always practical.

INSTRUMENTS OF THE ORCHESTRA, British Ministry of Education,
  film version of Benjamin Britten's *Young Person's Guide to the
  Orchestra.*

THE ORCHESTRA AND ITS INSTRUMENTS, Folkways 3602

SPOTLIGHT ON BRASS, Vox DL–300

SPOTLIGHT ON KEYBOARD, Vox DL–362

SPOTLIGHT ON PERCUSSION, Vox DL–180

SPOTLIGHT ON STRINGS, Vox DL–320

SPOTLIGHT ON WINDS, Vox DL–312

Additional experience in recognizing instruments, individually and in
various combinations, is provided by the examples suggested for listening in
the following chapter on mediums.

mediums

The voices and instruments surveyed in the previous chapter make music in many combinations. There are no restrictions on the types or numbers used together, and at one time or another music probably has been written for almost every conceivable group. Certain combinations by virtue of special qualifications are most prevalent. These are the common mediums of music.

Solo

Solo, literally, means alone. In music it is used both in its literal sense and in the sense of a piece or passage for one predominant instrument or voice with accompaniment. Unaccompanied solos occasionally are written for other instruments, but the only one which regularly appears by itself is the piano. The piano is adaptable to old music and new, to brief character pieces and extended major works. A *piano sonata* is a three- or four-movement work for piano alone. Because of the wealth of literature, the abundance of competent performers, and the availability of instruments, the piano undoubtedly is heard more than any other instrument or combination of instruments.

Sergei Rachmaninoff: *Fantasy Pieces, Op. 3* (1892)
(1873–1943)   2. Prelude in C-sharp minor   4:00
    Piano solo: piano alone

L. van Beethoven. *Piano Sonata in F Minor, Op. 2 No. 1* (1795)
(1770–1827)   1. Allegro   4:25
                                     2. Adagio   4:35

      3. Menuetto: Allegretto   3:00
      4. Prestissimo   4:10

Piano sonata: piano alone
This is the first of Beethoven's 32 sonatas for piano. Though composed early in his career, it is a classic example of the form.

Used in the sense of a piece for an instrument or voice with accompaniment, solo usually is modified by the name of the instrument or voice performing the solo part. It is generally safe to assume that the accompaniment unless otherwise indicated is played by the piano. Thus, a *vocal solo* or a *soprano solo* is a song for voice and piano; a *violin solo* is a piece for violin and piano, and so on.

Independent songs for solo voice and piano are called *art songs* or *lieder* (from the German word for songs). Composers using German texts produced a vast treasury of such songs during the 19th century. Franz Schubert (1797–1828) is credited with originating the form, Robert Schumann (1810–1856), Johannes Brahms (1833–1897), and Richard Strauss (1864–1949) contributed substantially to it. The foregoing composed extensively for other mediums, but the reputations of two composers, Robert Franz and Hugo Wolf are founded entirely upon their productions of lieder.

ROBERT FRANZ: *Widmung (Dedication), Op. 14 No. 1* (1850)   1:30
  (1815–1892)

HUGO WOLF: *Mörike Lieder* (1888)
  (1860–1903) 19. Verborgenheit (Secrecy)   2:15
    Art songs or lieder: voice and piano (*Widmung* in Westminster album WLE–104)

Instrumental solos with piano accompaniment are a common medium of musical expression. The solo literature is especially plentiful for instruments like the violin which are heard in solo recitals. Many concert artists add to their laurels by composing and arranging music for their own instrument. Sarasate and Kreisler were known primarily as violinists during their lifetimes, but their fame is perpetuated by their compositions.

PABLO DE SARASATE: *Introduction and Tarantella, Op. 43*   4:40
  (1844–1908)

FRITZ KREISLER: *Caprice Viennois (Viennese Caprice)*   3:40
  (1875–1962)
    Violin solos: violin and piano

Instrumental solos accompanied by orchestra most often fall in the concerto category. In a *piano concerto* the piano is elevated to the solo role, and the accompaniment is provided by the orchestra. The amount of orchestral participation in the presentation and working out of thematic ideas varies considerably from one concerto to another. The primary function of the orchestra in some is to provide background for the solo. Others are virtually symphonies with one predominant instrument. The following example is between these extremes.

EDVARD GRIEG: *Piano Concerto in A minor, Op. 16* (1868)
   (1843–1907)   1. Allegro molto moderato   12:20
      Piano concerto: solo piano and orchestra

Chamber Music

Chamber music is the general designation for instrumental ensemble music performed with one player on a part. Since there is only one player for each part in the music, the number of players is never large. A word indicating the number of players or parts (e.g., *duo* or *duet, trio, quartet, quintet, sextet, septet, octet,* or *nonet*) is often included in the title of chamber works. Music for more than nine players usually does not qualify as chamber music, and most chamber music is for groups of two to five players. Musical interest is distributed, more or less equally, between the parts. There is no soloist or leader, and opportunities for displaying individual virtuosity are purely incidental.

Duos or *duets* for two melody instruments are abundant in the teaching literature, but only a few are programmed. The following example is one of the exceptions. It is coupled on the current recording (Decca 8510) with the Mozart *Duo* for the same instruments.

BOHUSLAV MARTINU: *Three Madrigals for Violin & Viola* (1947)
   (1890–1959)   1. Poco allegro   3:50
      Duo: violin and viola

Sonatas for two instruments, usually a melody instrument and piano, conform to the basic definition given for chamber music, but they are not always included in the classification. This is because the solo-accompaniment relationship between the two instruments in some sonatas is inconsistent with the ideals of chamber music. Sonatas in which the primary function of the piano is to provide an accompaniment for the melody instrument perhaps belong in the solo category, but many are perfectly valid examples of chamber music.

Though sonatas have been composed for piano in combination with virtually every instrument, including another piano, those for violin and piano are most numerous. Both instruments may be named in identifying sonatas, or the piano may be taken for granted in sonatas as it is in solos. The chamber music classification of the following example and similar sonatas is substantiated by the absence of superficial technical display and by the participation of both instruments in the presentation of the musical ideas.

JOHANNES BRAHMS: *Violin Sonata No. 3 in D minor, Op. 108* (1888)
(1833–1897)   3. Un poco presto e con sentimento   3:00
              4. Presto agitato   5:40
    Violin sonata: violin and piano

A *trio* may comprise any three instruments, but the only combinations standardized to any degree are the *string trio*, consisting of violin, viola, and cello, and the *piano trio*, consisting of violin, cello, and piano. The piano trio is the only combination of three instruments for which a large and significant body of literature exists.

FELIX MENDELSSOHN: *Piano Trio No. 1 in D minor, Op. 49* (1839)
(1809–1847)   1. Molto allegro ed agitato   7:45
    Piano trio: violin, cello, and piano

The dearth of music for three instruments contrasts with the abundance of music for four. Any combination of four instruments may be used as a *quartet*, but the most usual combination consists of two violins, viola, and cello, the instrumentation of a *string quartet*.

The string quartet is an ideal medium, and practically every composer since Haydn (1732–1809) has written for it. This combination of instruments provides the composer a perfectly balanced, homogeneous medium with a wide range of pitches and dynamic levels. The sounds of a string quartet can be sonorous one moment and ethereal the next. If power and brilliance are limited, clarity and intimacy compensate. It has been said facetiously that "A string quartet is the highest form of art, but the lowest form of entertainment." Devotees of chamber music endorse just the first half of that statement, and only the uninitiated accept it *in toto*. The following example is one of the many masterpieces in the string quartet literature.

L. VAN BEETHOVEN: *String Quartet No. 16 in F, Op. 135* (1826)
   (1770–1827)   1. Allegretto   6:30
                                  2. Vivace   3:05
     String quartet: 2 violins, viola, and cello
     Beethoven wrote string quartets in each period of his creative life
     and devoted his last years to this form. This quartet is his final opus.

The plentiful literature for string quartet is balanced by a bounteous array of stellar performers. Renowned string quartets tour and record regularly and, by playing as a unit through many seasons, achieve perfection as ensembles. University faculty, student, and amateur string quartets, in addition, are numerous and often excellent. The literature and the performing groups are sources of reciprocal stimulation. String quartets are organized to perform the existing literature, and the active performing groups are a constant incentive for composers to write still more for them.

The instrumentation of the string quartet is accepted as the norm, and deviations from this combination are reflected in the designations for works and the groups required to play them. For example, a *piano quartet* consists of a violin, viola, cello, and piano, not four pianos as the name might imply. An *oboe quartet* consists of oboe, violin, viola, and cello. The name in each case is derived from the instrument which replaces one of the violins in the string quartet instrumentation. The piano quartet, particularly, is a standard and frequently heard ensemble. Several quartet combinations of three string instruments and one wind have been used effectively, but no combination of four instruments challenges the supremacy of the string quartet as a medium of musical expression.

Quartets of woodwind and brass instruments are also possible, though less common than those involving string instruments. The usual make-up of a *woodwind quartet* is flute, oboe, clarinet, and bassoon. There are several likely combinations of four brass instruments. A *brass quartet* can consist of two trumpets and two trombones; two trumpets, horn, and trombone; trumpet, horn, trombone, and tuba, or any group of four brass instruments, including those with cornets and baritones. Many brass quartet compositions can be played by more than one combination of instruments. Woodwind and brass quartets are not the perfect chamber music mediums that string quartets are. The tone quality of the various woodwind instruments is lacking in homogeneity, and the brass instruments by nature are less suited to the performance of intimate music.

A *quintet* often consists of a string quartet augmented by one additional instrument, in which case it is identified by the name of the added instrument. A *viola quintet* is a string quartet with an extra viola. A *cello quintet* is a string quartet with an extra cello, and a *clarinet quintet* is a string quartet plus clarinet. The most popular addition to the basic instrumentation of the string quartet is the piano, resulting in the *piano quintet*.

ROBERT SCHUMANN: *Piano Quintet in E-flat, Op. 44* (1842)
(1810–1856)   1. Allegro brillante   9:00
    Piano quintet: 2 violins, viola, cello, and piano

Woodwind quintet is a curious but usual way of referring to a group of four woodwind instruments and one brass. In the interest of accuracy the name is sometimes shortened to *wind quintet*. Both names apply to a group consisting of flute, oboe, clarinet, bassoon, and horn. This combination lacks the warmth of a string quintet and the power of a piano quintet, but it has greater diversity of tone color than either. Wind quintet music tends to be witty and clever rather than emotional or profound. Contemporary composers have found the medium attractive, and many have composed effectively for it.

JACQUES IBERT: *Trois Pièces Brèves (Three Short Pieces)* (1930)
(1890–1962)   1. Allegro   2:25
               2. Andante   1:20
               3. Assez lent—Allegro scherzando   3:00
    Woodwind quintet: flute, oboe, clarinet, horn, and bassoon

Chamber music has been written for groups of six (sextet), seven (septet), eight (octet), and nine (nonet) players. There is no standard instrumentation beyond the quintet, and the literature is not extensive. Isolated chamber works exist for larger ensembles, but the tendency with larger groups is to depart from the chamber music concept and to use more than one player on a part.

Vocal music is ordinarily excluded, by definition and custom, from the chamber music category. However, *madrigals* are a type of vocal ensemble music intended for performance (but not always performed) with one on a part, which qualifies them for consideration in this context. Madrigals of the most prevalent type are secular works for four to six voices, with five most usual. Four-part madrigals are for soprano, alto, tenor, and bass. Five-part madrigals usually call for an additional soprano; six-part madrigals for these five and another tenor. Madrigal writing flourished in Italy and England during the 16th and 17th centuries, and the name has been revived by contemporary composers.

THOMAS MORLEY: *Sing We and Chant It* (1595)   1:40
   (1557–1602)

AVERY CLAFLIN: *Lament for April 15* (1950)   5:50
   (1898–   )
      Madrigals: 2 sopranos, alto, tenor, and bass
      The text of the Claflin madrigal is taken from the U.S. Income
      Tax Form 1040, hence the intriguing title.

The performances of jazz combos are chamber music of a sort, startling as the idea may seem to purists. The small combos improvise intimate jazz with one player on a part. Emphasis is on group performance, but each member has opportunities to be in the spotlight. Classic chamber music designations—trio, quartet, quintet, and sextet—are common. The instrumentation in a combo is completely flexible, but the elements of melody, harmony, and rhythm must be represented. A recording of any small combo or Dixieland group will serve to illustrate this new style of chamber music.

Choirs

A *choir* is a group devoted to the singing of sacred music. A *choir* is also a group of instruments belonging to the same family. It is used here in both senses, though an instrumental choir within an orchestra or a band is usually called a *section*.

Vocal choirs have been an important adjunct to worship since the time men learned to sing together, and the magnificent sound of numerous voices did not go unnoticed by composers of secular music. Composers of both sacred and secular music have written copiously for voices since the beginning of the Renaissance. The enormous quantity of music for voices is in sharp contrast to the relatively meager amount for individual instrumental choirs. Choral music is normally written for soprano, alto, tenor, and bass voices. Each of these can be divided when the music requires more than four parts. Technically, a choir sings sacred music and a chorus secular music, but the distinction is not always observed. Church music was formerly for unaccompanied voices, and *a cappella* (meaning "for the chapel") is now a general designation for unaccompanied vocal music and the groups that perform it.

JOSQUIN DES PREZ: *Ave Maria*   5:45
  (1450–1521)

RANDALL THOMPSON: *Alleluia* (1940)   4:15
  (1899–)
    A cappella choir: sopranos, altos, tenors, and basses

Of the instrumental choirs, the string choir is the most versatile. It becomes the string section in an orchestra and a string orchestra when it performs independently. It includes all of the bowed instruments—several of each. Music for strings is normally written in five parts, two for violins and one each for violas, cellos, and basses. The cellos and basses at times play the same part, reducing the number to four. Oftentimes one or more of the five is divided to accommodate additional melodic lines or to provide fuller harmonies. Though the instrumentation of a string orchestra adds only basses to that of a string quartet, the larger number of players and the possibility of dividing the parts affects the style of writing and noticeably alters the tone quality. Tchaikovsky's *Serenade* would not be mistaken for a string quartet nor would the composer have written precisely the same way for the smaller ensemble.

P. I. TCHAIKOVSKY: *Serenade in C, Op. 48* (1880)
  (1840–1893)   2. Waltz   3:40
    String orchestra: 1st violins, 2nd violins, violas, cellos, and basses

Many passages in the symphonic literature are assigned exclusively to the woodwind section, but the woodwind choir is rarely, if ever, used independently. The Strauss *Serenade* will serve to illustrate the sound of the woodwind choir, though its score includes, in addition to a full complement of woodwinds, four horns.

RICHARD STRAUSS: *Serenade in E-flat, Op. 7* (1881)   9:10
  (1864–1949)
    Thirteen winds: 2 flutes, 2 oboes, 2 clarinets, 2 bassoons, contra-bassoon, and 4 horns

The brass section of an orchestra consists of trumpets, horns, trombones, and tuba. All of these instruments are heard in the following work, but the numbers are not the same as would be found in an orchestra.

NICOLAI BEREZOWSKY: *Brass Suite, Op. 24* (1939)
(1900–1953)   1. Fanfare & Gallop   1:45
                     2. Lullaby   3:00
                     3. Valse   1:50
                     4. Rondo   1:50

Brass choir: 2 trumpets, 2 horns, 2 trombones, and tuba

The remaining section of the orchestra is the percussion section. It is not customary to refer to it as a choir, perhaps because the number of players is small or perhaps because so few of its instruments produce definite pitches. At one time it might have been because percussion instruments were only heard in orchestras and bands, but this is no longer the case. Percussion ensembles are springing up all over the country (in other countries too, no doubt), and music is being composed for them to play. The percussion instruments seem to have a special appeal for contemporary composers.

CARLOS CHAVEZ: *Toccata for Percussion Instruments* (1942)
(1899–   )   1. Allegro, sempre giusto   4:35
                     2. Largo   3:40
                     3. Allegro un poco marciale   3:10

Percussion ensemble: large and small Indian drums, side (snare) drums, tenor drums, bass drum, timpani, large and small gongs, glockenspiel, xylophone, suspended cymbals, chimes, claves, and maraca—6 players

Band

Woodwind, brass, and percussion sections are combined in a band. The instrumentation in bands is not uniform. They are student groups predominantly, and their make-up is influenced in some cases and determined in others by the availability of players and instruments. Bands vary in size from fewer than 28 members, the normal complement of a military band, to well over one hundred. There is no "typical" band, but the Eastman Wind Ensemble, widely known for its recordings, gives some idea of the usual instrumentation and proportions.

FIGURE 14. *Eastman Symphonic Wind Ensemble, Frederick Fennell Conductor*

EASTMAN WIND ENSEMBLE INSTRUMENTATION

Woodwind

Piccolo	E-flat clarinet
Flutes (2)	Clarinets (8)
(Alto flute)	Alto clarinet
Oboes (2)	Bass clarinet
English horn	Alto saxophones (2)
Bassoons (2)	Tenor saxophone
Contrabassoon	Baritone saxophone

Brass

Cornets (3)
Trumpets (2)
French horns (4)
Euphoniums (baritones) (2)
Trombones (3)
Tubas (2)
—String bass (not a brass instrument, but used in conjunction
with the tubas)

Percussion

5 players (available for any percussion required by the score;
normally includes timpani, snare or tenor drum, and bass
drum)

The alto flute is available only if the piccolo player or one of the flute players shifts to that instrument. Other players also double providing flexibility in the instrumentation. Harp, piano, organ, harpsichord, solo string instruments, and chorus are added as required for special works.

In marching bands instruments like oboes, bassoons, and tubas that are ineffective outside or are difficult to carry are eliminated, and the brass, saxophone, and drum forces are augmented. The participation of marching bands in parades and football half-time shows has won them an exalted position in the realm of entertainment. Concert bands in recent years have been recognized by composers and audiences as a significant, new medium deserving their serious attention.

VINCENT PERSICHETTI: *Divertimento for Band, Op. 42* (1950)

(1915–)	1. Prologue	1:10
	2. Song	2:10
	3. Dance	1:00
	4. Burlesque	1:50
	5. Soliloquy	2:30
	6. March	1:40

Dance Band

The larger dance bands have three distinct sections.

Reed: saxophones, sometimes clarinets
Brass: trumpets and trombones
Rhythm: piano, string bass, drums, sometimes guitar

Striving for an individual style, a name band plays special arrangements exclusively, making a unique instrumentation both feasible and desirable. This concept is the exact opposite of that prevailing in symphonic literature. Symphonic composers do their own orchestration, and every orchestra plays the same version.

Reed sections have a minimum of four saxophones—2 altos, tenor, and baritone—often more. Most saxophone players also play clarinet, so the arranger has at his disposal four or more players to divide between saxophones and clarinets as he wishes. The distribution is not necessarily the same for all selections.

Brass sections vary from three trumpets and two or three trombones to as many as five of each, with the numbers approximately equal. The lowest trombone part is usually written for bass trombone.

The rhythm section provides the steady, underlying beat that renders the intricate rhythms of the other sections meaningful and makes the music danceable. Rhythm players, if they use music, read from parts containing chord symbols rather than complete notation, and they improvise on the harmonic framework indicated by the symbols. The drummer is surrounded by an impressive assortment of percussion instruments, known collectively as *traps*, which make him virtually a one-man band. The bass drum and a cymbal device are played with the feet, leaving both hands free for the snare drum and other instruments.

A dance band constituted along these lines is capable of tremendous volume, and arrangers capitalize on this feature. Maximum sound is produced by having each player on a different note and each chord complete in each section. This style of writing and this type of band were in vogue during the *swing* era of the thirties and forties. The legendary figures of that generation—Glen Miller, Benny Goodman, the Dorsey brothers, Artie Shaw, and Harry James, to name a few—are still heard on recordings. The "big band" sound has been revived by the "stage bands" currently popular in high schools and colleges.

Symphonic jazz arrangements sometimes include strings and other instruments borrowed from the orchestra, but this movement has not become widespread. Paul Whiteman, Duke Ellington, and Stan Kenton have evoked favorable, even enthusiastic, responses with innovations which combined symphonic and jazz elements, but their pioneering efforts have not led to enduring traditions.

Orchestra

An orchestra consists of four sections: woodwind, brass, percussion, and string. The string section, which distinguishes orchestras from bands, is always the largest. The instrumentation of symphony orchestras, having evolved gradually over an extended period, tends to be relatively stable. Therefore, the approximate distribution of instruments for orchestras of various sizes can be tabulated. The major professional orchestras have resources beyond those listed on the table, and extras are available for special requirements.

The seating plan of orchestras varies. The conductor stands front and center on the stage with the orchestra spread in a fan shape around his cen-

TABLE 4

DISTRIBUTION OF INSTRUMENTS IN THE ORCHESTRA

	Small Orchestra	Full Orchestra	Large Orchestra
WOODWIND			
Piccolo			1
Flute	1	2	2-3
Oboe	1	2	2-3
English horn			1
Clarinet	1	2	2-4
Bass clarinet			1
Bassoon	1	2	2-3
Contra bassoon			1
Total	4	8	12-17
BRASS			
French horn	2	4	4-8
Trumpet	1-2	2-3	3-5
Trombone	(1)	3	3-4
Tuba		1	1
Total	3-5	10-11	11-18
PERCUSSION	1-2	3	4
HARP AND PIANO		1	2-3
STRING			
1st Violin	4-8	8-12	14-18
2nd Violin	4-6	6-10	10-16
Viola	2-4	4-8	8-12
Cello	2-4	4-8	8-12
Bass	1-3	4-6	8-10
Total	13-25	26-44	48-68
Grand total	21-36	48-67	77-110

tral position. First violins are always on his left. The concertmaster, who leads the section and functions somewhat as an assistant conductor, is at the head of the first violins on the outside. The second violins may be next to the first violins, or they may be at the front of the stage opposite the first violins. Prevailing practice is to keep all of the violins together and to place the violas and the cellos on the conductor's right. The cellos may be on the outside and the violas on the inside, or vice versa. The string basses are at the side of the stage behind the cellos. The woodwinds are in front of the conductor. The French horns are usually between the woodwinds and the rest of the brass instruments. The trumpets, trombones, and tuba form a semicircle with the percussions section at the rear of the stage. Figure 15 shows the seating plan of the Philadelphia Orchestra.

FIGURE 15. *Seating Plan, Philadelphia Orchestra, Eugene Ormandy Music Director*

FIGURE 16. *New York Philharmonic with Leonard Bernstein in Philharmonic Hall*

FIGURE 17. *New York Philharmonic with Leonard Bernstein in Philharmonic Hall*

FIGURE 18. *New York Philharmonic with Leonard Bernstein in Philharmonic Hall*

Orchestral works composed before the middle of the 19th century typically are scored for pairs of woodwinds, a few brass instruments, timpani, and a modest body of strings. The late 19th and early 20th centuries saw the expansion of the orchestra to the dimensions of the large orchestra shown in Table 4 and the creation of works utilizing its full resources. Isolated works were written for still larger, gigantic orchestras. Composers are writing now for orchestras of all sizes, but practical considerations inhibit the use of extras beyond the standard large orchestra. The expansion which occurred during the last century and the first part of this one seems to have run its course.

The three examples suggested for listening are scored for representative small, full, and large orchestras. The Beethoven and Barber works are typical of their times and composers, but the selection by Wagner is unusually restrained and reflective for him and his age.

RICHARD WAGNER: *Siegfried Idyll* (1870)   17:35
    (1813–1883)

      Small orchestra: flute, oboe, 2 clarinets, bassoon, 2 horns, trumpet, and strings (usually a small section, but playable with one of each)

L. VAN BEETHOVEN: *Leonore Overture No. 3, Op. 72a* (1806)   12:10
(1770–1827)

> Full orchestra: 2 flutes, 2 oboes, 2 clarinets, 2 bassoons, 4 horns, 2 trumpets, 3 trombones, timpani, and strings
> Beethoven composed four overtures for his only opera, known first as *Leonore* but subsequently as *Fidelio*. The exact purpose and chronology of the overtures have been the subject of much speculation. This one is a revision of the one written for the first performance of the opera in 1805.

SAMUEL BARBER: *Symphony No. 1 in One Movement, Op. 9* (1936) 18:30
(1910–   )

> Large orchestra: 2 flutes, piccolo, 2 oboes, English horn, 2 clarinets, bass clarinet, 2 bassoons, contrabassoon, 4 horns, 3 trumpets, 3 trombones, tuba, timpani, percussion, harp, and strings (Page of orchestral score showing all instruments except harp, p. 301)

While the instrumentation of the Barber symphony is the largest that can be regarded as standard, much larger orchestras are called for on occasion. Stravinsky's ballet *The Rite of Spring* (see Chapter 5) is scored for 3 flutes, piccolo, alto flute, 4 oboes, English horn, 4 clarinets, bass clarinet, 4 bassoons, contrabassoon, 8 horns, 5 trumpets, 3 trombones, 2 tubas, timpani (2 players), percussion, and strings. Schoenberg originally scored his *Five Pieces for Orchestra, Op. 16* for woodwinds in 4's and 6 horns, but his subsequent revision, significantly, is for a standard, large orchestra. Additions to the woodwind and brass sections necessitate augmentation of the string section in proportion for balance. The added cost and difficulty of performing works for extraordinarily large orchestras restricts performances, a fact which composers must ponder before embarking on such projects.

Combined Groups

The orchestra is combined with voices in operas, oratorios, and cantatas. Some masses are for chorus and orchestra, and a few symphonies include voices. The combination of instruments and voices adds the vocal qualities and the capability of expressing a text to the already luxuriant resources of the orchestra. Together, the choral and orchestral forces afford the composer an unlimited range of power and nuances and the listener an unparalleled auditory experience. The full potential of this medium is exploited in *Belshazzar's Feast*. The text is Biblical, the music profane.

WILLIAM WALTON: *Belshazzar's Feast* (1931)   34:40
(1902–   )

> Chorus and orchestra with baritone solo

Hector Berlioz was an extremist in an age of extremes, so it is not surprising that one of his compositions is of Gargantuan proportions. His *Requiem* is scored for an enormous orchestra, a chorus to match, a section of timpani, and 4 brass choirs. To hear a live performance of this work is a memorable experience. Only a fraction of its magnitude can be captured on a recording, but its overpowering splendor is still apparent.

HECTOR BERLIOZ: *Requiem (Grande Messe des Morts), Op. 5* (1837)
   (1803–1869)   2. Dies irae   12:30
     Chorus, orchestra, and 4 brass choirs
     The 4 brass choirs enter in the *Tuba mirum* section, about 6 minutes after the beginning of the *Dies irae.*

the elements
of music

Individual sounds of varying pitch, loudness, color, and duration are combined simultaneously and in series to form the elements of music. The elements are not isolated in ordinary listening, but considering them separately facilitates study.

Rhythm and Meter

The most primitive element of music is *rhythm*. A dictionary defines rhythm as measured motion, the regular rise and fall of sounds, a symmetrical and regularly recurrent grouping of tones according to accent and time value. *Meter* is defined as systematically arranged and measured rhythm, rhythmical structure as concerned with the division into measures consisting of a uniform number of beats or time units. Rhythm and meter are slightly different but closely related aspects of the same element. In musical parlance, meter refers to the basic, underlying pulse—the fixed pattern of strong and weak beats to which one responds physically in marching, dancing, or in tapping the toe. Rhythm, properly, means the organized interplay of varied note values, including durations both longer and shorter than the beat. In practice, no such precision of usage is observed. The terms rhythm and meter are sometimes used interchangeably, and rhythm commonly is used to denote all aspects of duration, stress, grouping, and time value. No attempt to refine current terminology is made here.

Rhythm, unlike the other elements of music, can exist independently. Any sound, including noise, can establish rhythm. It is present in speech. Motion can be rhythmic, but rhythm usually implies organized sound. The sound of heels clicking on the pavement as a person walks creates a rhythmic pattern. The steps measure identical units of time, and these units are grouped in pairs by the alternation of left and right. The measured motion of walking has a direct counterpart in the rhythm of a march.

JOHN PHILIP SOUSA: *Sempre Fidelis* (1888)   3:30
 (1854–1932)

> This is one of Sousa's many stirring marches. Observe how easy it is to feel the pulse of this piece, as it is in all true marches. Tap your toe or wave your hand in time with the music as this or some similar march is played.

The pulse of music is called the *beat*. With certain types of music, marches among them, responding physically to the beat is almost a reflex action. When the beat is more obscure, tapping or clapping with it focuses attention on the rhythm and aids in sensing the beat.

Some instruments play with the beat, some faster than the beat, and some slower than the beat. In other words, music is made up of notes longer, shorter, and with the same duration as the beat. This does not disturb the perception of the beat or the regular pattern of the underlying rhythm. Quicker notes are heard in groups comprising beats, and slower notes are heard as combinations of beats. The drums and certain lower pitched instruments usually mark the beat in marches.

Musicians sometimes count with the beats as a teaching device. The counting for a march goes *ONE-two, ONE-two*. The beats in a march are alternately accented and unaccented. *ONE* coincides with the accented beats and *two* with the unaccented beats. The complete pattern, an accented beat plus an unaccented beat, constitutes a *measure* of music. In the interest of accuracy, it should be stated that marches also are written with a four-beat pattern, *ONE-two-three-four*. It simplifies the discussion to consider all march rhythms as two-beat patterns for the moment.

Listen to other traditional marches and compare their rhythm with that of some concert marches for band such as Barber's *Commando March* and Hanson's *March Carillon*. The beat in concert marches is not always as clear and regular as it is in street and military marches. It is common practice to adapt march and dance rhythms for use in concert music. Essential characteristics are preserved, but the music is not necessarily suitable for marching or dancing.

SAMUEL BARBER: *Commando March* (1943)   3:05
 (1910–   )

HOWARD HANSON: *March Carillon, Op. 19 No. 2* (1920)   2:00
(1896–   )

Stylized march rhythms also appear in works for orchestra and piano.

SERGE PROKOFIEV: *Opera, Love for Three Oranges* (1921)
(1891–1953)   March   1:40

FREDERIC CHOPIN: *Piano Sonata No. 2 in B-flat minor, Op. 35* (1839)
(1810–1849)   3. Funeral March: Lento   7:30
> These two works illustrate opposite poles of the march concept.
> The first is fast and gay; the second slow and somber. One must
> probe beneath the surface to detect the common rhythmic source
> indicated by the titles.

The *ONE-two* beat pattern found in marches also provides the rhythmic basis for much dance music. Like marches, dances are written in measures of four beats as well as in measures of two. The same steps are appropriate with either, and the sound is not affected noticeably by the difference in notation.

The *ONE-two* beat pattern is only one of numerous possibilities. Waltzes, for example, have a *ONE-two-three* rhythmic background. The lilting, supple rhythm of waltzes contrasts sharply with the angular, straightforward rhythm of marches. The traditional *oomp-pah-pah* waltz accompaniment highlights the waltz rhythm with the accented first beat in the low register and the unaccented second and third beats in a higher register. This figure establishes the rhythmic pattern and continues as an accompaniment for the melody in the following examples, as it does in most waltzes.

P. I. TCHAIKOVSKY: *Ballet, Swan Lake, Op. 20* (1877)
(1840–1893)   Waltz   4:00

JOHANN STRAUSS: *The Blue Danube, Op. 314* (1867)   9:50
(1825–1899)
> The nearly 500 works of Strauss include several operettas, but he is
> best known as a composer of waltzes. They were conceived as dance
> music but endure as concert music. This waltz, one of his most
> famous, is not a simple dance tune, but a series of sophisticated
> melodies elaborately scored for full orchestra. An introduction in
> another rhythm precedes the waltz proper, and in concert perform-
> ances the strict tempo of the dance is not preserved.

Just as march rhythms are found in music not intended for marching, waltz rhythms are found in music not intended for dancing. In the following example the name and the rhythm pattern of the waltz have been retained, but other connections with the dance have been severed.

FREDERIC CHOPIN: *Waltz in D-flat, Op. 64 No. 1, "Minute"* (1846) 1:25
(1810–1849)

> The familiar name of this delightful miniature suggests that it should be played in 60 seconds. Double that time is more realistic for most piano students, and the piece would still be too fast for dancing. Listeners hearing it played in the usual way tend to hear the beats in groups and the measure rather than the beat as the rhythmic unit. Concentrating on the typical waltz pattern of the accompaniment, instead of the melody, makes it easier to detect the waltz rhythm.

The rhythmic element is prominent and uncomplicated in marches and waltzes, so they make a logical point of departure for the study of rhythm and meter. The basic two-beat and three-beat patterns underlying the rhythm of marches and waltzes, respectively, are also found in music far removed from the parade and the ballroom. Music of widely divergent types may share a common rhythmic background. The rhythmic element in concert music is usually less obvious than in march and dance music, but in most instances the beats and groupings are readily perceptible. Try tapping and counting with the beats as you listen to the following examples illustrating various rhythms and meters.

W. A. MOZART: *Opera, The Marriage of Figaro, K.492* (1786)
(1756–1791)   Overture   4:00

> The rhythm of this dazzling piece has the same underlying *ONE-two* pattern as a march, but the style and character are totally different. This overture is frequently heard in symphony concerts apart from the opera.

FRANZ SCHUBERT: *Symphony No. 8 in B minor, "Unfinished"* (1822)
(1797–1828)   1. Allegro moderato   11:10

> This movement has a *ONE-two-three* rhythmic background, like a waltz. Conceivably one could dance to it, but the idea would hardly suggest itself. The innate beauty of the symphony and romantic legends about its "unfinished" state have combined to make it Schubert's best known orchestral composition. It consists of only two movements, instead of the customary four, but his untimely death at the age of thirty-one does not account for this fact. He lived six years after he presented the score of the two existing movements to

a music society as a condition of membership. During this time
he wrote another very large symphony (No. 9 in C).

Regular, recurrent patterns of two beats or three beats underlie the
rhythm of most music. In a two-beat pattern the first beat is accented and
the second unaccented. In a three-beat pattern the first beat is accented and
the second and third are unaccented. These are the basic beat patterns. Each
basic pattern may constitute a *measure* of music. Two or more basic patterns
are combined in larger measures. A measure of four beats, for example, consists of two groups of two beats. The first of the four beats receives a primary
accent. The third receives a lesser, secondary accent, and the second and
fourth beats are unaccented. This, at least, is the theory learned by young
musicians. From the standpoint of the listener, the distinction is not always
clear. The amount of accent is purely relative, and it is not always possible
or even desirable in performance to exaggerate the difference between the
stresses to the point where the primary and secondary accents are readily
distinguishable. As a result, many marches are written in four-beat measures
rather than in two-beat measures. When a march has a four-beat pattern,
the left foot comes alternately with the first and third beats of the measure,
the right foot with the second and fourth, but no one is disturbed by it. The
same is true of dance music, which is written both ways.

It must be noted that the possibility of confusion exists only for the
listener. Musical notation is explicit, and conductors are meticulous about
making appropriate gestures, the ones which players expect for a given notation, though such subtleties are lost in radio and recorded performances.

The following example is written in measures of four beats. The rhythmic element is pronounced, and no difficulty will be experienced in locating
the march-like beat. Distinguish if you can not only between accented and
unaccented beats but between primary and secondary accents. Once you have
located the primary accent, count with the rhythm *ONE-two-three-four*. A
certain sensitivity is required to differentiate between qualities of accent, but
a reasonable degree of accuracy can be achieved by careful listening when
performers are punctilious in their rendition. The distinction between two-
beat measures and four-beat measures is not so much a fact to be observed
as a suggestion to be sensed.

P. I. TCHAIKOVSKY: *Symphony No. 6 in B minor, Op. 74 "Pathetique"* (1893)
   (1840–1893)   3. Allegro molto vivace   9:35

From a standpoint of the written measure, the next example is the
same as the previous one, but the effect is totally different. The notated beat

of the Bach *Air* is so slow that what is written as a half beat is usually felt as the rhythmic unit. In effect this creates measures with a total of eight beats. Eight-beat measures quite logically can be heard as two four-beat measures or even as four two-beat measures. The possible dichotomy between the sound and the notation of rhythm is apparent, but only the former is of importance to the listener.

J. S. Bach: *Suite No. 3 in D for Orchestra, S.1068* (1730)
(1685–1750)   2. Air   5:30

> The bass line moves in a persistent rhythm, treading along in notes of equal duration. Over this soars one of the most inspired melodies in music. The unswerving rhythmic regularity of the bass provides an effective foil for the sustained, singing melody.

Just as rhythmic groups of two beats are combined in four- and eight-beat measures, rhythmic groups of three beats are combined in six-, nine-, and twelve-beat measures. In measures with six beats, the first receives the primary accent as always. The fourth receives the secondary accent, and beats two, three, five, and six are unaccented. The possibility of confusion between the primary and secondary accents and consequently between three-beat measures and six-beat measures is apparent. It is reassuring to note that appreciation is not seriously impaired by such minor discrepancies in perception and that professional musicians are not infallible in this regard. The following example is written in measures of six beats, but at least parts of it can be heard just as readily in independent groups of three.

W. A. Mozart: *Symphony No. 40 in G minor, K.550* (1788)
(1756–1791)   2. Andante   7:50

> The first note of a composition is not necessarily the first beat of a measure. Many works begin, as this one does, with a fraction of a measure. When the first measure of a piece is incomplete, the first note or group of notes is unaccented, and the first primary accent comes at the beginning of the first complete measure. This particular movement commences on the sixth beat of the measure. The second note of the melody comes on the first beat of a measure. See how long you can follow the six-beat pattern of the underlying rhythm. Later in the movement there is a theme which is almost waltz-like, but the written measures still have six beats.

In measures with nine beats, the first receives the primary rhythmic accent, the fourth and seventh secondary accents. The remainder are unaccented. This is the rhythmic foundation of the following example.

L. van Beethoven: *String Quartet No. 1 in F, Op. 18 No. 1* (1800)
(1770–1827)   2. Adagio affettuoso ed appasionata   10:00

> The pulse and pattern of the underlying rhythm are established
> by the accompanying instruments before the melody enters. The
> beat is slow and the motion stately, but as the work progresses,
> splashes of rapid notes appear against a throbbing background. The
> rhythm should continue in the imagination during momentary
> periods of silence in the music, called *rests*.

Measures of twelve beats are the most extended that are commonly
used. The primary accent falls on the first beat of the measure, secondary
accents on the first of each succeeding group of three beats. The following
example has twelve-beat measures.

Antonio Vivaldi: *L'Estro Armonico, Op. 3 No. 11 in D minor* (1712)
(1678–1741)   3. Largo e spiccato   3:15

> Except for a brief passage at the beginning and again at the end, the
> motion of the accompanying instruments coincides exactly with the
> beat. This accompaniment consists of repeated notes of equal dura-
> tion with four groups of three in each measure. Concentrating on
> the accompaniment orients the listener and the performer rhythmi-
> cally, but the interest and beauty of this work lie in its incomparable
> melody.

The underlying rhythmic pulses of music basically may be grouped
and divided into duple and triple patterns. These basic duple and triple patterns and combinations of them in measures of four, six, eight, nine, and
twelve beats constitute the conventional metric units of familiar music.
Conceivably six- and twelve-beat measures can result from combinations
of either two- or three-beat patterns, but usually they are derived from three-
pulse groups. The rhythmic possibilities of measures with five, seven, ten,
and eleven beats and asymmetric divisions were not exploited until recent
times. These possibilities open new vistas for composers and listeners alike.
Tchaikovsky was one of the first to use five-beat measures in a symphonic
composition.

P. I. Tchaikovsky: *Symphony No. 6 in B minor, Op. 74, "Pathetique"* (1893)
(1840–1893)   2. Allegro con grazia   7:15

> The five-beat rhythmic pattern of this music may not feel quite as
> "comfortable" as the more usual patterns, but one soon becomes
> accustomed to its regular, though asymmetric groupings. Five-beat

measures usually are heard as a group of two followed by a group of three or vice versa. The unequal length of the groups and the irregular spacing of the accents produces an effect quite unlike that of symmetric rhythms.

Asymmetric divisions of a more complex genre are found in the works of many contemporary composers, among them Bela Bartok. This feature appears not only in his major orchestral and chamber works but also in small pieces for one and two instruments. The latter provide ideal examples as they are both concise and varied.

BELA BARTOK: *Mikrokosmos* (1926–1937)
(1881–1945)   Six Dances in Bulgarian Rhythm

148.	4 plus 2 plus 3	1:50
149.	2 plus 2 plus 3	1:10
150.	2 plus 3	1:20
151.	3 plus 2 plus 3	1:25
152.	2 plus 2 plus 2 plus 3	1:13
153.	3 plus 3 plus 2	1:40

Each of the dances makes use of a different asymmetric meter. The beats within measures are grouped as shown. The pace in some is too fast for individual units to be discerned, but the effect of the irregularity is unmistakable. The fact that these rhythms are derived from Bulgarian folk music suggests that they perhaps are newer to us than to some other peoples. These six dances are the last of a group of progressively graded piano pieces. The total collection, published in six volumes, is a virtual encyclopedia of contemporary devices.

It is but a short step from the use of asymmetric meters to the abandonment of fixed rhythmic patterns. The constant patterns and regular accents which regulated the rhythmic flow in music of the past are no longer universal. Many works of this century have irregular accents defining unpredictable groupings of beats and notes. The old sense of rhythmic stability and security is replaced by a sense of freedom and excitement. Symmetric rhythms, while still used, can no longer be taken for granted. Contemporary composers have added a new dimension to rhythm and have used it with skill and imagination. As a result, rhythm has been elevated from a role of subservience, a mere handmaiden of melody and harmony, to that of an equal in the hierarchy of musical elements. One of the first to grasp the potential of rhythm for attracting attention and sustaining interest and to feature it in extended passages was Igor Stravinsky.

IGOR STRAVINSKY: *Symphony in Three Movements* (1945)
(1882–   )   I. ♩ = 160 (♩ = 80)   9:45

> Stravinsky provides no clue to the style of this movement but only
> specifies the number of beats per minute as shown. The fact that
> he gives the rate for two units, one twice as fast as the other, suggests
> that either may be taken as the beat. Considering the shorter of the
> two time units (160 per minute) as the beat, measures of 4, 3, 2, 6,
> 5, 1, and 1½ occur in that order. Irregular measures and shifting
> accents figure conspicuously in the rhythmic plan of the work. In
> some passages almost every measure has a different duration than its
> neighbors. In others the measures are fairly constant, but accents
> occur in unexpected places. Sometimes there is silence where an
> accent is anticipated. All of this adds up to rhythm which is as com-
> plex and high-tensioned as the age in which it was composed. Its
> intricacies are a challenge to performers and listeners alike. Many
> are attracted to this music immediately. Others have to learn to like
> it, but very few are tempted to sleep through it.

Accents and obvious rhythmic groupings are not mandatory in music.
Notes can be played and sung without perceptible accents or divisions, though
this possibility is largely ignored. The tendency to organize sounds in groups
seems to be innate. It emerges spontaneously in the writing of composers and
in the playing and singing of performers. Listeners are inclined to attach significance to the slightest hint of stress or division and to organize sounds into
patterns even where none are intended. Furthermore, it is impossible in
modern musical notation to avoid suggestions of division. Bar lines, originally
introduced as an aid to reading, are drawn between measures, and they have
an acquired rhythmic significance which musicians are trained to observe.
It is difficult for them to overcome this conditioning in the few passages where
it is not appropriate. The net result is that few passages and fewer performances are lacking in stresses and groupings, but stresses should not be regarded as perpetual necessities. No music exists without flow and motion,
but the obvious type of accent and grouping heard in marches and dances
diminishes to the vanishing point at the opposite end of the rhythmic spectrum. The following examples, essentially lacking accents and stresses, are
drawn from the periods when this type of rhythm is most likely to be
found, before 1600 and after 1900.

G. P. DA PALESTRINA: *Pope Marcellus Mass* (1567)
(1525–1594)   Benedictus   3:50

> Metric accents are foreign to Palestrina's style. The stressed syllables
> of the text are associated with longer rhythmic values and with
> leaps in the vocal lines. The stresses in the various parts, unlike

metric accents, are largely independent of each other. This rhythmic concept is remote from that underlying most concert and popular music. It contributes to an ethereal style, free from any suggestion of the profane and ideally suited to the expression of religious sentiments. This work is often cited as a model of Catholic liturgical music.

SAMUEL BARBER: *Adagio for Strings, Op. 11* (1936) 6:10
   (1910–   )

> This work was written as the slow movement of a string quartet, but it is better known in this arrangement by the composer for string orchestra. It and the *Pope Marcellus Mass*, composed 369 years earlier, display certain rhythmic similarities in their free-flowing lines and unhurried tranquillity. Compulsive regularity is absent in both works, and the pulse is pliable. Though Barber's rhythms may echo the past, his lush harmonies and soaring strings are uniquely of the present.

At the beginning of each piece of music and wherever changes in the rhythmic framework occur, there is a *time signature*, also called a *meter signature*. The time signature most often consists of two Arabic numerals, one written above the other in the manner of a fraction. The lower number shows which note symbol is used to represent the beat. The upper number indicates the number of beats in each measure of the music. The measures are marked in musical notation by vertical lines called *bar lines*. Vestiges of an older system of rhythmic notation persist in two time signatures which have a symbol in place of the two numbers. A large "C" is the equivalent of a 4/4 time signature, and the same symbol with a vertical line through it is the equivalent of a 2/2 time signature.

Conductors, with their right hand or a baton, describe stylized patterns in the air appropriate to the various time signatures. Each conductor makes personalized modifications in the designs, but sufficient uniformity is preserved to make the beats intelligible to players. A stroke straight down directly in front of the conductor is used for the first beat of each measure. For this reason, the first beat of a measure is referred to as the *down beat*. If there are two beats in the measure, the second is indicated by an upward motion roughly parallel with that of the down beat. A three-beat pattern approximates the shape of a triangle—down, right, and up to the point of origin. The conductor's beat for four-beat measures is down, left, right, and up. The motion for six-beat measures is down, left, left, right, right, and up. Unaccented beats at the end of measures come on the up stroke of the conductor's beat and are referred to as *up beats*. Measures with more than six beats usually are conducted with motions following one of the contours mentioned with subdivisions as necessary. When the beats are too fast to be conducted individually, one gesture is used for a group of beats. Conversely, when the notated beat is very slow, it may be divided and conducted with two or three motions.

What aspects of rhythm should listeners be able to discern? Distinguishing between two-beat and three-beat patterns presents no formidable problem. Recognizing combinations of basic groups is more difficult, and infallibility cannot be expected. However, attentive listeners will be aware of extended measures in the more obvious examples. Sensitivity to shifting accents, to changes of meter, and to the absence of rhythmic stresses should be cultivated. Rhythm is the foundation of the musical edifice. The realm of listening experience is extended by an awareness of its patterns and functions.

Tempo

Tempo refers to the rate of speed in music. In 1816 Johann Maelzel constructed a device using the pendulum principle capable of marking units of time, and hence the tempo of music, with absolute precision. Called a *metronome*, it could be set to swing and tick at any selected rate in a range exceeding the requirements of practical music. Metronome markings are expressed in terms of the number of units per minute. The marking M.M. = 60 indicates 60 rhythmic units per minute or one per second. Often a note symbol is used in place of the abbreviation M.M. Thus ♩ = 72 indicates 72 quarter notes (the symbol shown) in a minute or that one quarter note has a duration of 1/72 of a minute, 5/6 of a second.

Beethoven was intrigued by the possibilities of the metronome, and he provided his symphonies with metronome markings. Contemporary composers are more inclined to use metronome markings than were composers of the period immediately following its invention. Perhaps composers object to the mechanical nature of the metronome, for they continue to use Italian terms introduced early in the 17th century as tempo indications. These terms lack the precision of metronome markings, but they convey implications of style as well as of pace. Combining Italian words with metronome markings is a common practice which secures the advantages of both.

Tempo indications would be of no particular concern to the listener except that they are used to designate the various movements of multimovement works and sometimes figure in the titles of compositions. This makes familiarity with at least the more common ones desirable. Arranged from the slowest to the fastest with approximate English equivalents, they are:

Largo: broad, large	*Moderato*: moderate
Lento: slow	*Allegro*: cheerful
Adagio: comfortable, easy	*Vivace*: lively, quick
Andante: going along, walking	*Presto*: very fast, rapid

Derivative forms of these terms provide shades of meaning. *Larghetto*, a diminutive form of *Largo* indicates a tempo slightly less slow. *Allegretto*, a diminutive form of *Allegro*, indicates a tempo slightly less fast. There is disagreement on the interpretation of *Andantino*, the diminutive form for *Andante*. Some regard *Andante* as a slow tempo and *Andantino* as somewhat faster. Others class *Andante* as a fast tempo and consequently consider *Andantino* to be a little slower. No less a personage than Beethoven was puzzled by this question. Though the precise meaning of *Andantino* is in doubt, the confusion about its significance establishes the fact that *Andante* falls at the center of the scale of tempos and on the dividing line between those classified as fast and those classified as slow. *Prestissimo* is a superlative form of *Presto* meaning extremely fast. Diminutive and superlative forms of other terms also are used.

To provide more explicit and descriptive directions, tempo indications are modified with additional Italian words and phrases such as:

Agitato: agitated	*Grazioso*: with grace
Animato: animated	*Ma*: but
Appassionato: passionately	*Maestoso*: majestically
Assai: very	*Marcato*: marked
Cantabile: singing	*Molto*: very, much
Con brio: with spirit	*Non*: not
Con fuoco: with fire	*Non troppo*: not too much
Con moto: with motion	*Piu*: more
E or ed: and	*Poco*: little
Espressivo: expressively	*Sostenuto*: sustained

Many combinations of these and other terms are used in identifying the examples. See the glossary for additional definitions.

In addition to the words and phrases for rates of speed, there are indications for gradual and sudden changes, both faster and slower. Listeners should be alert to changes of pace, a significant means of musical expression.

Composers from time to time abandon Italian terminology in favor of the vernacular, but this practice has not become general. It is more prevalent now than formerly, but it has two disadvantages. Italian words and phrases through long usage have developed connotations difficult or awkward to express in other languages, and musical terms in Italian are more universally understood than any other.

There are no absolute limits on musical pace, but practical considerations regulate extremes. Sustaining accuracy in extremely slow tempos is difficult. Equally difficult is conducting, counting, and playing extremely fast tempos. Tempos related to the physiological rhythm of the heartbeat seem most natural. These encompass rates between approximately 60 and 80 per minute. Tempos outside these limits are perceived as slow or fast. The tendency is to divide or combine units to bring them within this range, though the points at which this occurs vary with individuals, both performers and listeners.

Tempo is a major factor in setting the mood of music, and it is a prime source of variety. Contrast of tempo is sought between sections of larger works, between movements of multimovement works, and between selections on programs. The usual order of tempos in a four movement symphony is: fast—slow—moderate or moderately fast—fast, the last usually faster than the first. There are, of course, many modifications of and exceptions to this plan. A typical sequence of tempos is illustrated in Mozart's *Haffner Symphony*.

W. A. MOZART: *Symphony No. 35 in D, K.385, "Haffner"* (1782)

(1756–1791)	1. Allegro con spirito	5:00
	2. Andante	4:00
	3. Menuetto	3:20
	4. Presto	3:25

This symphony was written in honor of Siegmund Haffner, the son of Salzburg's mayor, at the time he was elevated to the nobility. No tempo indication is given for the minuet (*menuetto* in Italian), a practice of the period that leads to diverse interpretations. Originally a rustic dance, the minuet made its way into the French court and thence into concert music. The dance was characterized by grace and dignity, but the minuets in symphonies are often played in a sprightly style. The most usual tempo marking, when one is given, is *Allegretto*.

Schumann's brief *Scenes from Childhood* (*Kinderscenen*) provide an interesting study in tempo. Each editor (and performer, too, no doubt) has different ideas regarding interpretation. Tempo markings of three editions are given for comparison. The Schirmer edition is edited by Harold Bauer. It is the only one to use descriptive terms in conjunction with the metronome markings. The Kalmus edition is "edited according to manuscripts and from her personal recollections by Clara Schumann," wife of the composer and a concert pianist. Conrad Kuehner is editor of the Litolff edition which gives two figures as shown. English translations of the original German titles are from the G. Schirmer publication.

ROBERT SCHUMANN: *Scenes from Childhood, Op. 15* (1838)

(1810–1856)	1. About Strange Lands and People	1:30
	2. Curious Story	1:00
	3. Blindman's Buff	:35
	4. Pleading Child	:50
	5. Perfectly Contented	1:10

6. Important Event   1:00
7. Reverie (Traumerei)   2:10
8. At the Fireside   :45
9. The Knight of the Rocking-horse   :40
10. Almost too Serious   1:10
11. Frightening   1:30
12. Child Falling Asleep   1:25
13. The Poet Speaks   1:30

		Schirmer	*Kalmus*	*Litolff*	
1.	Andante	72	108	108	(84)
2.	Allegro giojoso	132	132	112	(132)
3.	Allegro scherzando	116	120	138	(108)
4.	Moderato	60	88	138*	(124)*
5.	Allegro moderato	84	72	132*	(152)*
6.	Allegro marziale	120	120	138	(126)
7.	Adagio espressivo	56	80	100	(84)
8.	Allegretto grazioso	104	108	138	(104)
9.	Allegro con brio	176	76†	80†	(66)†
10.	Moderato, poco rubato	100	104	69‡	(108)
11.	Poco allegro	96	108	96	(80)
12.	Lento non troppo	44	80*	92*	(88)*
13.	Adagio espressivo	88	92	112	

* For a notated value one half as long
† For a notated value three times as long
‡ For a notated value twice as long

It is interesting to compare the tempos of recorded performances with these markings.

Unless a composer gives a metronome marking, he merely suggests an approximate tempo, and no two conductors or players will give identical interpretations. Some performers choose to ignore even precise directions. Fast, brilliant tempos are favored by some while others are partial to slower, more deliberate paces. Both schools of thought have many partisans, and "correct" tempo is a frequent subject of debate among musicians.

Melody

Melody is that inscrutable, magical element of music that captures the imagination and lingers in the memory to be recalled, hummed, and whistled long after words and accompaniments have been forgotten. Melody and music are almost synonymous. It is strange, therefore, that countless textbooks are devoted to harmony, counterpoint, and form but few to melody. One reason may be that dissecting and analyzing melodies is not very illuminating. Melody, perhaps more than the other elements of music, is dictated by inspiration and appreciated by instinct. Some questions about melody, however, can be posed and answered objectively.

What is a melody? How are melodies conceived? What are the characteristics of a good one? How are melodies recognized and remembered? These are questions inquisitive listeners might ask. The first is the easiest to answer.

A melody is a succession of musical tones conveying an impression of continuity—a series of pitches arranged in a logical sequence. Random sounds are not perceived as melodies, nor are tones unduly separated in time, register, or color. As usually construed, melodies have definite points of beginning and ending, the latter attended by a sense of completion. The proportions of individual melodies are modest, and most compositions have more than one. Extended works have many, though probably only a few of them are remembered vividly. An essential art of composition is to delineate separate melodies without disturbing the flow and continuity of the whole.

Most melodies are played or sung in their entirety by the same instrument, voice, or group. This is not mandatory, but it is suggested by the requirement of continuity. It also serves the purpose of making the melody easier to follow. Exceptions to this occur in repetitions after a melody is familiar. Then various instruments may share a single statement for variety. In orchestral compositions, contrasting melodies usually are assigned to different instruments.

The principal melody more often than not is higher in pitch than the accompaniment and secondary melodies. This, however, is something which changes with the period, the style, and the form. Occasionally the main melody is assigned to the bottom or middle of the musical texture. At other times melodic interest is divided between all the parts. Composers and performers subtly direct the listener's attention to the most important melodic line when it departs from its accustomed position. This is done by making it louder, faster, slower, or different in color from the background.

The exact mechanism by which a person is able to remember and recognize hundreds of different tunes is a mystery, but musical memory is not much different from any other. It is aided by repetition and association. It improves with use and retains best that which it finds most pleasant. Musical memory and musical enjoyment are closely linked. There is satisfaction in hearing familiar melodies and in anticipating well-known strains. Extending the scope of one's listening experience to include both more and better music develops the musical memory and in the process broadens the foundations of musical enjoyment. The full potentials of memory and appreciation are realized when music one initially finds intriguing is heard repeatedly under agreeable circumstances.

Remembering melodies, like remembering words, names, addresses, and telephone numbers requires the ability to recognize familiar arrangements of a limited number of components—twelve tones in the case of music. Melodies are nothing more than distinctive arrangements of pitches selected from the twelve available. Few melodies make use of all of them. More important than the selection and order of tones in melodic recognition is contour. Melodic contour results from the interplay of pitches and durations.

A graph of the melodic contour of *Who Is Sylvia* is given as an aid in visualizing that aspect of melody. Follow it during the performance. The melody is heard three times with different words.

FRANZ SCHUBERT: *Who Is Sylvia, Op. 106 No. 4* (1826)   2:47
(1797–1828)

> Observe the balance between ascending and descending motion and between conjunct and disjunct movement. Notice also the distribution of high and low points in the line. Small rhythm and pitch patterns, which are repeated literally and varied, provide unifying elements. Schubert demonstrates infallible intuition in achieving these desirable melodic characteristics. (Notation p. 302)

Knowing that a composer draws his material from a fundamental stockpile of twelve notes and that his melodies can be represented by graphs may make composing sound like fitting pieces of a jigsaw puzzle into suitable patterns of up and down, long and short. This obviously is not the case. What about inspiration? Its role is not as decisive as popular legends would lead one to think. Composers do not experience a powerful emotion and dash wild-eyed to the piano to create, spontaneously, an immortal masterpiece. In reality the creative process is much less romantic and more arduous, but not a mechanical or perfunctory task.

Composition begins with an idea—call it inspiration if you will. Ideas may come out of the blue, but far more often inspiration strikes the composer while he is pursuing it, pencil in hand. Each composer develops a personal approach to composition, but with most the initial germ is born in the mind without recourse to any instrument. The idea is abstract, conceived mentally, but immediately it is translated into symbols and perhaps into sounds as well. Most often the initial idea for a composition is a motive or a melody, occasionally a rhythm, a chord, or a harmonic progression. A unique fragment envisaged in a flash may contain the seed of an entire symphony, but infinite skill, patience, and imagination are required to bring it to fruition. This is the craft of the composer.

If inspiration dictates any aspect of music, it is melody, but even the most inspired melody rarely springs from the composer's mind full blown

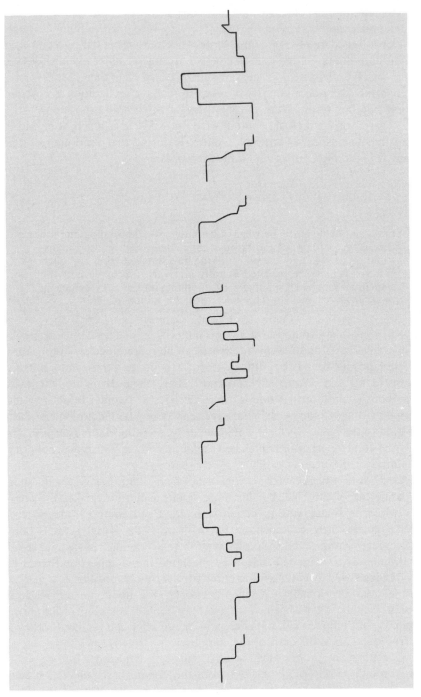

FIGURE 19. *Melodic Contour Graph: Who Is Sylvia* (Notation p. 302)

86

and perfect. More often initial melodic conceptions require reworking and polishing. When a composer applies technique to his inspiration, he strives for those melodic characteristics illustrated in the Schubert example: balance between unity and variety and between high and low points. His own artistic instinct serves as the sole arbitrator of what constitutes *balance*, and his success or failure as a composer depends in large measure upon his ability to make such decisions in a manner acceptable to discerning audiences. Immortal masterpieces and rejected manuscripts are made from the same raw material.

The dividing line between good and bad melodies, like that between good and bad music generally, is blurred by subjective judgments. Beauty and ugliness, order and chaos, and the like are not states of being but reflections of personal opinion. Such opinions are supported more by emotional convictions than by logic, and logic at best is not easily brought to bear upon aesthetic matters. The result is that great disparity exists in melodic and musical preferences, in likes and dislikes. This is not only inevitable, but essential. Except for differences in taste, there would be only one kind of music, and what could be more dreary? The vitality of the art is in a large measure a product of its diversity, but the diverse melodic styles illustrated will not prove equally attractive to everyone. Personal inclinations as well as differences in conditioning dictate otherwise. The appeal of some melodies is immediate and almost universal, but the taste for others, like the taste for green olives, must be acquired.

A melody, as most listeners would define the term, is a lyric, flowing, and song-like series of musical tones. Melodies of this sort are found in the music of all periods. Romantic composers added to these qualities their own special kind of sensuous emotion to write soaring melodies of breath-taking beauty and grace. Though Sibelius lived and composed well into the present century, he was a great melodist in the romantic tradition. His music is imbued with lyricism and copiously supplied with singing and singable melodies.

JEAN SIBELIUS: *Violin Concerto in D minor, Op. 47* (1903)
(1865–1957) 2. Adagio di molto 8:30

> The only concerto by Sibelius was for the instrument he played, the violin. His intimate knowledge of the instrument undoubtedly stimulated his rare melodic gift as he conceived this movement. The solo violin at times leaves the principal melodic material to the orchestra and spins a delicate filligree around it.

In the late 18th century, melodies typically were also lyric, flowing, and song-like, but they were inclined toward classic simplicity, clarity, and purity rather than sensuousness. Melodies of this type are more akin to folk songs. They are expressive, but the emotions they express are subdued and restrained. They are more elegant than dramatic, more charming than poignant. The melodies of Haydn, Mozart, and their contemporaries fall into this category.

W. A. Mozart: *Clarinet Concerto in A, K.622* (1791)
   (1756–1791)   1. Allegro   12:50
> The availability of the fabulous clarinetist, Anton Stadler, induced Mozart to write several works involving clarinet, including this, one of his most significant instrumental compositions.

Another type of melody, instrumental in character but found also in vocal music, is active and athletic rather than lyric. Insistent rhythms bordering on perpetual motion progress mostly along scale lines, relieved by skips along chord lines. The supple curves of the styles previously illustrated are supplanted by rugged and vigorous contours. Melodies of this type are characteristic of the early 18th century and appear frequently in the works of Bach and Handel.

J. S. Bach: *Magnificat in D, S.243* (1723)
   (1685–1750)   7. Deposuit   2:00
> This aria for tenor aptly illustrates the bustling, continuous melodic motion typical in fast movements, both instrumental and vocal, of the period. The text of the song is, "He hath put down the mighty from their thrones and hath exalted the lowly."

Twentieth-century composers have been energetic in expanding melodic concepts beyond the types illustrated thus far. Singable melodies are no longer considered essential. Melodies with wide ranges, angular leaps, and disjunct contours are in vogue. Contemporary rhythmic and harmonic resources have exerted strong pressures on melodic designs. The combined effect of these influences has altered recent melodic invention to the point where modern music is accused of being tuneless by some schooled exclusively in the old traditions. A blanket indictment is not justified, though isolated pieces of evidence can be cited to support it. Modern melodies depart radically from traditional means, but their objectives remain the same. The intent of contemporary composers is to achieve greater interest and expressiveness by abolishing arbitrary restrictions and exploiting new freedoms. They may at times sacrifice ordered regularity, tonal stability, the clarity, the simplicity, and the sensuousness of the previous melodic styles in their quest for melodic materials more suitable to their requirements, but they are still striving for successions of musical sounds conveying impressions of continuity and logic.

The old ways of achieving these ends have not been discarded, but many new ones have been added. The melodies of Hindemith's *Kleine Kammermusik* are certainly recognizable as melodies, yet they have a thoroughly contemporary flavor. They are capricious, brittle, and fresh.

PAUL HINDEMITH: *Kleine Kammermusik Op. 24 No. 2* (1922)
1.	Lustig (Merry)	2:30
2.	Walzer (Waltz)	2:00
3.	Ruhig und einfach (Quiet and simple)	4:45
4.	Schnelle (Quick)	:45
5.	Sehr lebhaft (Very lively)	3:00

> The mocking humor in this gay and witty piece is not to be taken too seriously. The clever melodies sparkle, with no pretensions of profundity. Not until the third movement is there a hint of traditional melodic lyricism.

Harmony

Different pitches sounding together produce harmony. The smallest elements of harmony are *intervals*, which consist of two tones. The harmonic effect of an interval depends upon the relationship between the vibrating frequencies of the two tones comprising it. In general, simple ratios are more harmonious; complex ratios more discordant. The Table of Intervals, Table 5, shows the intervals above *C* in relation to the piano keyboard and lists them in order of complexity. The ratios are only approximate because of minor discrepancies between the natural ratios and modern tuning. The descriptive terms given for the quality of the intervals are purely subjective.

To hear the effect of all the intervals, find the note *C* near the center of the piano keyboard (see Table 5), and play each interval, progressing from the smallest to the largest. Then play the intervals in order of complexity, as they are listed at the bottom of the Table of Intervals. After this, you may wish to substitute your own descriptive terms for those given.

Intervals are classified as perfect consonances, imperfect consonances, and dissonances. According to this classification, unisons, octaves, fourths, and fifths are perfect consonances. Thirds and sixths are imperfect consonances. Seconds, sevenths, the augmented fourth and diminished fifth are dissonances.

There is a tendency to regard consonant intervals as pleasant and dissonant intervals as unpleasant. This is unfortunate. No musical sound or combination of sounds is intrinsically unpleasant. A more valid association can be made between dissonance and tension and between consonance and repose. Dissonance generates tension which is relieved by consonance. This

TABLE 5

TABLE OF INTERVALS

Notes	Interval	Ratio	Description
C-C	Unison	1:1	amplifies sound only
C-C	Octave	1:2	white, transparent
C-G	Fifth, perfect	2:3	barren, open, hollow
C-F	Fourth, perfect	3:4	barren, open, hollow
C-E	Third, major	4:5	clear, bright
C-E♭	Third, minor	5:6	somber, dark
C-A	Sixth, major	3:5	clear, bright
C-A♭	Sixth, minor	5:8	somber, dark
C-D	Second, major	8:9	mildly discordant, rough
C-B♭	Seventh, minor	9:16	mildly discordant, rough
C-B	Seventh, major	8:15	sharply discordant, harsh
C-D♭	Second, minor	15:16	sharply discordant, harsh
C-F♯	Fourth, augmented	{ 17:24 }	strident, unstable
C-G♭	Fifth, diminished		

(different ways of notating the same relationship)

* Or half step.
** Or whole step.

is analogous to the conflict in a novel produced by problems which are resolved at the end. Consonances and happy endings are meaningful artistically only in terms of the dissonances and conflicts that precede them. Dissonant intervals and chords should not be regarded as distasteful but as the harmonic elements which render consonant intervals and chords imperative. The interaction of consonance and dissonance in the composer's matrix gives substance and direction to his musical thought.

The various intervals provide several shades of consonance and dissonance. The range of consonance and dissonance is expanded to infinity when the number of tones sounding together and the relationships between them are unrestricted. The music of different styles and periods operates on entirely different harmonic planes. Just as drama runs the gamut of human emotions from the comparative tranquillity of Arcadian idylls to the intensity of Greek tragedies and the horror of murder mysteries, music explores the extremes from purest consonance and complete repose to ear-shattering dissonance and electrifying tension. Any harmonic sound can be meaningful and appropriate in the proper frame of reference.

Most harmonies contain three or more tones. Three or more tones sounding together make a *chord*. The foundation structures of harmony are three-note chords built from alternate notes of a scale, C-E-G for example, called *triads*. The three notes of a triad may be arranged in any order and doubled in various octaves without causing the triad to lose its identity, but every detail of order, spacing, doubling, and scoring modifies the sound somewhat. A triad may be constructed on any note, and each one has a distinctive quality and function in relation to the others.

Clear examples of unadulterated triad harmony are not plentiful. During the period when triad harmonies were used exclusively, all of the parts in the prevailing style were conceived melodically, not harmonically. The melodies combined to form triads at strategic points, but between these points notes not belonging to the triad were used. Also, one part sometimes arrived at its triad note slightly after or before the other parts. In listening to such music the ear is attracted to the melodic lines by their independent rhythms, and the harmonic foundation governing the melodic movement goes unnoticed. The triad harmonies are unusually clear at the beginning of the following example, where the style is least typical of Palestrina and his contemporaries.

G. P. DA PALESTRINA: *Missa Brevis (Short Mass)* (1570)
   (1525–1594)   Gloria   3:20

> After the initial clear triad harmonies, the voices begin to move independently, and the chords they form are obscured by the melodic motion. Triads are the only chord structures recognized

in the music of this period, but other notes occur melodically as the voices move from one triad tone to another.

The harmonic materials of music are never static, and it was inevitable that additions to triad structures would be made almost as soon as composers started to think of music in terms of chords and chord progressions rather than in terms of combined melodies. Four-note chords constructed in the same way as triads, from alternate scale tones, began to make tentative appearances early in the 17th century. If the numbers 1-3-5 are used to represent triad formations, the numbers 1-3-5-7 would represent the components of these four-note chords, called *seventh chords*, a seventh being the interval between 1 and 7. Seventh chords were assimilated gradually into the harmonic vocabulary during the 17th and 18th centuries but never threatened the supremacy of the triads. The bulk of music now performed was written during the period when triads and seventh chords were the accepted chord structures. This period encompasses the greatest names in music—Bach, Haydn, Mozart, Beethoven—and the most universally appreciated music, but the suggested example is drawn from a lesser composer, Rameau, who codified the principles of traditional harmony.

J. P. RAMEAU: *Les Indes Galantes (The Gallant Indies)* (1735)
   (1683–1764)   Act II.   Clair flambeau du monde   4:30
                      (Bright torch of the world)

> This aria, besides illustrating triad harmonies with occasional seventh chords, shows evidence of Rameau's systematic use of chords to accompany one predominant melody. Rameau is remembered primarily as a theorist rather than as a composer, but the dramatic works of this contemporary of Bach aroused the highest enthusiasm when they were presented on the French stage during his lifetime. *Les Indes Galantes* combined elements of ballet and opera in an elaborate, costumed spectacle with dancing, singing, and staging, but very little plot, a format not unknown in Hollywood.

In some works composed during the second half of the 19th century, seventh chords displaced triads as the most prevalent chord structure. Concurrently, a predilection for chromaticism (that is, the use of the five tones not included in the scale or key of the piece) emerged. Extensive use of seventh chords and chromatic (color) notes led to highly colorful and expressive harmony. Richard Wagner pioneered this trend. Criticized as an undisciplined radical by some of his contemporaries, he now is acclaimed as one of the great innovators in the history of music.

RICHARD WAGNER: *Opera, Tristan and Isolde* (1859)
(1813–1883)   Prelude   10:45

> Nowhere are Wagner's revolutionary harmonic ideas employed
> more effectively than in his *Prelude* to *Tristan and Isolde*. After
> more than a century, this music is unsurpassed for sheer sensuous-
> ness, and the harmonies still have an aura of strangeness. The first
> performance must have been astounding.

Adding another note, the second note above the seventh, to a seventh
chord produces a *ninth chord*. Ninth chords are both too rich and too cumbersome for a steady diet, but they contribute added spice to the musical
fare. Claude Debussy exploited ninth chord sonorities around the turn of
the century. Later, jazz composers and arrangers discovered these sounds
and soon put a blight on them by excessive use.

CLAUDE DEBUSSY: *Nocturnes* (1899)
(1862–1918)   2. Fêtes (Festivals)   5:45

> Ninth chords are used freely, but by no means incessantly, in this
> atmospheric work. Debussy's tone painting is devoted more to con-
> veying impressions than details, but his depiction of a procession,
> first approaching and then departing, is unmistakable.

Continuing the process of building chords from alternate scale tones
beyond the ninth produces *eleventh chords* and *thirteenth chords*. Eleventh
chords are fairly common, especially in popular songs of the Broadway
musical variety. Thirteenth chords, which contain all of the notes of a
seven-tone scale, are somewhat less useful and less used. One hesitates to
suggest a specific selection from the popular field, because most of them are
short-lived. Almost any sophisticated arrangement of a popular song will
provide examples of this type of harmony. Gershwin's *Rhapsody in Blue* is
a more enduring work in a similar vein.

GEORGE GERSHWIN: *Rhapsody in Blue* (1924)   16:10
(1898–1937)

> Jazz elements of the period when it was written dominate the
> rhythms, melodies, and harmonies of this work. Seventh chords are
> the most prevalent harmonic ingredient, but ninth chords, eleventh
> chords, and occasionally more complicated harmonic structures
> occur. Gershwin was a composer of popular music primarily, but his
> few ventures into larger forms—this work, the *Piano Concerto in*

F, An American in Paris, and the opera *Porgy and Bess*—achieved
immediate and apparently enduring success.

By the time eleventh and thirteenth chords were accepted into the harmonic vocabulary, other methods of constructing chords were being explored. Clusters of consecutive scale tones were sounded together. Chord structures were derived from every third or fourth scale tone as well as from alternate scale tones. Simple chords, such as triads, were combined, and tones from different, even remote, keys were joined together. These are the harmonic materials of our time. The era was inaugurated with a bang in 1913 when Stravinsky's *Rite of Spring* was first performed in Paris. It is still a startling and exciting work after more than half a century.

IGOR STRAVINSKY:	*Ballet, The Rite of Spring* (1913)	29:45
(1882–)	The Adoration of the Earth	
	Introduction	:00
	Dances of the Adolescents	3:00
	Game of Abduction	6:05
	Spring Rounds	7:25
	Games of the Rival Towns	10:10
	Cortege of the Sage	12:00
	Adoration of the Earth (The Sage)	12:30
	Dance of the Earth	12:50
	The Sacrifice	
	Introduction (Pagan Night)	14:00
	Mystic Circle of the Adolescents	17:35
	Glorification of the Chosen One	20:15
	Evocation of the Ancestors	21:45
	Ritual Action of the Ancestors	22:25
	Sacrificial Dance (The Chosen One)	25:20

Every measure of *Le Sacre du Printemps,* to use its French name, contained innovations when it was written, and it breached all of the conventional boundaries with its harmonic complexity and rhythmic intricacy. The materials and procedures Stravinsky employed were ideally suited to portraying the primordial fertility ritual of spring with all its primitive compulsion. The titles of the sections give clues to the stage action, but the musical impact is not dependent upon dramatic values. The music alone is capable of evoking the pagan atmosphere and making believable the dance to death of the chosen virgin. The "Dances of the Adolescents" and the "Sacrificial Dance" are particularly appropriate for illustrating complex harmonies, but time permitting, this 20th-century masterpiece should be heard in its entirety. Sections are not always clearly delineated, so approximate elapsed times are given.

Harmonic tension and dissonance approached the saturation point in *The Rite of Spring*. It marks a turning point in the evolution of music after which composers diverted much of their attention from harmony to other considerations.

Tonality and Mode

Tonality is that phenomenon which causes organized musical sounds to gravitate to a single focal point. This tendency exists both in melodies and in harmonic progressions. The tone which emerges as the center of the tonal system is designated the *tonic* or *keynote*. The letter name of the keynote is the *key* of the piece or passage.

There is no obvious reason for the supremacy of one tone and the subservience of others, but this orientation around a central pitch occurs spontaneously. The function of all other tones and chords is ordained by their relation to the tonic.

Tonality is an elusive quality, difficult to define but easy to demonstrate. Start singing the first stanza of *America* and stop on the word "I." Notice the sensation of being "up in the air." The impression is stronger if the harmony is added. The phrase demands completion which is accomplished by adding the tonic note and chord with the word "sing." At the end of the stanza, the tonic on "ring" is approached differently, but stopping short of it produces the same effect. A variant of this experiment is to lift the stylus from a recording before the final chord. In each case a feeling of finality is demanded which only the tonic can supply. The interaction of tonal relationships which creates this situation is *tonality*.

Any pitch may serve as the tonic. The relation of other tones to it determines the *mode*. Between octaves of the tonic, there are eleven different pitches. Together with the tonic they comprise a *chromatic* scale of twelve tones. Commonly, music is based on scales of seven tones selected from these to form certain patterns of whole steps (major 2nds) and half steps (minor 2nds). Numbering the scale degrees up from the keynote, the most prevalent pattern has half steps between 3-4 and 7-8, whole steps elsewhere. This is the pattern associated with the syllables *do, re, mi, fa, sol, la, ti, do*. It forms a *major scale*, and music derived from it is in a *major mode* or *key*. *America, The Star Spangled Banner, Home on the Range*, and most familiar songs are in major keys.

After major, the next most common scale pattern is that of *minor*. Natural minor is a seven-tone scale with half steps between 2-3 and 5-6. *When Johnny Comes Marching Home* is a well-known song in minor. The major mode has been so predominant, elements of it customarily are incorporated in pieces which are fundamentally minor. This has led to scale resources referred to as forms of minor but which actually are hybrids combining elements of the two modes. The essential difference between major and all forms of minor lies in the 3rd degree of the scale. It is a major 3rd above the keynote in major and a minor 3rd above the keynote in minor.

Contrast the sound of the two following examples—one major, the other minor. Both pieces end with a strong return to the keynote in the melody. See if you can sing the keynote at the conclusion of the performance.

FREDERIC CHOPIN: *Preludes for Piano, Op. 28* (1839)
   (1810–1849)   No. 7 in A major   :45
                            No. 4 in E minor   1:50

The bulk of music written since 1600 is either major or minor. The ability to distinguish between major and minor and to discern the keynote at the end of compositions and at critical points during the course of a work is evidence of perceptive listening.

Though familiar music is preponderantly major or minor, these are not the only modes. Rich and varied scale resources of earlier periods fell into disuse when the major-minor system gained ascendency around 1600. The music of previous centuries was based on the *church modes* (or *ecclesiastical modes*), a complete system of scales that evolved over hundreds of years. The church modes are seven-tone scales like major and minor, but the half steps are in different locations. As the name suggests, early church music was derived from these modes exclusively.

GREGORIAN CHANT (Codified 590–604)
   Tract: Domine non secundum   3:10
   Sequence: Sancti spiritus assit nobis gratia   1:10

     Melodies based on the church modes, as these are, sound somewhat strange to modern ears accustomed to hearing only major and minor. The displacement of the half steps, in relation to the more familiar scale patterns, reduces the tendency of certain tones to progress in a prescribed direction and makes the contour to the melodies less predictable, less bound by conventions. These examples are included in *The History of Music in Sound* Volume II, RCA Victor LM–6015.

Prior to 1600 all Christian liturgical music was modal, but the use of the church modes was never restricted to sacred music. The modes were also used in the secular music of the period, and they have been preserved to the present time in folk music. Two Carolina folk songs, *The Winter's Past* and *Wayfaring Stranger*, each derived from a different church mode, are the source of the melodies in the following work.

WAYNE BARLOW: *The Winter's Past* (1938)   5:10
  (1912–   )

> The folk tunes are essentially intact in this contemporary setting. The quaint flavor of the melodies stems from their church-mode derivation. The harmonies exhibit a curious but delightful mixture of old scale resources and new structures. This is one of the pieces of *American Music for Solo Winds and String Orchestra* on Mercury record 50076.

After nearly 300 years of neglect, the church modes were rediscovered by composers and adapted to current usage. Contemporary applications have little in common with Gregorian chant, but modal influences abound in 20th-century music. Ravel's *String Quartet* is one of many recent works in which modal scale resources are exploited deliberately.

MAURICE RAVEL: *String Quartet in F* (1903)
  (1875–1937)   1. Allegro moderato—Très doux   7:30

> The composed modal melodies of this quartet are unlike the chants or folk songs with which they share scale materials. The modal influence does not extend to the harmonies, which are typical of Ravel and turn-of-the-century French music.

Toward the end of the last century composers seem to have come to the conclusion that the possibilities of musical invention within the major-minor system were approaching exhaustion. In any event the exploration of other scale resources dates from about this time. Besides reviving the church modes, composers devised and exploited new scales. One of the most distinctive of the new scales was the *whole tone scale*. In contrast to major and minor scales and the church modes, whole tone scales have no half steps and only six tones. The following composition draws its material, except for a brief passage in the middle, entirely from a whole tone scale.

CLAUDE DEBUSSY: *Preludes for Piano, Book I* (1910)
   (1862–1918)   2. Voiles (Sails or Veils)   2:45

    The whole tone scale is ideal for creating the nebulous atmosphere
of this piece.

    Fascinating as the whole tone scale is, there are definite limits to its
usefulness. Melodies and harmonies derived from it have a certain sameness
of sound, and the very striking quality which initially attracts both composers
and listeners soon leads them to tire of it. Contemporary composers have
utilized many other scale formations, but the prevailing trend has been to
reject the concept of selective scales.

    Composers in this century have come to regard the limitations of selec-
tive scales as arbitrary. Whereas composers previously were inclined to draw
their basic tonal material from a preconceived scale of seven tones and to
use the remaining five tones incidentally, contemporary composers are more
apt to regard all twelve tones as equal in status and accessibility. The net
result of this is that the previous hierarchy of tones is abolished, and the
available tonal resources are expanded and freed from restraint.

    Renouncing selective scales and according equal status to all twelve
tones does not automatically eliminate the possibility of tonality. Tonal
centers can be established which include in their orbit all eleven remaining
tones, rather than the customary six that gravitate to a conventional tonic.
Distinctions between major and minor disappear, and the tonality of such
music is vague. However, alert listeners can detect the tonal centers in music,
like the following example, which embodies the principles of this expanded
tonal concept.

DMITRI SHOSTAKOVICH: *Symphony No. 1 in F, Op. 10* (1925)
   (1906–   )   1. Allegretto   9:25

    The tonal centers in passages of this 20th-century symphony are
    almost as obvious as they are in 18th-century works, yet all twelve
    tones are used with equal freedom. A contemporary flavor is attained
    without undue complexity. Judicious balance between the old and
    the new have made this symphony a favorite with listeners who are
    a little tired of the standard repertory but not quite ready to embrace
    more radical new music.

    Some modern music is in two or more keys at the same time. This is
called *polytonality*, a device that appeals to some composers of our time,
Darius Milhaud among them. Polytonality is not a technique that can be used
exclusively with good effect, but it produces a delectable piquancy in brief

compositions and isolated passages. The sense of tonality is never strong when two keys are used together. The perception of polytonality is usually based on the recognition of its peculiar quality rather than on the actual identification of dual tonal centers.

DARIUS MILHAUD: *Saudades do Brasil* (1921)
   (1892–   )   7. Corcovado   1:35

> Milhaud spent two years in Brazil as a French diplomat. The twelve pieces of the *Saudades* are souvenirs of his visit. Each depicts some colorful district of Rio de Janeiro—this one the "hunchback" mountain which is one of its landmarks. The tonal center implied by the melody is often different from that of the accompaniment.

Many 20th-century composers have made the final break with tradition, as far as tonality is concerned, and write music which has no key center. Music without a tonal center is said to be *atonal*. Proponents of this type of music eschew the term, but it is descriptive. Arnold Schoenberg evolved a system of "composition with twelve tones related only to one another" which assures the equal use of all twelve tones and eliminates the possibility of any tone inadvertently asserting itself as a tonic, or tonal center. A *series* of tones comprising all twelve notes in a fixed order, with none repeated, serves as the basis for a complete work. The series, subjected to specified manipulations and modifications, is repeated throughout the composition. No note is used except as it occurs in its prescribed order in the series. Actually, there is a good deal more to the philosophy and the technique of the system than this, but a detailed description is beyond the scope of a music appreciation book.[1]

Serial music, as music written according to Schoenberg's principles is commonly called, is not designed for easy listening, but it must be considered by anyone seriously interested in the music of our time. Some of the greatest creative minds of 20th-century music regard serial organization as the most viable, if not the only valid, compositional procedure. Every living composer is familiar with the system and, it seems safe to generalize, is influenced by it to some degree. No composer active at the present time could, or would choose, to insulate himself from such a significant development, though many do not subscribe to the method. Composers on the whole have been more intrigued by serialism and atonality than have performers and listeners. Performers find it difficult and frequently ungrateful to play. Listeners are rarely able to detect the high degree of organization implicit in

---

[1] For additional information see Leon Dallin, *Techniques of Twentieth Century Composition*, second edition, Dubuque: Wm. C. Brown Company Publishers, 1964.

the system and are perplexed by the absence of familiar tonal functions. The preceding examples illustrate various kinds of tonality. The following example contrasts with these and demonstrates the difference between music which has a tonal center, however vague, and that which has none.

ARNOLD SCHOENBERG: *String Quartet No. 4, Op. 37* (1936)
   (1874–1951)   1. Allegro molto, energico   8:10

> This music is atonal. Unless you have previously heard music by Schoenberg or one of his disciples, you probably have never heard any like it before. It is not performed often, for it is extremely difficult to play. Until recently, there were few performances or recordings of music like this. You will not find singable melodies, toe-tapping rhythms, or sonorous harmonies in it. The melodic motion is disjunct, the rhythm irregular, and each part obstinately independent. Kaleidoscopic convolutions reflect the turmoil of the age which gave this music birth. In listening to it, try to put aside preconceived notions about what music should be, and accept this music on its own terms. It will not recall fond memories, and you will not go away whistling its tunes. It does provide a provocative and stimulating listening experience.

Modulation

The same melodic and harmonic devices which cause one note to emerge as a tonal center are used to shift the center from one pitch to another. This process is called *modulation*. Any change of key is a modulation.

Modulation is a constant source of variety in music and a feature of musical form. Excursions to other keys are invariably followed by a return to the original tonic in traditional compositions. One must be aware of changes in tonality, especially the departure from and return to the original key, to comprehend musical structures and procedures completely. The perception of tonality and modulation may be on the subconscious level, but static tonality produces conscious monotony.

Modulations may be made between any two keys, but most often they occur between *related keys*. Related keys are those keys which have five or more of their seven notes in common. Keys with fewer than five notes in common are *foreign* or *remote keys*, and modulations to them are *foreign* or *remote modulations*. Pairs of keys, one major and one minor, which have all seven notes in common but a different keynote are *relative keys*. The major key and the minor key with the same keynote are *parallel keys*.

Modulations are reckoned according to the relationship of the new tonic to the old. In describing key relationships the Roman numerals and the names associated with each scale degree are useful. In scale order, they are:

I—Tonic
VII—Subtonic (Leading tone)
VI—Submediant
V—Dominant
IV—Subdominant
III—Mediant
II—Supertonic
I—Tonic

Either the name or the numeral indicating the scale degree can be used in referring to modulations. For example, a modulation to the dominant key or to V would indicate that the fifth scale degree of the old key would become the new tonic. Modulations throughout a composition are related to the original tonic key established at the outset. Modulations to the dominant key are most common, followed by modulations to the subdominant (IV), supertonic (II), relative major (III), and relative minor (VI). These are closely related keys having six or all seven of their tones in common.

Modulations are illustrated in the examples of Part II in connection with the study of musical form.

Dynamics and Color

Dynamics and tone color, or timbre, cannot be ignored in a discussion of musical elements. They are not elements in the same sense as rhythm, melody, and harmony, but they are nonetheless essential components of the composer's expressive material.

Dynamics have to do with degrees of loudness and softness, prime ingredients of emotional intensity in music. Dynamic level is determined by the number and kind of instruments used and by the manner of playing. Instruments and voices are capable of wide dynamic variations, and the composer's intentions are conveyed to the players by means of signs which are a part of musical notation. There are signs for several degrees of loudness and for changes both gradual and sudden. Dynamic indications are relative, and very loud for a violin is quite different from very loud for a trombone or full orchestra. However, composers learn what to expect from each instrument and combination and score accordingly. The inbalance of tone produced by certain categories of instruments is compensated for somewhat by the numbers used. For instance, string instruments produce much less sound than brass instruments, but there are many more of them in an orchestra. In this regard it is noteworthy that doubling the number of players does not double the amount of tone. Two violins playing with equal intensity are only 1.3 times louder than one. Ten are required to double the sound of one. Securing proper dynamic levels and balancing the sound of opposing sections in larger ensembles is a strategic function of conductors.

Color in music results from the fusion of pitches and timbres. Each note on every instrument has a unique sound, even ignoring pitch differences. With various pitches and timbres mingled, the color possibilities are infinite. The art of orchestration (scoring music for orchestra) and the quest for orchestral color have been carried to new heights during the last century. This trend has been encouraged by mechanical improvements in instruments and by the astounding technical proficiency of large numbers of performers. Performances of scores which would have been deemed impossible to play before the turn of the century are commonplace today. The perfection of instruments and the artistry of players have stimulated composers to write ever more demanding scores and to tap hidden instrumental resources for new colors. Fresh orchestral colors have been produced by instruments playing in extreme registers—very high and very low. Mechanical devices have been used in and on instruments to modify their tone coloring. Unusual ways of producing tones, like strings playing with the wood rather than the hair of the bow, have been used for special effects. These variegated tints added to the normal rich coloring of the orchestra provide the composer with a tempting palette.

Recent composers have taken full advantage of bounteous and relatively stable instrumental resources. They have made penetrating studies of instrumental possibilities, limitations, and peculiarities and have cultivated an idiomatic way of writing for each instrument which utilizes its capabilities to the fullest and minimizes its shortcomings. This facet of composing was largely ignored by earlier composers who were inclined to be indifferent toward instrumentation. Many of their scores do not specify the instruments to be used, an unthinkable omission in recent times. Lack of standardization in both instruments and instrumental combinations fostered the practice of writing, on occasion, parts which could be played by any of several instruments. These circumstances, coupled with the preoccupation of composers for an extended period with problems of melody, harmony, and form, delayed the full flowering of orchestral color. Ferreting out latent instrumental possibilities, skillful and colorful orchestration are hallmarks of the late 19th and 20th centuries.

Harmony also is a source of musical color. Some combinations of notes are rich, others stark. Some are bright, others dark. Some harmonic progressions are iridescent and some are achromatic. Words are inadequate to describe them, but the hues of harmony are apparent to all who listen.

The full range of dynamic levels from whispering to thundering and the full spectrum of orchestral color from infrared to ultraviolet are exploited in the following examples.

RIMSKY-KORSAKOV: *Capriccio Espagnol, Op. 34* (1887)

(1844–1908)	1. Alborada	1:15
	2. Variations	4:30
	3. Alborada	1:15
	4. Scene and Gypsy Song	4:45
	5. Fandango of the Asturias	3:00

The composer's intention was to create a piece which would "glitter with dazzling orchestral color." He was satisfied with his accomplishment, as well he might have been! He took issue with critics who praised the *Capriccio* as a magnificently orchestrated piece and preferred to think of it as a brilliant composition for the orchestra, a subtle but in his mind an important distinction. The first, third, and fifth movements share thematic material. The fourth and fifth are played without interruption.

OTTORINO RESPIGHI: *The Pines of Rome* (1924)   19:15

(1879–1936)   The Pines of the Villa Borghese

The Pines near a Catacomb

The Pines of the Janiculum

The Pines of the Appian Way

This descriptive work in four connected sections utilizes the full color and dynamic range of the modern symphony orchestra.

texture

There are three basic kinds of musical texture, *monophonic, polyphonic,* and *homophonic.* Phonic by itself is an adjective meaning *of or pertaining to sound.* Mono- is a combining form meaning *one, single, alone.* Poly- is a combining form signifying *many, much, several.* Homo- is a combining form denoting *common, joint, like.* These terms have special connotations in music.

Monophonic Texture

Monophonic texture, or *monophony* to use the noun form, is music consisting of a single, unaccompanied melodic line. It is the most ancient of the three types. Monophonic music occupies such an insignificant position in our culture that it is difficult to realize the large span of music history devoted to its development and how large it still looms on the universal musical scene. Primitive music and that of ancient civilizations, early church and court music, and Oriental music to the present day are essentially monophonic. Most of this music was little known beyond its own time and sphere of influence until musicologists and ethnologists combined their skills with the marvels of recording to discover, collect, recreate, and disseminate music from the distant past and from the far corners of the world.

Acquaintance with old and exotic music has increased recognition of its value. Freedom and interesting detail of line in monophony compensate for its sparseness of texture. It is refreshing to discover the beauty of single lines—rediscover would be more exact. The systematic sounding together of different pitches, dating back only a little over a millennium, is a comparatively recent development.

The largest single body of monophonic music is found in the liturgy of the Catholic Church. There are nearly 3000 chant melodies in the repertory, a treasury no proper study of music can ignore. Music of the remote past should not be equated with familiar styles. The very old, like the very new, must be accepted on its own terms. Its quaint sound, unaccompanied simplicity, and unmeasured rhythm must not be taken as tokens of inferiority.

GREGORIAN CHANT (Codified 590–604)
  Alleluia: Vidimus stellam   2:00

> The musical ritual of the Catholic Church crystallized during the pontificate of Gregory the Great (590–604), from whom the chant takes its name. The origins of some of the chants can be traced back to antiquity, while others postdate Gregory. This example is recorded on Haydn Society 9038, *Masterpieces of Music before 1750.* (Notation p. 302)

Instrumental melodies are rarely unencumbered in Western music. The following examples are selected from the isolated instances in which composers have lavished their talents on a single instrumental line. In these selections the melody does not have to compete with harmony or counterpoint for attention, and listeners are free to concentrate on the details of pure melodic invention.

J. S. BACH: *Partita No. 2 in D minor for Violin, S.1004* (1722)
  (1685–1750)   4. Gigue   4:00

> String instruments are capable of playing double notes and chords, but this movement from the *Partita* for unaccompanied violin is an example of pure monophonic texture.

CLAUDE DEBUSSY: *Syrinx* (1912)   2:35
  (1862–1918)

> This work for flute is one of the very few for an unaccompanied wind instrument. Syrinx is the Greek name for panpipes, a primitive wind instrument attributed to the god Pan. It consists of a graduated series of pipes fastened together and played by blowing.

Few works on modern concert programs are limited to a single melodic line, but monophonic passages are common in all styles, periods, mediums, and forms. These examples demonstrate that an unaccompanied melody can capture and hold a listener's attention, but the primary function of monophonic texture is to provide variety in works which are essentially homophonic or polyphonic.

Polyphonic Texture

At an early date melodies and chanting were accompanied by stamping, clapping, and percussion instruments. The second part in such cases is lacking in pitch and the other attributes of tone, so it does not, strictly speaking, represent a combination of musical sounds. The first real departures from monophony probably resulted from minor discrepancies committed by accident or intent in the performance of a single line. The sounding together of slightly discrepant versions of the same melody produces *heterophony*. Heterophony occurred in ancient Greek music, and it persists in the music of Africa, Java, China, and particularly Japan. Neither heterophony nor percussion-accompanied melody is common in recent Western music, though there are isolated instances of both. These styles are featured only in primitive and exotic music.

Another early step toward polyphony came as a result of combining male and female or boys voices. The natural pitch of adult male voices is about an octave lower than that of preadolescent and female voices. When the two sing the same melody together, they normally sing in octaves. That is, they sing identical melodic contours and notes with the same letter names, but different pitches. The ratio of vibration between the two parts is constantly 1:2. Two pitches with this ratio blend so perfectly that they are barely distinguishable, and the sound is more like an amplification of one pitch than a combination of two. This pitch relationship results automatically in community singing by mixed groups. It also is common between the principals in dramatic musical works.

RICHARD RODGERS: *The King and I* (1951)
  (1902–   )   We Kiss in a Shadow   3:20

> First the tenor and then the soprano sing alone. Then, in a pattern familiar in this type of musical production, they sing the melody together in octaves. The orchestral background, of course, would not figure in primitive examples of this type of texture.

The incidental and almost spontaneous combinations of sound such as percussion-accompanied melody, heterophony, and octave doubling which occur in ancient and primitive music did little to pave the way for subsequent development. This was delayed until pitches were combined systematically and preserved in notation. The oldest specimens with these qualifications date from the 9th century. At first the added parts duplicated the contour and rhythm of the original melody, but this stage did not last long. Soon the intervals between the parts were varied, and not long after the parts became rhythmically independent. The effect was no longer that of one line with a shadow but that of autonomous parts. These early experiments sound crude to modern ears, but the significance of this innovation cannot be exaggerated. The pace of musical development quickened with this breakthrough, and it has been gaining momentum ever since.

EARLY POLYPHONY (10th and 11th centuries)
Sit Gloria Domini	:15
Alleluia: Surrexit Christus	3:00
Regi Regum Glorioso	2:00

> The first example is the earliest and most primitive. It consists of a melody doubled by a parallel part a fourth lower and duplication of both parts at the octave. The second example, taken from a manuscript dated about 1100, shows marked progress. Two-part music alternates with monophonic passages. The added part no longer parallels the other voice, but frequently moves in the opposite direction. Though the two parts are rhythmically identical, the combination of different melodic contours has been accomplished. The third example employs procedures similar to those of the second except that the two parts are continuous and there are instances of momentary rhythmic independence. These examples are in *The History of Music in Sound* Volume II, RCA Victor LM–6015.

Music conceived as a combination of melodies is *polyphonic* or *contrapuntal* in texture, the terms being used interchangeably. The art of combining melodies and the study of contrapuntal music is *counterpoint*.

Polyphonic music is, generally speaking, more demanding on the part of both listeners and performers than monophonic or homophonic music. The listener must follow the interweaving of multiple lines, and the performer must play them in a manner which makes this feasible.

Contrapuntal texture can be created in three basic ways: (1) by overlapping statements of the same melody started at different times, (2) by joining melodies which have common material and share motives but have independent contours and rhythms, and (3) by combining melodies related only by association. Polyphonic texture more often than not is an amalgamation of the three types.

A part which duplicates the rhythm and contour of a previously stated musical idea is said to be in *imitation*. The number of beats or measures between entrances is the *distance of imitation,* and the difference in pitch between starting notes is the *interval of imitation.* These terms are applicable to the first type of polyphonic texture and to the second in passages where material passes directly from one part to another within the space of a few measures. They are not appropriate for the third type which is *nonimitative* or *free counterpoint*.

The composer writing imitative counterpoint is confronted with the special problem of fitting together predetermined melodic lines, but examples of this type of polyphony occur in rudimentary sources. Rounds such as *Are You Sleeping, Three Blind Mice*, and *Row, Row, Row Your Boat* are perfectly valid examples of polyphonic texture and continuous imitation. The limitations of continuous imitation are too severe for most art music, but it is used in many short compositions and in brief passages of longer works. The usual procedure is for imitation to be used for the entrance of a part and then abandoned. Another common practice is to exchange motives between parts without systematic or extended imitation. Bach exploits all of these possibilities in his *Two-Part Inventions*.

J. S. BACH: *Two-Part Inventions, S.772/786* (1720)

(1685–1750)	No. 2 in C minor	1:25
	No. 3 in D major	1:10
	No. 7 in E minor	1:25

The two parts of *Invention 2* are in strict imitation at the interval of an octave and at the distance of two measures (eight beats) during most of the invention. The imitation is interrupted briefly in the middle and just before the end. The lower voice imitates the upper for the first half of the piece, and the upper voice imitates the lower in the last half.

In *Invention 3* the second voice enters in imitation two measures (six beats) after and an octave lower than the first voice. The imitation is dropped after two measures and not resumed, though the two parts exchange motives on several occasions. (Notation p.303)

Invention 7 is organized around motives which pass from one part to the other carrying the burden of interest.

Attentive listening and repeated hearings are usually necessary before the individual lines of imitative counterpoint can be followed and fully appreciated. The interchange of motives between parts is less difficult to perceive. Perhaps the most common type of contrapuntal texture is that involving exchanges of material between the parts and imitation of limited duration. *Fugues* are prime examples of this type of counterpoint.

The structure of fugues is considered in greater detail in Chapter 9, but basically a fugue is a musical form in which each part enters imitatively with the same theme or *subject* and in which subsequently the subject is combined with itself and with other melodies. Melodic interest is distributed between all of the parts, and recognizing the themes wherever and whenever they appear is essential for comprehension of the musical design. The subject is announced alone at the beginning of a fugue. Hearing the subject by itself a few times facilitates recognition of later entrances when it is associated with other melodic lines.

J. S. BACH: *Fugue in G minor, "Little," for Organ* (1700)   4:50
(1685–1750)

> Bach brought the fugue to its highest perfection, and this is a classic example of the form. Counting the statements of the subject as they appear is one way to determine whether or not all of them are being detected.

Though fugue form was perfected in Bach's time, it has been adapted to changing styles through the years and is still in use. The following example in comparison with the previous one demonstrates that the fugue idea has diverse applications.

JAROMIR WEINBERGER: *Opera, Schwanda the Bagpiper* (1927)
(1896–1967)   Polka and Fugue   7:30

> The opera *Schwanda* tells the tale of a jolly bagpipe player who defeats the devil himself with his magical music. The complete opera is seldom given in this country, but this excerpt is a favorite. The *Polka* is fundamentally homophonic, though countermelodies are introduced at times. It comes to a close in just over two minutes, and the violins by themselves announce the fugue subject. From this point on the fugue subject or fragments of it are passed from one section of the orchestra to another in typical fugue fashion, and the texture becomes polyphonic. Toward the end of the fugue, elements of the fugue subject and the polka theme are combined.

The next example might be regarded as a sort of 20th-century counterpart of the Bach *Two-Part Inventions*. The two violin parts are conceived melodically, rather than harmonically, so the texture is polyphonic but for the most part nonimitative. Listen for the independent melodies in the two parts and for the features mentioned in the description.

BELA BARTOK: *Duos (44) for Two Violins* (1931)
(1881–1945)   1. Teasing Song   :53
                   2. Maypole Dance   :36
                   3. Menuetto   :58
                   4. Summer Solstice Song   :52

5.	Slovakian Song No. 1	:52
6.	Hungarian Song No. 1	:52
7.	Walachian Song	:40

The melodic lines are essentially independent in the first two duos. The little figure with which the upper part enters in No. 3 also appears in the lower part, but this is the extent of the common material. No. 4 begins imitatively, but soon the two parts pursue their separate paths, sharing only rhythmic figures. The parts of No. 5 are related only by association. There is imitation in No. 6, but it is rhythmically altered and will probably go undetected. The plan of No. 7 is for the two players to trade parts at the half-way point and play an embellished version of the first half. The exchange of parts, however, will not be apparent in a recorded performance. At the very end one part echoes the other.

When you can detect the entrances of the subject in a fugue and follow the lines of two-part counterpoint with ease, you are ready for more demanding listening experiences. The next example is a challenge for even the most attentive listener. Three independent melodies ultimately are combined in a magnificent specimen of polyphonic texture.

RICHARD WAGNER: *Opera, Die Meistersinger (The Mastersingers)* (1868)
 (1813–1883)   Prelude   9:00

The piece and the first theme begin together with an incisive rhythmic motive followed by an ascending scale line. A new rhythmic motive and full chords in the brass and woodwind sections signal the beginning of the second theme (1:35). The first theme returns (2:20) transformed into a lyric melody. The mood changes, and the third theme, the famous "Prize Song" of the opera, enters quietly (3:35). After extensive development, all three themes are combined in the final section (6:25). The "Prize Song" theme is the principal melody. Both versions of the first theme are used in the bass, and the second theme provides the harmonic background.

Homophonic Texture

The texture is homophonic when the melodic interest is concentrated in a single part, usually the highest, and the remaining parts serve primarily to provide an accompaniment. Supporting parts in homophonic music are designed to form a suitable rhythmic and harmonic background for the predominant melody.

The homophonic and polyphonic approaches to music, though differing in point of view, are not mutually exclusive. The difference is one of emphasis. An accompanying part in homophonic music creates a linear sequence of tones in going from one chord tone to another, but the composer strives for complete chords and smooth, unobtrusive lines rather than for engaging contours. In polyphony each part is conceived as a melody, but the melodic tones sounding together form chords. One melody is supreme in homophonic music, and all other parts cooperate to provide a setting favorable to its unfolding without competing for attention. All parts are melodies in polyphonic music, and though the center of interest may shift, one never becomes subservient to another. Except for the one melody, homophony is vertically oriented, and harmonic progression is of primary importance. Polyphony is horizontally oriented, and linear movement is of primary importance. Conversely, the lines of accompanying parts in homophony and the harmonic progressions resulting from polyphony are secondary considerations.

Ideally, the vertical and horizontal aspects of music—the chords and lines—should be in balance. Their conflicting requirements are reconciled by composers of genius with no apparent compromises. Few compositions are purely homophonic or polyphonic. One type of texture may predominate, but rarely to the exclusion of the other. The dividing line between homophonic and polyphonic texture is not always sharp, and borderline cases are probably more prevalent than clear examples of either.

The development of multipart music was melodic rather than harmonic until about 1600 when a group of poets and composers attempting to recreate Greek drama laid the foundations for both the homophonic style and opera, neither of which was implicit in their model. One aim of the group was to provide dramatic texts with musical settings that would permit the words to be clearly understood. The polyphonic style did not satisfy this requirement. Their solution was to project a single melodic line against a background of slower-moving harmonies, and the concept of homophonic music was born. Claudio Monteverdi was the most distinguished of its early practitioners.

CLAUDIO MONTEVERDI: *Opera, Orfeo* (1607)
(1567–1643)   Tu se' morta (Thou art perished)   2:35

> This is a *recitative*, a passage in declamatory style for solo voice with a simple harmonic accompaniment. The recitative style dominated the first operas and persisted between more lyric sections of operas, oratorios, and cantatas into the 19th century.

The recitative style, in which a simple melodic line is accompanied by relatively static harmonies, is one type of homophonic texture. Another type of homophonic texture results when all of the parts, including the melody, move together in block chords. This type of homophonic texture is found in hymns, chorales, carols, patriotic songs, and the like when they are sung in parts with the rhythm and the words of the accompanying voices coinciding with those of the tune. The following examples are representative of chordal, homophonic texture.

MICHAEL PRAETORIUS: *Lo, How a Rose E'er Blooming* (1609)   1:05
   (1571–1621)

ANONYMOUS: *God Rest You Merry, Gentlemen*   1:00
   Congregational and community singing is generally in a chordal, homophonic style. This style is preserved in the recording of these songs on RCA LM–2139, *Christmas Hymns and Carols.*

The third and most prevalent type of homophonic texture involves, like the others, a single predominant melody but with a rhythmically animated accompaniment. This is the style of most solo songs and practically all instrumental music, both popular and serious for large groups and small, which is not contrapuntal in nature. The most obvious means of motivating otherwise static harmony is to repeat the chords in a rhythmic pattern. This not only adds interest and movement, but, in the case of the piano, provides a way of sustaining the sound at equal intensity. The repeated notes in *The Erl-King* accompaniment serve both purposes.

FRANZ SCHUBERT: *The Erl-King, Op. 1* (1815)   4:00
   (1797–1828)
   This is Schubert's most famous song and one of the best and best known in the entire literature. In addition to a narrator, there are three characters in the song, a father, his son, and the Erl-King, a symbol of death. Singers ordinarily vary their vocal quality to represent the different characters. The rapid repeated notes in the piano accompaniment graphically portray the frantic night ride of the father holding his dying son in his arms.

Another way to motivate harmony is to have the notes of the chords sound one at a time in succession, typically in consistent rhythm and pitch patterns. The keyboard music of the last half of the 18th century is replete with accompaniment figures fitting this stereotype. Mozart was one of the composers who used this method of motivating harmonies in a basically homophonic texture.

W. A. MOZART: *Piano Sonata No. 15 in C, K.545* (1788)
   (1756–1791)   1. Allegro   3:00

        2. Andante   4:00
        3. Allegretto grazioso   1:25

Each movement of this sonata contains accompaniment figures current in Mozart's time. The patterns are varied and interrupted to avoid monotony, but the real interest is in the melody above the accompaniment.

Similar accompaniments are also possible in nonkeyboard works. Haydn, a contemporary of Mozart, wrote one for strings.

JOSEPH HAYDN: *String Quartet in F, Op. 3 No. 5* (1763)
  (1732–1809)   2. Andante cantabile   5:55

An ingratiating melody in the first violin is accompanied by the other three instruments playing pizzicato (plucked) in a consistent pattern.

Harmonic progression and motivation were both highly stylized in this period leaving composers free to concentrate on melodic invention and organization, a circumstance which contributed to the tremendous fecundity of men like Mozart and Haydn without noticeably impairing the quality of their music. Men of lesser talent relying excessively upon these devices produced a quantity of undistinguished music which is no longer performed.

Another attribute of accompaniment figures, aside from those already mentioned, is their capacity to create the illusion of full chords with few notes. This combines the advantages of satisfying harmony with simplicity and clarity. There is no confusion or obscurity in the Mozart sonata, for much of the time only two notes are sounding, one melody tone and one tone of the accompaniment pattern. This fact is camouflaged by the figuration and the use of the sustaining pedal of the piano.

Composers of the next century were less inclined to settle for stereotyped patterns and harmonies. Their accompaniments generally are more elaborate and imaginative, sometimes approaching the status of secondary melodies, but still serving the same purposes as those of their predecessors. Their harmonies are more colorful, partially as a result of the fancier accompaniment patterns and partially as a product of natural evolution. Chopin was a luminary in this generation of composers.

FREDERIC CHOPIN: *Preludes for Piano, Op. 28* (1839)
  (1810–1849)   No. 3 in G   :55

Chopin was a master in conceiving brilliant piano figurations. His music ushered in a style of piano writing which remains at the apex of piano literature. It is a rare piano program on which he is not rep-

resented. This *Prelude* is a small sample of the piano style upon
which his reputation is based.

Accompaniment patterns related to those found in piano music are also
found in music for other mediums, but less obviously and extensively. One
reason is that most instruments, unlike the piano, are capable of sustaining
tones, so it is not necessary to repeat or change pitches to maintain volume.
Another reason is that repeated chords and figures submerged in the total
sound of an orchestra or a large ensemble are less apparent than the same
devices played on the piano. In writing for soloists, chorus, and orchestra
Mendelssohn supports single melodic lines with all three types of homophonic
accompaniment—sustained chords, rhythmically animated chords, and
block chords moving synchronously with the melody.

FELIX MENDELSSOHN: *Oratorio, Elijah, Op. 70* (1846)

(1809–1847)	3. Ye people, rend your hearts	1:00
	4. If with all your hearts	2:40
	15. Cast thy burden upon the Lord	1:35

No. 3 is a recitative with sustained chords in the orchestra accompanying a declamatory vocal line. The style is similar to the chrono-
logically earlier recitative of Monteverdi. The homophonic texture
of No. 4, an aria, consists of a melody for solo tenor plus an accompaniment in the orchestra of chord figures, rhythm patterns, and
repeated chords. No. 15 is a chorale in which the words of the text
occur synchronously in four-part chords formed by the voices. The
orchestra provides bridges between phrases of the chorale and
brings it to a close. The big choral numbers in *Elijah* are too contrapuntal to be appropriate examples in this context, but including
one or more in the listening gives a more complete picture of the
work. (Vocal parts of No. 15, p. 304)

Composers of the present century shun everything that smacks of pattern
or stereotype and consequently are not attracted to the homophonic accompaniment patterns. Finding substitutes for them magnifies the problems of
composition and reduces output, but most composers now seem to feel that
the added effort is not only justified, but necessary. Composers continue to
write homophonic music, but their rejection of ready-made devices requires
them to devote their creative energies as much to the settings as to the melodies and themes. Popular music is the one area where standardized accompaniments remain the rule rather than the exception.
   The evolution of music has gone from monophony through polyphony
to homophony, but the advent of a new type of texture has not meant the
supplanting of the old one. Since 1600, and to some extent even before, the

three types of musical texture have flourished side by side. The usual procedure is to vary the texture within a work, emphasizing first one type and then another. Extended works particularly are apt to make use of at least two types of texture, if not all three, for variety. Polyphonic and homophonic texture appear in almost equal proportion along with glimpses of monophonic texture in the finale of Mozart's *String Quartet.*

W. A. MOZART: *String Quartet No. 14 in G, K.387* (1782)
  (1756–1791)   4. Molto allegro   4:00

PART II

The Forms
of Music

small homophonic forms

Form in music can be defined as design or structure. It results from the patterns of repetition and contrast. Form refers to the logical organization of musical elements in a sequence of time.

Musical form has points in common with architecture, language, and literature. The structure of music can be likened to the structure of an edifice. The sounds of music create patterns in time as the shapes of material create patterns in space. Phrases and sentences in language have counterparts denoted by the same terms in music. Musical ideas enter, unfold, develop, and reach climaxes in the manner of novels and plays.

In spite of certain similarities to speech and the other arts, musical organization is essentially unique. It does not convey concrete meanings, so it is free from syntactical rules. Its formations are not restricted by the pull of gravity or the necessity of bearing weight. It exists only in time. Its perception is dependent upon remembering and relating a sequence of musical events. Elusive though it may be, form is a primary concern of the composer, the performer, and the listener. Music is not fully comprehended unless its plan of organization is perceived.

The forms of music cannot be regarded as molds into which the composer pours pitches and rhythms until they are full. In a very real sense each musical idea dictates its own form, and no two are identical. However, in the evolution of music certain recurrent patterns have crystallized. Without being the same they are sufficiently uniform to yield to systematic study. Not every work is cast in a traditional form, but the traditional forms influence even the musical designs they do not determine.

The Building Blocks

Musical organization begins with a note, but a single note cannot be related to a specific work. The smallest identifiable musical unit is a *motive*. A motive may be a rhythm, a pitch pattern, a combination of these, or less often a harmonic progression. Motives are the cells which coalesce into an organic whole. The most useful motives are those easily recognized in manifold modifications and readily adapted to multiple functions. Often they serve like mortar in binding together the other elements. Motives serve to link contrasting ideas, and they may figure in accompaniments as well as in melodies. Motives are particularly useful in *sequences*, that is, repetitions at other pitch levels of rhythmic, melodic, or harmonic patterns. Some themes are constructed by expanding and extending motives sequentially. The opening motive of Beethoven's *Fifth Symphony* fulfills all of these functions and in its many guises permeates the entire first movement.

L. VAN BEETHOVEN: *Symphony No. 5 in C minor, Op. 67* (1808)
(1770–1827)   1. Allegro con brio   6:00

> The first four notes introduce the motive which consists initially of three short notes on the same pitch followed by a longer note a third lower. The rhythm approximates the letter "V" in Morse code used during World War II as a victory motto. The statement of the motive is followed immediately by a repetition of its rhythm and contour at a slightly lower pitch. Different versions of the motive then are strung together in sequence to form a theme. The motive is still in evidence during a transitional passage, and when a lyric melody enters, it moves to the accompaniment. The rhythm of the motive is always recognizable no matter how its shape is bent or where it appears in the texture. The motive is a primary unifying element of the *Symphony* and the germ from which this movement springs. (Motive p. 305)

The structural unit of music just larger than a motive is a *phrase*, borrowing a term from language. More than one phrase is generally required to complete a musical idea, so the musical idea in a single phrase is usually incomplete. The standard phrase length is four measures, but longer and shorter phrases are uncommon only in dance-inspired music. The setting of each of the following familiar lines is one phrase long. The phrases vary in length from three to six measures, as shown by the number in parentheses at the end of each line. Observe that two or three phrases of text may be set to a single phrase of music and that sometimes there are perceptible subdivisions within a musical phrase.

O say! Can you see, by the dawn's early light, (4)
O beautiful for spacious skies, for amber waves of grain, (4)
Come, Thou almighty King! (3)
My country, 'tis of thee, sweet land of liberty, of thee I sing. (6)

Each phrase ends with a *cadence*, the musical equivalent of the vocal inflections in spoken language associated with the end of phrases and sentences. The cadence effect is achieved by appropriate melodic, harmonic, and rhythmic formulas. The strength of cadences varies from a momentary pause within a musical idea to absolute finality at the end of a composition. The cadences within a musical idea are *incomplete cadences*. The cadences at the end of complete ideas and works are *complete cadences*.

Homophonic music, like language, grows by a cumulative process. In language the two parts of a compound sentence are joined to express a complete thought. Similarly, in music the incomplete ideas of two or more phrases are combined to express a complete musical thought. The resulting unit of musical form is a *sentence*, also called a *period*.[1] Sentences in music most often consist of two phrases. The first phrase in two-phrase sentences ends with an incomplete cadence, and the concluding phrase ends with a complete cadence. Interrelationships between the phrases comprising a sentence are the norm.

The most concrete way to examine typical sentence structures is to sing some familiar melodies illustrating them. Several are suggested. The phrase structure of each sentence is described and diagramed. A line under the words extends to the end of a phrase. The diagonal stroke at the end of a phrase line signifies a cadence, incomplete if the abbreviation i.c. appears below the line and complete if the abbreviation c.c. appears below the line. Phrases are identified by lower-case letters. A letter in parentheses following an identifying letter indicates a closely related phrase.

The phrases in two-phrase sentences typically have a question-answer relationship. The two phrases may begin alike and be very similar right up to the cadence points, but the cadences are different. The first phrase closes with the rising inflection of a question and an incomplete cadence. The second phrase closes with the falling inflection of an answer and a complete cadence. Stephen Foster's famous melody begins with this type of sentence.

Sentence: Two phrases beginning alike

Way down upon the Swannee River, far, far away,/
a   i.c.

---

[1] Among musicians *period* is the more prevalent term, but *sentence* seems preferable for nonmusicians.

There's where my heart is turning ever, there's where the old folks stay./
b (a)   c.c.

In the other type of two-phrase sentences the two phrases begin differently, as in the following example. The question-answer effect results from the contrasting contours of the two phrases. The ascending motion of the "a" phrase is answered by the descending motion of the "b" phrase. Unity is achieved by the repetition of a rhythmic pattern that occurs three times in each phrase. Observe that the meaning of the words and the punctuation have no bearing on the question-answer relationship of the two phrases.

Sentence: Two phrases beginning differently

Should auld acquaintance be forgot, and never brought to mind?/
a   i.c.

Should auld acquaintance be forgot, and days of auld lang syne?/
b   c.c.

Sentences are predominantly of the two-phrase variety with the phrases either beginning alike, like *Old Folks at Home*, or differently, like *Auld Lang Syne*. Less common are sentences of three, four, or more phrases.

In a three-phrase sentence the first two phrases end with incomplete cadences and the third with a complete cadence. The entire melody of *Silent Night* is a three-phrase sentence.

Sentence: Three phrases, all different

Silent night, holy night, all is calm, all is bright./
a   i.c.

Round yon virgin mother and Child, holy Infant so tender and mild./
b   i.c.

Sleep in heavenly peace, sleep in heavenly peace./
c   c.c.

In sentences of three or more phrases, two of the phrases may be the same. Of the four phrases in the first sentence of *Flow Gently, Sweet Afton*, the first and third are the same except for one note. Modifications, such as this, which do not obscure the identity of a part or alter its function are indicated by adding a prime sign (′) to the identifying letter or number. The second and fourth phrases begin alike but end differently. Only the last phrase of a sentence has a complete cadence.

Sentence: Four phrases, first and third alike

> *Flow gently, sweet Afton, among thy green braes;/*
> a   i.c.

> *Flow gently, I'll sing thee a song in thy praise;/*
> b   i.c.

> *My Mary's asleep by thy murmuring stream,/*
> a'   i.c.

> *Flow gently, sweet Afton, disturb not her dream./*
> c (b)   c.c.

The sentence structures of most music can be related to one of these four patterns illustrated from familiar songs. There are exceptions, of course, and in extended works and especially in developmental and transitional passages the divisions are apt to be vague and the phrases irregular.

Motives, phrases, and sentences—these are the building blocks of the homophonic forms.

One-Part Form

A *one-part form* differs from a sentence only in that a one-part form is complete in itself, whereas a sentence is usually part of a larger whole. All one-part forms, naturally, are sentences, and any sentence which stands by itself as a complete entity is also a one-part form. *Silent Night*, cited as an example of a three-phrase sentence, is also a one-part form. The melody of *When Johnny Comes Marching Home* is a four-phrase sentence and, likewise, a one-part form.

One-part form:

> *When Johnny comes marching home again, hurrah, hurrah!/*
> a   i.c.

> *We'll give him a hearty welcome then, hurrah, hurrah!/*
> b (a)   i.c.

> *The men will cheer, the boys will shout, the ladies they will all turn out,/*
> c   i.c.

> *And we'll all feel gay when Johnny comes marching home!/*
> d   c.c.

Other familiar one-part forms are: *America the Beautiful, Stars of the Summer Night, Abide with Me,* and *Anchors Aweigh.* One-part forms are common in folk, traditional, patriotic, and children's songs and in hymns. They are relatively rare, but not unknown, in art music. Several of Chopin's *Preludes*, for example, are one-part forms.

FREDERIC CHOPIN: *Preludes for Piano, Op. 28* (1839)
(1810–1849)   No. 1 in C   :35
One-part form:

a   i.c./ b (a)   i.c./ c   i.c./ d (a)   c.c./

An agitated rhythmic figure persists throughout the piece, not even interrupted at the cadence points. This makes the phrase divisions difficult to hear but contributes to the "oneness" of the form.

Two-Part Form: Binary

Binary is the customary designation for musical forms consisting of two distinct parts. Each part consists of a sentence or equivalent and ends with a complete cadence. The first complete cadence comes toward the middle of the form and ends the first part. The second complete cadence closes the second part and ends the work. Binary form is found in the same categories of familiar music as one-part form. The melodies of *Auld Lang Syne, Sweet and Low,* and *Aura Lee* are binary. The first sentence of *Aura Lee* is the setting for the verses, and the second sentence is the setting for the refrain. In all ensuing form diagrams musical sentences and parts with sentence function are identified by capital letters.

Binary form:

As the blackbird in the spring, 'neath the willow tree,/
A-a   i.c.

Sat and piped, I heard him sing, singing Aura Lee./
A-b (a)   c.c.

Aura Lee, Aura Lee, maid of golden hair,/
B-a   i.c.

Sunshine came along with thee, and swallows in the air./
B-b   c.c.

In concert music binary form is almost peculiar to the baroque period (1600–1750). It is the traditional form of the dance movements in the suites of that era. As used in the suites the form is known more specifically as *baroque binary.*

Baroque binary form is highly stylized. The tonic key is firmly established at the beginning of the first part, and then a modulation is made to a related key, ordinarily the dominant or relative major. A cadence in the new key concludes the first part. It is repeated immediately. The material of the second part is derived from and closely related to that of the first. There is no contrast of style, mood, or tempo. Frequently the only difference between the beginnings of the two parts is the change of key. The second part begins in the new key to which the first part modulated. Sometimes the second part starts as an inversion, that is, an up-side-down version of the first part. After beginning in the related key the second part modulates back to the original key, sometimes passing through one or more other tonalities enroute making it somewhat longer than the first part. A complete cadence in the tonic key concludes the second part. It, too, is repeated immediately. Though repeats are invariably indicated, they are not always observed by performers. Examples of baroque binary form are legion in the suites of Bach and his contemporaries. The ones in the *French Suites* are exceptionally concise and clear.

J. S. BACH: *French Suite No. 4 in E-flat* (1722)·
(1685–1750)   6. Gigue   2:30
     Binary form:

A	Starts with a lilting figure in one voice, other two enter imitatively, ends with complete cadence in dominant key.
A	Repeated. :30[2]
B	Starts with single voice like "A" but theme inverted and in dominant key, ends with complete cadence in tonic key. 1:00[2]
B	Repeated. 1:45[2]

(Themes p. 305)

Immediate repetitions of parts or sections do not affect the basic designations for the forms. The AB pattern of *Aura Lee* and the AA BB pattern of a typical baroque binary dance movement are both binary.

Three-Part Form: Ternary

A three-part design comprising statement-departure-return, represented by the letters ABA, is the most prevalent pattern of musical organization. It occurs in works of all sizes, small and large. When each of the three parts consists of a single idea, the form is simple *ternary*. Many familiar songs and practically all popular songs are ternary in form. Ternary design is most obvious when there are no repetitions and the three parts are of equal dura-

---

[2] Approximate elapsed time to the beginning of the part.

tion, as they are in the following example. After the basic ternary design is completed, a brief closing section, called a *coda*, ends the piece.

ROBERT SCHUMANN: *Scenes from Childhood, Op. 15* (1838)
   (1810–1856)   13. The Poet Speaks   1:40
       Ternary form:

> A   Sentence of two phrases ending with a complete cadence in minor.
>
> B   Four fragments together equalling sentence length but ending with an incomplete cadence.   :30
>
> A   Exactly as before. 1:00
>
> Coda Brings the piece to a close with a complete cadence in major. 1:30
>
>   (Themes p. 305)

A *coda* is a section sometimes added to the basic design of a form to bring a composition to a more conclusive or satisfactory close. *Codetta* is a diminutive form of the term meaning "small coda" but frequently used, as in this book, to designate a closing section appended to a principal part within a work. Codas are not usually found in one-part or binary forms but are common in ternary and all of the larger forms.

The function of the "B" section in a ternary form is to provide contrast with the "A" section which precedes it and to create a need for the return of "A" to round out and complete the design. The degree of contrast between the "A" and "B" sections varies considerably. In simple, concise examples of ternary form like *The Poet Speaks*, the thematic material of "B" may be derived from and very similar to that of "A" and the degree of contrast slight, just sufficient to establish a feeling of departure and return. In other examples of the form, especially more expansive ones, the material of "B" may be completely new, and the style may contrast sharply with that of "A" as it does in Chopin's *Nocturne No. 4*. The larger dimensions of this ternary form result from the expansion of the sections. Each of the three parts contains several phrases but only one complete idea. The high degree of contrast between the parts eliminates the necessity for decisive internal cadences.

FREDERIC CHOPIN: *Nocturne No. 4 in F, Op. 15 No. 1* (1833)   4:05
   (1810–1849)
       Ternary form:

> A   Slow tempo, lyric theme in major, last phrase extended to lead directly into "B."
>
> B   Fast tempo, dramatic theme in minor, extension of last phrase prepares for return of "A." 1:25

> A′   Slow tempo, lyric theme in major as before but ending
>   altered to arrive at a complete cadence.   2:20
>   (Themes p. 305)

All of the homophonic forms are routinely expanded by repetition. According to an established principle the immediate repetition of a part or group of parts does not alter the analysis of the underlying form. For example, an AB pattern and an AA BB pattern are both regarded as binary. One explanation for this is that a literal repetition is usually indicated by a sign, and the music is only written out once. Baroque binary forms with an AA BB pattern are written:

$$\|\!: \quad A \quad :\|\|\!: \quad B \quad :\|$$

The underlying structure of a piece with repeats is more apparent to one examining the music on the printed page than to one hearing it performed. Though immediate repetitions do not change the designation or the basic organizational plan, they do alter the actual sequence of musical events and complicate the aural perception of the form. However, familiarity with the conventional patterns of repetition simplifies the problem. Literal repetitions of complete parts are relatively rare in recent music, and the repeat signs prevalent in older music are not always observed in contemporary performances. These developments are perhaps a reflection of our accelerated pace of living.

In ternary forms the first part is repeated more often than not. When only the first part is repeated, the resulting pattern is AA B A. This design with each part an eight-measure sentence is standard for popular songs. It is also the design of *Träumerei*.

ROBERT SCHUMANN: *Scenes from Childhood, Op. 15* (1838)
(1810–1856)   7. Träumerei (Reverie)   2:10

Ternary form:

> A   Two phrases beginning alike, the second ending with a
>   complete cadence in a new key, but the rhythmic motion
>   continues in the bass.
>
> A   Repeated.   :30
>
> B   Closely related to "A," two phrases with similar contours,
>   the second higher, both cadences incomplete.   1:00
>
> A′   First phrase the same as before, second phrase modified
>   to remain in tonic key and to cadence conclusively.   1:30
>   (Themes p. 306)

All of the phrases in this piece begin with the same melodic contour. Emphasis is upon unity rather than variety, which is usual in small forms.

In ternary forms the first sentence frequently modulates and cadences in a new key, as it does in *Träumerei*. When this occurs, the return of "A" is modified to remain in the tonic key, and the piece ends in the same key as it began. It is traditional to begin and end compositions in the tonic key and to explore other tonalities in between. Thus the formal principal of departure and return applies to tonality as well as to thematic material.

Any of the parts of a ternary form may be repeated individually, but the usual practice when there are two repeats is to repeat the first part by itself and to repeat the second and third parts together as a unit. The pattern then becomes AA BA BA, but the form is still regarded as simple ternary. The ternary design is apparent when the repetitions are indicated by repeat signs.

‖: A :‖: B A :‖

The returns of "A" may be modified or abbreviated, and sometimes "B" is a phrase or a group of phrases rather than a sentence. The following is an example of a ternary form with an AA BA BA pattern of repetitions in which "B" is a phrase.

ROBERT SCHUMANN: *Scenes from Childhood, Op. 15* (1838)
  (1810–1856)   1. About Strange Lands and People   1:30
    Ternary form:

A	Opening melodic motive appears three times in succession in this sentence.
A	Repeated. :15
B	Almost as long as "*A*" but just a phrase. :30
A	First note different but otherwise as before. :45
BA	Repeated together. 1:00

(Themes p. 306)

Between the end of one part of a musical form and the beginning of the next there may be a *transition*. A transition is a passage that functions as a bridge between two structural units of a form. For this reason transitions are also called *bridge passages*. A modulation (change of key) normally occurs within a transition, and transitions also serve to prepare the way for changes of tempo, mood, and style. Transitional passages are usual between the parts of the larger musical forms; less usual but not uncommon between the parts of ternary forms. The transition in the following ternary form leads from the end of the "B" section in a contrasting key back to the tonic key and the return of the "A" theme.

P. I. TCHAIKOVSKY: *Nutcracker Suite, Op. 71a* (1892)
(1840–1893)   4. Russian Dance (Trepak)   1:05
    Ternary form:

A   Four phrases with an a-b-a-c(b) pattern.
A   Repeated with somewhat fuller scoring.
B   Melody moves to the bass, four phrases with the same design as "A."   :24
Transition based on motive common to the two parts.
A′   First three phrases essentially as before, last phrase extended several measures without a cadence until the end.   :43
               (Themes p. 306)

    The following 20th-century work is a relatively sophisticated example of ternary form. In it the return of "A" is substantially modified from the original statement, and the two transitions plus the coda (concluding section) account for approximately half of its duration.

PAUL HINDEMITH: *Mathis der Maler (Matthias the Painter)* (1934)
(1895–1963)   2. Grablegung (Entombment)   4:05
    Ternary form:

A   Three phrases of which the first and third are related.
Transition   :45
B   Oboe and then flute and oboe play two related phrases accompanied by pizzicato strings.   1:20
Transition using elements of both "A" and "B."
A′   First phrase of "A" modified and extended.   2:15
Coda 2:50
               (Themes p. 306)

Compound Binary Form

    Just as phrases are joined in sentences and sentences are combined in binary and ternary forms, binary and ternary forms are united at the next level of musical organization. The resulting forms have specialized applications, and there is no universally accepted terminology for them. *Compound binary* is a descriptive designation for the musical form consisting of two parts, each of which is simple binary or ternary. This form is typical of marches and rarely encountered elsewhere, so *march form* is another name for it.

    The first part of a compound binary form in march style is sometimes referred to as the *march* (as it is in the following diagram) to distinguish it from the second part, which is customarily labeled and called the *trio*. There is no logical reason for calling the second part a trio, but the usual explanation is that the corresponding part in a minuet is called a trio. March trios are traditionally in the subdominant key, and the trio concludes the form. Marches, therefore, are the one consistent exception to the rule that a piece ends in the same key as it begins. The trios in marches are usually lyric in style. Their lyricism is sometimes interrupted by a contrasting middle section, after which the lyric style returns.

Marches often begin with a brief *introduction*. An introduction is a passage that precedes the main body of a form. Introductions are useful in capturing the attention of listeners, in establishing the tempo, mood, and key of the piece, and in preparing for the entrance of the first thematic idea. *Hands Across the Sea* is a march in compound binary form which begins with an introduction and adheres to the conventional march plan throughout.

JOHN PHILIP SOUSA: *Hands Across the Sea* (1899)   2:35
    (1854–1932)

> Compound binary form:
> March: Binary
>> Introduction, one phrase.
>> A   Four phrases.
>> A   Repeated.
>> B   Four phrases.   :35
>> B   Repeated.
>
> Trio: Ternary
>> A^3 Lyric melody in subdominant key, four phrases. 1:05
>> A   Repeated.
>> B   Begins with low and high instruments sounding alternately. 1:35
>> A'   Embellished return of "A."
>> BA'   Repeated together, ends in subdominant key.   2:05
>> (Themes p. 307)

Composers of marches generally follow the basic plan of organization utilized by Sousa. The march proper is nearly always binary, and the trio is usually binary or ternary but is occasionally one part. It is traditional in marches for each sentence to be repeated.

---

[3] The letter "A" represents the first sentence (or passage with sentence function) in each part of a multipart-form diagram.

Compound Ternary Form

A form with an over-all A B A design in which each part individually is a simple binary or ternary form is a *compound ternary* form. Compound ternary is the usual form for minuets (French, *menuet*; Italian, *menuetto*). Each part of a minuet is most often ternary. The middle part, like the second part of a march, is a trio. The trio designation apparently originated when it was the practice to write the middle part of minuets for three instruments. The name persisted long after the reason for it had disappeared. The word *minuet* is used in two ways—to identify a complete piece or movement and more specifically to refer to the parts of a minuet that precede and follow the trio. Minuet-trio-minuet is the sequence of parts in a complete minuet. The first appearance of the minuet and the trio ordinarily have a full complement of repeats, and the return of the minuet has none, producing the following pattern.

Minuet	Trio	Minuet
‖: A :‖‖: BA :‖	‖: A :‖‖: BA :‖	ABA
(AA BA BA)	(AA BA BA) (CC DD CC)	

The third movement in classic four-movement sonatas, symphonies, and quartets typically is a minuet, as it is in Beethoven's *Piano Sonata No. 11*.

L. VAN BEETHOVEN: *Piano Sonata No. 11 in B-flat, Op. 22* (1800)
(1770–1827)   3. Menuetto   3:00

Compound ternary form:

Minuet: Ternary, major.

A	Two-phrase sentence.
A	Repeated.
B	Contrasting style, two-phrase sentence.
A	As before.

Codetta based on motive from "A."

BA-Codetta repeated together.

Trio: Ternary, minor.   1:30

A	Running figure in bass, two-phrase sentence.
A	Repeated.
B	Rhythmic motion continues, one phrase.
A'	Reduced to a phrase.
BA'	Repeated together.

Minuet: Ternary, as before but without repeats.   2:15

A	As before.
B	As before.
A	As before.
Coda	Same as previous codetta, now serves to conclude the movement.

(Themes p. 307)

Starting with Beethoven the minuet in multimovement works was sometimes replaced by a *scherzo*. Scherzos have the same form and meter as minuets but differ in tempo, which is faster, and style, which is less graceful. Scherzo is an Italian word meaning "joke" or "play." In keeping with the name, scherzo movements may contain elements of whimsy, humor, and surprise in their bustling rhythms. The following is an extremely concise but perfectly valid example of scherzo form and style.

L. VAN BEETHOVEN: *Violin Sonata No. 5 in F, Op. 24, "Spring"* (1801)
(1770–1827)   3. Scherzo: Allegro molto   1:05

Compound ternary form:

Scherzo: Ternary
    A   Piano alone.
    A'   Material repeated but violin added.
    B   Just a phrase, full chords in piano.
    A'   First phrase only.
    BA'   Two previous phrases repeated together, slightly extended.

Trio: Binary   :25
    A   Running figure in both violin and piano.
    A   Repeated.
    B   First phrase has running figure in piano, second phrase has running figure in violin.
    B   Repeated.

Scherzo: Ternary   :45
    A   As before.
    A'   As before.
    B   As before.
    A'   First phrase only but slightly extended as it was previously after the repetition of BA' together, which is now omitted.

(Themes p. 308)

There are a few scherzos with two trios. The plan then becomes:

Scherzo—Trio I—Scherzo—Trio II—Scherzo

The *Scherzo* in Schumann's *Symphony No. 1* has two trios, as does the *Scherzo* in his *Quintet for Piano and Strings*.

When the return of the minuet or scherzo after the trio is literal and complete except for the repeats, it is not necessary for it to be written again. This repetition is indicated by the sign *D.C.*, abbreviation for the Italian words *da capo* meaning "from the beginning." On seeing this sign performers go back to the beginning and play to the end of the minuet or scherzo proper (up to the trio), where the word *fine*, meaning "end," appears. Repeat signs are ignored when playing a "da capo."

In vocal music compound ternary structures are found in the *da capo arias* of cantatas, oratorios, and operas. Da capo arias are songs for solo voice with instrumental accompaniment in which the first part returns, sometimes with improvised vocal embellishment, after a contrasting section. The return of the first part corresponds to the return of the minuet or scherzo after the trio. The repetition of Part I is indicated by the abbreviation for da capo, giving the form its name. Da capo arias were common in the music of the past. The fact that their musical design required repetitions which were not implicit in the text perhaps contributed to the failure of works in which they were prominent to achieve a permanent place in the repertoire. *He was despised* is one of the two da capo arias Handel wrote in *The Messiah*, but they are not always performed in their entirety.

G. F. HANDEL: *Oratorio, The Messiah* (1741)
   (1685–1750)   23. He was despised   12:20
      Compound ternary form:

        Part I: Ternary, major.
            A   Orchestra introduces the thematic material of Part I.
            A′   Voice enters, first phrase like orchestral statement, second phrase altered and extended, modulates to new key, orchestra adds a concluding phrase.
            B   Same text and motives as "A," starts in new key but returns to tonic for cadence. 2:40
            A   Orchestra. 4:50
        Part II: Binary, minor.
            A   Contrasting style and mode, agitated rhythmic figure in accompaniment. 5:30
            B   Background figure continues without interruption to vocal declamation, part ends with two chords in orchestra. 6:10
        Da capo: Ternary, as before from the beginning. 6:50
                (Themes p. 308)

The following recordings of *The Messiah* have this aria complete with the da capo: London 4357, stereo 1329 and Westminster 3306, stereo 306. On some recordings of this aria Part II and the da capo are omitted.

Some small homophonic compositions have unconventional structures which, though not unique, are relatively uncommon. Small forms that depart from the usual binary and ternary designs are generally classified as *free part forms*. In this category are patterns such as A B C A, the form of Chopin's *Mazurka No. 41 in C-sharp minor* (Op. 63 No. 3) and *Mazurka No. 42 in G* (Op. 67 No. 1).

Additional Examples

One-Part Form

    CHOPIN: *Preludes Op. 28*
                No. 4 in E minor
                No. 7 in A major

Binary Form

    HANDEL: *Concerto Grosso Op. 6 No. 1 in G,* last movement
    BRAHMS: *Waltzes Op. 39, No. 3 in G-sharp minor*
    BACH: *French Suite No. 5 in G,* all movements

Ternary Form

    BRAHMS: *Waltzes Op. 39, No. 2 in E*
    CHOPIN: *Mazurka No. 24 in C, Op. 33 No. 3*
    RACHMANINOFF: *Prelude in C-sharp minor, Op. 3 No. 2*

Compound Binary Form

    SOUSA: *Manhattan Beach*
             Fairest of the Fair
    GOLDMAN: *Cheerio*

Compound Ternary Form

    HAYDN: *Symphony No. 104 in D, "London"*
             3. Menuetto: Allegro
    MOZART: *Symphony No. 39 in E-flat, K.543*
             3. Menuetto: Allegretto
    BEETHOVEN: *Symphony No. 3 in E-flat, Op. 55, "Eroica"*
             3. Scherzo: Allegro vivace

Free Part Form

    SCHUBERT: *Moment Musical in F minor, Op. 94 No. 3*

CHAPTER 8

large homophonic forms

The terms *large* and *small* are relative as applied to musical forms. A fast, terse large form may be of shorter duration than a slow, diffuse small form. A greater number of parts and a higher degree of organization distinguish the large forms from the small forms.

Rondo Forms

There are certain similarities between rondo forms and poetic forms which have a refrain. Both have a fixed element which returns after each departure. In a poem the constant element is a refrain; in a rondo form the recurrent idea is the *rondo theme*.

The most obvious application of the rondo principle occurs in *old rondo* forms in which the rondo theme is a one-part form. Old rondos begin and end with the rondo theme. There is no fixed number of parts, but the rondo theme returns after each digression. Bach's *Gavotte en Rondeau* (Gavotte in Rondo Form) is a perfect example of old rondo form. It has four contrasting sections and a total of nine parts, each of which is a sentence ending with a complete cadence.

J. S. BACH: *Partita No. 3 in E for Violin, S.1006* (1722)
   (1685–1750)   3. Gavotte en Rondeau   2:50
      Old rondo form:

           A   Rondo theme, tonic key, major.
           A   Repeated.
           B   Contrasting sentence in relative minor key.   :25

A   As before.
C   Contrasting sentence in dominant key.   :50
A   As before.
D   Contrasting sentence in supertonic key.   1:25
A   As before.
E   Contrasting sentence in mediant key.   2:05
A   As before.
                    (Rondo theme p. 308)

This Partita is numbered "6" when Bach's Sonatas and Partitas for solo violin are numbered together. A partita is a group of movements with dance characteristics. A gavotte is a dance in duple meter and a moderate tempo which first became popular in France during the 17th century.

The archaic old rondo form was superseded by the classic rondo forms. The parts in classic rondos, as compared with those in old rondos, tend to be fewer in number and larger in size. Classic rondos have five or seven parts, and the individual parts frequently have a binary or a ternary design, sometimes with repeats. Transitions between parts are common, and they may be extensive. Classic rondos customarily end with a coda.

The classic rondo form with five parts, called a *five-part rondo* or a *simple rondo*, has a basic A B A C A design. Since the parts, or themes, in a rondo are generally larger than a sentence, they are represented in the form diagrams by Roman numerals, and they are sometimes known by descriptive names, as follows:

A   Theme I   Rondo theme
B   Theme II   Subordinate theme I
A   Theme I   Rondo theme
C   Theme III   Subordinate theme II
A   Theme I   Rondo theme

The second movement of Mozart's *Eine Kleine Nachtmusik* (A little Night Music) is a typical example of five-part rondo form.

W. A. MOZART: *Serenade in G, K.525, "Eine Kleine Nachtmusik"* (1787)
    (1756–1791)   2. Romanze: Andante   6:10
    Rondo form, five-part:

    Theme I (Rondo theme), ternary.
        A   Sentence of two phrases.
        A   Repeated.
        B   Contrasting phrase.   1:00

A′ Reduced to a phrase.

BA′ Repeated together.

Theme II, two parts. 2:05

A Phrase which ends with a complete cadence.

A Repeated.

B Material derived from preceding phrase, dissolves without a cadence.

Transition

Theme I (Rondo theme), reduced to one part. 3:10

A As before.

Theme III, two parts. 3:40

A Phrase which ends with a complete cadence like II-A, contrasting mood in minor.

A Repeated.

B Material derived from preceding phrase, dissolves without a cadence like II-B.

Transition

Theme I (Rondo theme), ternary. 4:35

A As before.

B As before.

A′ As before.

Coda Three chords, then final reference to rondo theme. 5:35

(Themes p. 309)

Compositions and movements that are labeled "rondo" by the composer usually have seven parts. *Seven-part rondo* form is also known as *rondo-sonata* form and *sonata-rondo* form, because it has features in common with sonata form, discussed next. Seven-part rondos theoretically have two more parts than five-part rondos but have the same number of themes. The two additional parts come from a return of theme II (subordinate theme I) transposed to the key of the rondo theme (the feature derived from sonata form), and an extra statement of the rondo theme. In practice the final statement of the rondo theme is usually merged with the coda. The basic plan of a seven-part rondo form is:

A Theme I (Rondo theme), tonic key.

B Theme II (Subordinate theme I), related key.

A Theme I (Rondo theme), tonic key.

C Theme III (Subordinate theme II), new key or keys. (sometimes replaced by a development section)

A Theme I (Rondo theme), tonic key.

B′ Theme II (Subordinate theme I), transposed to the key of theme I, tonic.

A This statement of theme I is usually incorporated in the coda, tonic key.

Seven-part rondo form is frequently used for the final movements of sonatas and concertos. Beethoven ends his *Piano Sonata No. 2* characteristically with a clear example of the form.

L. van Beethoven: *Piano Sonata No. 2 in A, Op. 2 No. 2* (1795)
(1770–1827)   4. Rondo: Grazioso   5:45
Rondo form, seven-part:

Theme I (Rondo theme), ternary.
    A   Soaring figure begins both phrases of this sentence.
    B   Contrasting phrase.
    A′   Reduced to a phrase.
Transition, running figures modulate to dominant key.

Theme II, one part.   :45
    A   Extended sentence in the dominant key.
Transition, undulating figure in low register.

Theme I (Rondo theme), ternary.   1:10
    A   Slightly embellished.
    B   As before.
    A′   As before.

Theme III, ternary.   1:40
    A   Loud and vigorous, starts in parallel minor key and modulates to its relative major.
    A   Repeated.
    B   Continues style of preceding sentence.
    A′   Modified and shortened version of "A."
    B   Same material as before but now the style is soft and smooth.
    A′   Partial return which dissolves into. . . .
Transition, single descending line leads to return of. . . .

Theme I (Rondo theme), ternary.   3:05
    A   With additional embellishment.
    B   Embellished.
    A′   Soaring figure filled in but otherwise as before.
Transition, same material as that following first statement of rondo theme, but this time it does not modulate.

Theme II, one part.   3:50
    A′   Transposed to the tonic key but otherwise essentially as before.

Theme I (Rondo theme) and coda merged.   4:10

> This section, which is developmental in character, functions as. the final statement of the rondo theme and as the coda. Ornate versions of the rondo theme at the beginning and end of this section are separated by contrasting material derived from theme III.

(Themes p. 309)

Sonata Form

A certain amount of confusion about the term *sonata* is inevitable, since it has different meanings in different contexts. Originally, sonata simply meant a "sound piece" which was played, as opposed to a *cantata* which was sung. This usage is no longer current, but sonata is still used to designate (a) a multimovement work for one or two instruments, and (b) a specific plan of musical organization within one continuous unit. *Sonata form* proper comes under the second heading.

Sonata form, like most musical forms, evolved over an extended period, borrowing elements from existing forms, modifying and adding to them. It emerged as a distinct form around the middle of the 18th century and was in general use by 1780. A high percentage of all larger musical compositions written since that time have fulfilled the essential conditions of sonata design. The form is ideally suited to the requirements of the classic era and readily adaptable to the changing styles of subsequent periods down to the present.

Sonata form seems to have evolved from binary form, but its broad outline is essentially ternary. The three large sections of a sonata form are concerned in turn with the presentation, the working out, and the return or summing up of its thematic material. The three sections are the *exposition*, the *development*, and the *recapitulation*, respectively.

In the exposition at least two and generally three thematic ideas are stated. The *first theme* is the *principal theme;* the *second theme* is the *subordinate theme;* and the *third theme* is the *closing theme*. The principal theme and the subordinate theme differ in character and tonality to provide the essential element of contrast. The principal theme is commonly but not invariably dramatic and masculine in nature, and the subordinate theme lyric and feminine. The closing theme may be little more than a series of cadential formulas bringing the exposition to a close, or it may be a group of thematic ideas equal in scope and importance to the first two themes. When the closing theme has distinct parts, it may be called a *closing group*. Some composers, notably Beethoven, are fond of recalling motives of the principal theme at the end of the exposition in the closing theme. The exposition traditionally is repeated before proceeding to the development.

The development section, as the name implies, is concerned with combining the themes, placing them in new settings, manipulating them, and working them up to a climax.

In the recapitulation readily recognizable versions of the three themes return in their original order. The significant difference between the recapitulation and the exposition is in the keys of the second and the third themes. A transition following the first theme in the exposition modulates to the new key of the second theme, and from that point on the tonic key is avoided until the recapitulation. The beginning of the recapitulation is signaled by the obvious return of the first theme in the tonic key. The tonality is essentially tonic throughout the recapitulation, with the second and third themes transposed and the transitions adjusted as necessary.

A coda, which may amount to a second development section, customarily follows the recapitulation. First movements in sonata form frequently have an introduction. If the introduction is more than a few measures long, it normally is in a slow tempo, contrasting with the fast tempo of the body of the movement.

Beethoven's *Piano Sonata No. 8,* the *"Pathetique,"* is one of his best known works and an unmistakable masterpiece. The first movement provides a perfect introduction to sonata form.

L. van Beethoven: *Piano Sonata No. 8 in C minor, Op. 13* (1799)
 (1770–1827)   1.   Grave—Allegro di molto e con brio   6:30
   Sonata form:

   Introduction
      Slow tempo, somber mood.
   Exposition
      Principal theme (I) 1:20
         Fast tempo, ascending phrase answered by descending
         phrase in first sentence, second sentence begins like first
         but ends differently.
      Transition
         Partially based on first phrase of principal theme.
      Subordinate theme (II)   1:55
         Three related sentences, the third extended to lead
         directly into closing theme.
      Closing theme (III)   2:30
         A   Repeated notes in the bass and soprano with a
                busy figure between.
         B   Running figure in high register.
         C   Reminiscent of principal theme.
      (The repeat sign in the score at this point is rarely observed
      in modern performances.)

    Development   3:10
        Section 1
            Brief return to tempo and material of introduction.
        Section 2
            Fast tempo, principal theme developed to a climax.
            Transition
                Rapid single line.
    Recapitulation
        Principal theme (I) 4:25
            One sentence exactly as in exposition, partial repetition
            dissolves into transition.
        Transition
            Based on second phrase of principal theme, only
            the last two measures are like the exposition.
        Subordinate theme (II)   4:45
            Transposed but otherwise as in the exposition.
        Closing theme (III)   5:15
            Transposed to the tonic key but otherwise all three
            parts return essentially as in the exposition.
  Coda   5:50
        Section 1
            Tempo and material of introduction.
        Section 2
            Final reference to principal theme.
                 (Themes p. 310)

    The design of sonata form is such that many details can be varied without destroying the identity or the logic of the plan. A theme may consist of a single idea, a group of related ideas, or be cast in the mold of a small form. The transitions may be perfunctory or as attractive and imaginative as the themes. Repeat signs are no longer written at the end of expositions, and those in older works are not always observed in modern performances. New material may be introduced in the development section, or the development section can be omitted, in which case the form is abridged and the exposition is followed immediately by the recapitulation. In the recapitulation the order and tonality of the themes may be changed. All of these variations are possible within the broad concept of sonata form. Most of them are illustrated in the Additional Examples listed at the end of the chapter.

    A standardized modification of sonata form attributed to Mozart occurs regularly in the first movements of classic concertos. The special adaptation of sonata form used in concertos has a *double exposition* instead of a repeated exposition. In the first exposition the orchestra presents the thematic material all in the tonic key. After remaining silent during the first exposition, the solo instrument makes an ear-catching entrance to begin the second exposition, and thereafter dominates the musical scene. In the second exposition, which takes the place of the usual repetition, the key relationships and the order of the themes are normal for sonata form. The development and recapitulation are perfectly regular, but at the end of the recapitulation where a cadence is anticipated, the progress of the movement is interrupted to provide an opportunity for the soloist to exhibit his virtuosity. This passage for the solo instrument unaccompanied is a *cadenza*. Originally improvised spontaneously on themes of the movement, cadenzas are now composed, but the free, improvisatory style is preserved. After a brilliant cadenza a mundane coda would be anticlimactic, so the movement usually ends summarily. Mozart's *Piano Concerto No. 27* begins, like his other concertos, with a movement in modified sonata form which has a double exposition and a cadenza.

W. A. MOZART: *Piano Concerto No. 27 in B-flat, K.595* (1791)
   (1756–1791)   1. Allegro   12:25
     Sonata form, double exposition:

         Exposition I
            Orchestra, tonic key.
         Exposition II   2:15
            Solo and orchestra, usual sonata form key relationships.
         Development   5:15
            Solo and orchestra, typical developmental procedures.
         Recapitulation   7:10
            Solo and orchestra, tonic key as usual in the form.
         Cadenza   10:40
            Solo, brilliant passage work using thematic elements.
         Coda   12:05
            Orchestra

    In 20th-century examples of sonata form the order of the themes in the recapitulation frequently differs from that of the exposition. Sometimes the order of the themes is reversed, producing an A-B-C—development—C-B-A design. This form is regarded by some as a modification of sonata form, by others as a distinct *arch form* or *bow form*. Arch forms also exist with a middle theme in place of the development section and with just five parts, A-B-C-B-A.

Additional Examples

Rondo Form

        BARTOK: *Three Rondos on Folk Tunes, No. 1* (Five parts)
        BEETHOVEN: *Bagatelle in A minor, "Für Elise"* (Five parts)

BEETHOVEN: *Piano Sonata No. 10 in G, Op. 14 No. 2*
    3. Allegro assai (Five parts, long coda)

MOZART: *Violin Sonata No. 10 in B-flat, K.378*
    3. Rondo: Allegro (Five parts)

BEETHOVEN: *Violin Concerto in D, Op. 61*
    3. Rondo (Seven parts)

BRAHMS: *Symphony No. 4 in E minor, Op. 98*
    3. Allegro giocoso (Seven parts with development)

SAINT-SAENS: *Introduction and Rondo Capriccioso, Op. 28*
    (Seven parts)

Sonata Form

HAYDN: *Symphony No. 94 in G, "Surprise"*
    1. Adagio cantabile—Vivace assai

MOZART: *String Quartet in G, K.387*
    1. Allegro vivace

BEETHOVEN: *Symphony No. 8 in F, Op. 93*
    1. Allegro vivace e con brio

MOZART: *The Marriage of Figaro, K.492*
    Overture (Without development)

TCHAIKOVSKY: *Nutcracker Suite, Op. 71a*
    Overture Miniature (Without Development)

BEETHOVEN: *Violin Concerto in D, Op. 61*
    1. Allegro ma non troppo (Double exposition)

HINDEMITH: *Mathis der Maler*
    1. Engelkonzert (Order of themes changed in recapitulation)

BARTOK: *String Quartet No. 5*
    1. Allegro
    5. Finale: Allegro vivace
    (Both movements with inverted recapitulations, making them arch forms)

polyphonic forms

Both homophonic and polyphonic forms are based on the principal of repetition, but the applications of the principal are different. In the homophonic forms repetitions of previously stated thematic elements alternate with contrasting material to establish patterns. In the polyphonic forms immediate repetition in another part (imitation) produces patterns of interlacing thematic entrances.

Polyphonic forms are conceived for a fixed number of parts, all of which participate in the unfolding of the thematic material. The number of parts dictates certain critical aspects of the organization, so the integrity of the various voices is maintained. Conflicting requirements of clarity, fullness, and freedom of movement restrict the number of parts in truly polyphonic music to a narrow range. Two-part texture tends to be sparse and harmonically incomplete. Four-part texture is more cumbersome, and following four individual melodic lines taxes the listener's ear. Three seems to be the ideal number of parts for polyphonic music, though single lines and passages in more than four parts have their place in the polyphonic forms. Rests are distributed through the parts in most polyphonic music, reducing the number of parts actually sounding together at a given instant below the total number participating. Polyphonic forms written for more than five parts are rare, but this does not preclude their being scored for orchestra and the larger ensembles. Any number of instruments can play a given part.

Canon

Continuous imitation between two or more parts produces a *canon*. Strict canonic imitation is the most rigid formal procedure in music, and even the momentary lapses allowed within the definitions of the form do not appreciably loosen the bounds. The severe limitations of canonic form make it unsuitable for extended works, but it is effective in short compositions and in brief passages of larger forms.

The part that begins a canon is called the *leader*, and those that imitate are called *followers*. The followers imitate the leader continuously at a fixed distance and interval up to a cadence point, where a momentary lapse may occur and where the leader and followers may change positions.

The following example shows the use of a canon as one part of a compound ternary form. The minuet proper (excluding the trio) is a strict and obvious two-part canon.

JOSEPH HAYDN: *String Quartet in D minor, Op. 76 No. 2, "Quinten"* (1798)
(1732–1809) 3. Menuetto: Allegro ma non troppo 3:05

> Overall, this minuet is in a regular compound ternary form. Individually, the minuet proper and the trio are simple ternary forms. In addition, the minuet is a canon in two parts with exact imitation throughout. The violins play the leader in octaves, and the viola and the cello play the follower in octaves, starting a measure (three beats) later and an octave lower. The trio is purely homophonic, but the canon is resumed on the return of the minuet. Haydn's fusion of polyphonic and homophonic form is a stroke of genius.

Canons in which the end leads back to the beginning are *round canons*, *perpetual canons*, or *rotas*. All three names are used. Round canon or just *round* is most familiar because of its association with children's songs like *Are You Sleeping, Lovely Evening, Three Blind Mice*, and *Row, Row, Row Your Boat*. While problems of notation delayed the development of other types of polyphonic music for a time, notation presented no serious barrier to early composers of rounds. Rounds could be, and were, written as single line melodies with just an indication of the point at which the second and subsequent voices were to enter. As a result the form was highly developed at an early date. The following example is remarkable for its sophisticated handling of complex texture at an early date.

ANONYMOUS: *Sumer Is Icumen In (Summer Is Coming In)* (1240) 1:15

> This is the oldest piece of secular music available in modern editions and still performed. It is an isolated example of this period and style, but its perfection attests to considerable prior development. Two distinct canons, a longer one in four parts and a shorter one in two parts, are combined for a total of six parts. The short two-part canon is repeated continuously against the more extended melody of the four-part canon. The combined rounds can be repeated infinitely, and no real ending is provided. The complete structure can be diagramed as follows:

FIGURE 20. *Structural Diagram: Sumer Is Icumen In*

Sumer is Icumen In is recorded in *The History of Music in Sound*
Volume II, RCA Victor LM–6015, and a facsimile of the original
manuscript is shown in the accompanying booklet.

In the absence of a composed ending, rounds and canons conclude
after an indefinite number of repetitions as each voice comes to the end of the
melody and drops out until none is left. Canons may be accompanied by free
melodic lines or by chords. It is not a requirement that all parts participate
in the imitation.

Certain manipulations of melodic lines traditional in contrapuntal music
can be illustrated succinctly in canons. Interest in these manipulations is re-
newed because of their extensive application in 20th-century music. The
theory is that melodic lines preserve their identity when played backwards,
upside down, in longer or shorter rhythmic values (but the same proportions), and in any combination of these. Musicians have precise names for
these transformations. They are:

> *Retrograde, crab*, or *cancrizans*—played from the end to the begin-
> ning.
> *Inversion* or *mirror*—contrary motion or as seen in a mirror.
> Ascending lines become descending lines and vice versa. Skips
> become equivalent skips in the opposite direction.
> *Retrograde inversion*—a combination of retrograde and inversion.
> *Original* or *rectus*—original or unmodified form of a melody.
> *Augmentation*—increased rhythmic values, usually doubled.
> *Diminution*—decreased rhythmic values, usually halved.

Most of these devices figure in the canons of Bach's *Musical Offering*.

J. S. BACH: *Musical Offering, S.1079* (1747)
(1685–1750)   Perpetual canon on the royal theme   1:25
                      Diverse canons on the royal theme
                            1. Two parts   :45
                            2. For two violins at the unison   :45

3. Two parts in contrary motion	:50
4. Two parts in augmentation and contrary motion	2:15
5. Two parts	2:35
Canonic fugue	2:00
Two-part canon in inversion (two versions)	2:35
Four-part canon	4:50
Perpetual canon	1:30

(Royal theme p. 310)

(The canons are listed in the order of the *Collected Edition*. The sequence is altered in some recordings.)

While one of J. S. Bach's sons, Philipp Emanuel, was employed as a musician in the court of Frederick the Great, the elder Bach was invited to the Potsdam palace to display his fabled powers of improvisation. Frederick provided a theme upon which Bach extemporized. After returning to Leipzig, he worked out and wrote down these canons and three other works which together constitute his "musical offering" to the king. The "royal theme" is present in all of the canons, sometimes as part of the canon and sometimes as a free voice. The canons have two voices in imitation and one free except the two-part canons, which have no free voice, and the four-part canon which has all four parts in imitation. Bach took the liberty of altering and embellishing the king's theme, so it is not always apparent. Canons involving inversion and retrograde forms of the theme are virtually impossible to detect without access to the score. Imitation of this sort serves to unify and organize musical sounds even though it functions largely on a subconscious level. Do not be disturbed if you are not consciously aware of it.

Canons are most effective when used for passages within a larger framework. Canonic imitation figures prominently in many development sections. Occasionally it is used in thematic statements. One such instance is in the Franck *Sonata for Violin and Piano*.

CESAR FRANCK: *Violin Sonata in A* (1886)
(1822–1890) 4. Allegretto poco mosso 5:25

The theme with which this movement opens is stated as an accompanied canon. In its first appearance the piano plays the leader and the accompaniment while the violin plays the follower. Each entrance of this theme is imitated canonically, with the violin and piano sometimes exchanging roles as leader and follower. The other themes of the movement are either homophonic or in free, nonimitative counterpoint.

Fugue

Fugue form occupies the same position of eminence in the baroque period (1600–1750) as sonata form does in the classic period (1750–

1825). It is the form in which composers of the time cast many of their most exalted musical ideas. Fugue form embodies the principle of imitation, but in a much more imaginative and flexible manner than does canon.

The germ cell of a fugue is a pithy thematic idea called a *subject*. Fugue subjects typically contain one or more motives which are readily recognized and capable of sustained development. The subject is announced alone in one voice. It is answered immediately in another. The answer is not an exact repetition of the subject. It is on different pitches, and sometimes the shape is altered slightly, but for listening purposes the subject and answer may be considered the same and are so regarded in this discussion. Each voice of the fugue enters in turn with the subject. If it is a three-voice fugue, there will be three such entrances. If it is a four-voice fugue, there will be four. Regardless of the number, each enters in its assigned register. When all of the voices have stated the subject, the first section or main exposition is concluded.

The next section consists of a series of expositions in different keys separated by passages without the complete subject called *episodes*. Episodes normally contain fragments of the subject or of counterpoints associated with the subject.

In the final section there is a return to the tonic key and traditionally a passage with overlapping statements of the subject called a *stretto*.

A fugue is, strictly speaking, a monothematic form, but sometimes a counterpoint consistently associated with the subject achieves the status of a secondary thematic idea and is designated a *countersubject*. Following the diagram of a typical fugue while it is being played does more to explain the form than multiplying words. A structural diagram of a very regular Bach fugue is provided for this purpose.

J. S. BACH: *The Well-Tempered Clavier, Vol. I, S.846* (1722)
    (1685–1750)   16. Fugue in G minor   2:00
                  (Subject and countersubject p. 310)

Works other than fugues often contain fugal passages. These are called *fughettas*, meaning "little fugues." Fughettas are usually similar in structure to the main exposition of a complete fugue.

Additional Examples

Canon

    BACH: *Goldberg Variations, S.988* (Every third variation is a
             two-part canon, most with one free voice)

    BARTOK: *Duos (44) for Two Violins*
            22. Dance of the Fly

BARTOK: *Mikrokosmos Vol. I, Nos. 28, 30, and 31*

Fugue

BACH: *The Well-Tempered Clavier, S.846/93*, any of the 48
  fugues

BACH: *The Art of Fugue, S.1080*

HINDEMITH: *Ludus Tonalis*

Structural Diagram: Well-Tempered Clavier, Fugue 16

Main Exposition /Episode /Relative Exposition
```
      SSSSSSS.....ccccc.................          SSSSSSS....ccc
SSSSSSScccccc..........                 SSSSSSS............... SSS
                  SSSSSSS...........  ccccc..ccccc.............
            SSSSSSScccccc...........    SSSSSSScccccc...SSSSS
```

/Epis/Subdominant Exposit./Episode /Tonic Stretto
```
cc  ..........SSSSSSS..ccccc............  .....   ....  ............
SSSS......ccccc......SSSSSSS.............SSSSSSS  .....SSSSSSS.......
..   ..SSSSSSS..ccccc.......          SSSSSSS.....      SSSSSSS
SS......                   ............  SSSSSSS.....ccccc.......
```

Subject: SSSSSSS   }
Countersubject: ccccc } Notation p. 310
Free counterpoint: ....

FIGURE 21.

variation forms

Variation is ever present in the music of virtually all periods and styles, but only a small group of forms are organized around the variation principle. Variation forms are unified by one or more constant elements such as melody, bass line, harmony, or structure. Interest is sustained by modifying the remaining elements. The type of variation is determined by the choice of fixed elements, the kinds of alteration made in the variable elements, and the manner of connecting or separating the variations.

A theme stated at the beginning of a variation form introduces the constant elements. The theme may be original with the composer or it may be borrowed from a preexistent source. *Theme and variations* is a more complete title appropriate for many sets of variations. The theme is announced in a simple, direct fashion calculated to impress its characteristics on the mind of the listener. The variations follow, ranging in number from one to more than thirty, each with a direct though sometimes obscure relationship to the theme. A set of variations may conclude with a restatement of the theme or with a final section departing from the variation principle such as a fugue or coda.

Sectional Variations

Sectional variations begin with a theme which usually is a simple tune in binary or ternary form, sixteen to thirty-two measures in length. The parts of the theme may be repeated, and the repetitions, if any, normally are preserved in the variations. The theme comes to a full close, and there is a momentary interruption between it and the first variation and between all subsequent variations. Each variation duplicates the structure of the theme, and pauses between them divide the work into segments of equal length, though duration may vary with changes in tempo.

Variations in which the melody is preserved more or less intact are the easiest to hear. Changes are restricted to the setting of the theme and to the registers and instruments in which it appears. The possibilities for variation are limited, so the number of variations is small. The Haydn example, with four, is typical.

JOSEPH HAYDN: *String Quartet in C, Op. 76 No. 3, "Emperor"* (1798)
   (1732–1809)   2. Poco adagio, cantabile   6:10
     Theme and variations:

       Theme—Poco adagio, cantabile
       Variation I   1:10
       Variation II   2:05
       Variation III   3:15
       Variation IV   4:30
                   (Theme p. 311)

> This quartet receives its familiar name from the theme of these varia-
> tions, which was the Austrian national anthem. The theme was not
> borrowed, however, for Haydn composed the anthem. The theme
> is a five-phrase sentence with an a-a-b-c-c design. The plan of the
> variations is simple. The first violin states the theme, and then it is
> assigned to a different instrument in each of the four variations, re-
> turning in the final one to the first violin. Changes in the harmony
> and counterpoint maintain interest through the five appearances of
> the theme melody. A slight extension at the end of the last variation
> brings the movement to a close.

A more flexible type of variation results when the melody of the theme is grouped with the variable elements. The same general plan of the previous example is followed, but the melody is embellished, altered, broken into fragments, and at times all but disappears. The structure and harmonic scheme remain as fixed elements, and the influence of the melody often is sensed even when it cannot be heard and isolated. The key center usually is constant, though changes back and forth between major and minor are common. The variation movement of Beethoven's *Piano Sonata Op. 26* falls in the category just described.

L. VAN BEETHOVEN: *Piano Sonata No. 12 in A-flat, Op. 26* (1801)
   (1770–1827)   1. Andante con Variazioni   7:10
     Theme and variations:
       Theme—Andante
       Variation I—Un poco piu mosso   1:15

Variation II—Piu animato, ma non troppo   2:30
Variation III—Piu sostenuto (minor)   3:30
Variation IV—Con moto   4:30
Variation V   5:35
Coda   6:40
(Theme p. 311)

The theme is ternary. The melody is suggested in each of the variations, but it is never restated in its original form. The structure and
cadence pattern of the theme are retained in all of the variations.
Within phrases the harmonies are sometimes varied, and tempo is
another variable element. In the absence of a tempo indication for a
variation, the previous tempo prevails.

In some sectional variations only the structure and broad harmonic
outline are constant. Details of harmony are changed, and allusions to the
theme melody may be so vague that they go undetected by all but the initiated.
The theme serves as a point of departure for almost free composition, but
enough of its spirit is preserved to assure the necessary unity. Brahms excelled in writing variations of this type. For him the theme functioned as a
fount of inspiration, never as a millstone on his creative imagination.

JOHANNES BRAHMS: *Variations on a Theme of Haydn, Op. 56a* (1873)
    (1833–1897)   17:00
    Theme and variations:
        Theme—Andante
        Variation I—Andante con moto   2:00
        Variation II—Vivace (minor)   3:15
        Variation III—Con moto   4:10
        Variation IV—Andante (minor)   5:50
        Variation V—Poco presto   7:45
        Variation VI—Vivace   8:35
        Variation VII—Grazioso   9:45
        Variation VIII—Poco presto (minor)   12:30
        Finale—Andante   13:30
                (Theme p. 312)

This work exists in two structurally identical versions, Op. 56a for
orchestra and Op. 56b for two pianos. The St. Anthony Chorale
melody upon which the variations are based is an old hymn of unknown origin. Brahms copied it from the second movement of a
Divertimento in B-flat for wind instruments by Haydn.

The theme is a ternary form with repeats, giving it an AA BA′ BA′
design. The structure of the theme, including the repeats and the
characteristic extension at the end, is retained in all of the variations. The bass line and the melody of the theme figure in the variations, but not in a way that inhibits their striking originality.

The finale is a set of continuous variations (discussed in the second part of this chapter) over a constantly reiterated five-measure motive freely derived from the theme melody. The motive is stated several times in the bass before migrating to the soprano. A final statement in the bass gives way to a triumphant return of the chorale melody and a brief coda, which conclude the work. It is a tribute to Brahms' ingenuity that the repeated motive never becomes obtrusive. On the contrary, it may not even be detected by melody-oriented listeners who do not know about it in advance.

The ultimate freedom in sectional variation form is displayed when the variations depart from the structure of the theme. In variations of this type the theme serves as a source from which the composer draws thematic material. The variations have at least a subsurface unity by virtue of their common ancestry, but they may be only "kissing cousins" with highly individual personalities. Such is the case in Rachmaninoff's *Rhapsody on a Theme of Paganini*. It is significant that the work is titled rhapsody rather than variations, though the techniques are those of free sectional variation form.

SERGEI RACHMANINOFF: *Rhapsody on a Theme of Paganini, Op. 43* (1934)
(1873–1943)   21:45

Introduction, theme, 24 variations, and coda (Theme p. 312)

This work differs in several respects from the previous examples of variation form. It is characterized by less strict adherence to constant elements derived from the theme, and a secondary theme is introduced. The rhapsody begins with a short introduction based on a motive from the theme. A skeletal outline of the theme, which perhaps should be regarded as the first variation, follows immediately. The theme proper comes next. As conceived by Paganini it is sixteen measures long with an a-a-b-c pattern of four-measure phrases. Rachmaninoff repeats the last eight measures, b-c, to extend the theme to twenty-four measures. Most of the variations are longer than the theme, but a few are shorter. Well-defined cadences separate some variations, some are fused together, while others are linked by cadenza-like passages. The tonic key and minor mode predominate, but other keys, including some major and very remote ones, are explored in variations 12 through 18. Rachmaninoff adds a melody from the Requiem Mass, *Dies Irae* (Day of Wrath), to the original theme in variations 7 and 10 and again in the coda.

Procedures used by Rachmaninoff in his *Rhapsody*, such as using more than one theme, fusing variations, and delaying the statement of the theme, have been used in other recent variations. Liberties such as these have released variation form from confining limitations and preserved it as a viable means of musical expression for contemporary composers and listeners.

Continuous Variations

In contrast to sectional variations, *continuous variations* flow from one into another without interruption. The requirement of continuity influences the choice of fixed elements, or perhaps the other way around, the selection of certain fixed elements is conducive to continuity. In any event, the persistent feature of continuous variations is either a bass line or a scheme of harmonic progressions rather than the melody or structure typical of sectional variations.

A *ground, ground bass,* or *basso ostinato* (literally, obstinate bass) are designations for short melodic phrases repeated over and over in the bass as a foundation for continuous variations. The possibility of transferring the phrase to a part other than the bass is not precluded, but it is exceptional. The finale of Brahms' *Variations on a Theme of Haydn* illustrates the procedures of continuous variation over a ground. Similar procedures are employed in the closing scenes of many early operas, among them the final aria in *Dido and Aeneas*, known variously as *When I Am Laid in Earth*, *Dido's Farewell*, *Lament*, and *Thy Hand, Belinda*.

HENRY PURCELL: *Dido and Aeneas* (1689)
   (1659–1695)   Act III. When I am Laid in Earth   4:00

> A descending chromatic bass line five measures long typical of 17th and early 18th-century grounds is heard a total of eleven times, first alone and then supporting full harmonies. This accompanies an independent melody with an AA BB design in the voice. (Ground p. 312)

Passacaglia and *chaconne* are names for specific types of continuous variation forms. Their origins are shrouded in mystery, and attempts to distinguish between them have not met with success. The themes of both are traditionally in the minor mode, eight measures long, and in triple meter. The theme may be a melody introduced in the bass or a series of harmonies. Bach wrote one of each type. He called the one with a continuously repeated line initially heard in the bass a passacaglia and the one which starts with an eight-measure pattern of chords a chaconne, but this distinction is not always observed by other composers. It is of no great importance, for bass and harmony are closely related. In the period when these two forms developed, a prescribed bass line would exert strong influence on the chord structures erected above it, and a prescribed harmonic progression would almost determine the choice of bass tones.

As with sectional variations, continuous variations may end with a section which departs from the variation process. Bach's *Passacaglia and Fugue in C minor*, as the title suggests, ends with a fugue.

J. S. BACH: *Passacaglia and Fugue in C minor, S.582* (1705)   13:45
  (1685–1750)
               (Theme p. 312)

> The passacaglia begins with the theme by itself. Becoming thoroughly familiar with it is a great help in following the variations. The end of the theme leads directly back to its beginning, and there is no break in the continuity between its twenty varied appearances. The passacaglia reaches a climax, which subsides suddenly for the start of the fugue about two-thirds of the way through the work. The subject of the fugue is the bass theme of the passacaglia with the ending changed. Since the subject is already known, the countersubject enters with the first statement of the subject, unlike most fugues in which the subject is stated initially alone.

Additional Examples

Sectional Variations

> PAGANINI: *Caprices for Violin, Op. 1, No. 24*
>
> BRAHMS: *Variations on a Theme by Paganini, Op. 35*

> These sets of variations are of particular interest because they, like the Rachmaninoff *Rhapsody on a Theme of Paganini* previously cited, are based on the same theme. Paganini conceived the theme and used it as a basis for eleven variations and a finale for solo violin.

Continuous Variations

> BACH: *Partita No. 2 in D minor for Violin, S.1004*
>   5. Chaconne
>
> BACH: *Mass in B minor, S.232*
>   16. Crucifixus (Ground bass)

CHAPTER 11

multimovement forms

The forms considered thus far have been closely knit entities performed, except for the brief pauses between sectional variations, without interruption. The cumulative process continues, and these separate entities are united in more expansive musical projects. The individual units retain their identity, however, for they close with final cadences and in performance are separated by periods of silence. The individual parts of these combined forms are movements. Random associations of movements are conceivable, but the orderly sequences prescribed by convention are the rule.

Complete Sonata Form

The emergence of sonata form proper together with the plan for the complete sonata marked an epoch in the history of music. These interrelated schemes have been the supreme form of musical expression from that day to this. Untold numbers of masterpieces have been spawned in the matrix of the complete sonata form. The durability of this mode of musical organization through the radically changing styles of the last 175 years attests to its adaptability and vitality.

Complete sonata form embraces far more works than those which bear its name. A trio, speaking now of the form and not the medium, is a sonata for three instruments. Likewise, a quartet is a sonata for four instruments; a symphony is a sonata for orchestra; and a concerto is a sonata for a solo instrument with orchestra. These works are variously titled according to the performing medium, but structurally they are all essentially the same.

A complete sonata, regardless of medium, consists basically of three movements with a fast-slow-fast tempo scheme. A fourth movement is often inserted between the slow and fast movements. The first movement is, with rare exceptions, a sonata form, and certain forms are associated by tradition with the other movements.

Movement	*Tempo*	*Form*
First	Fast	Sonata
Second	Slow	Compound ternary, sonata, variation, or rondo
Third (Optional)	Moderate-fast	Compound ternary
Last	Fast	Rondo or sonata

Haydn favored a four-movement plan with a minuet as the third movement. Mozart ordinarily included a minuet in symphonies and quartets but not in sonatas. Beethoven was partial to scherzos, which he included as the third of four movements, but reverted on occasion to the older minuet. Brahms was committed to the four-movement plan, but his third movements usually are without dance or scherzo connotations. There are, of course, many exceptions to the basic plans. One, which is fairly common when the first movement tends toward the slow side, is to reverse the order of the second and third movements, placing a faster rather than a slower movement after the opening movement.

A sonata, a quartet, a symphony, and a concerto will illustrate various types of complete sonata form as written for the different mediums by composers of widely separated periods.

W. A. MOZART: *Piano Sonata No. 17 in D, K.576* (1789)

(1756–1791)	1. Allegro—Sonata form	4:45
	2. Adagio—Compound ternary form	5:25
	3. Allegretto—Rondo form	4:10

The pattern of tempos and forms is typical for three-movement complete sonatas, but the internal structure of the first and third movements is somewhat irregular. The first two themes of the first movement begin with the same motive, and the order of the second and third themes is reversed in the recapitulation. The third movement structure is like a seven-part rondo with the second return of the rondo theme supressed, a modification of rondo form used by Mozart in other works. The thematic design is A B A C B′ A. The same motive is prominent in each of the three themes, producing a highly integrated movement.

JOSEPH HAYDN: *String Quartet in D minor, Op. 76 No. 2* (1798)

(1732–1809)	1. Allegro—Sonata form	4:40
	2. Andante o piu tosto allegretto—Compound ternary form	5:00

    3. Menuetto: Allegro ma non troppo—Compound ternary form   3:05

    4. Finale: Vivace assai—Sonata form   3:45

The nickname of this quartet, "Quinten," comes from the interval of a fifth which is prominent in the themes of the first movement. The quartet as a whole follows closely the traditional plan of complete sonata forms with four movements. In the second movement the third part is elaborately embellished in the manner of a variation rather than a literal return of the first part. The menuetto was cited previously as an example of canon.

SERGE PROKOFIEV: *Classical Symphony in D, Op. 25* (1917)

(1891–1953)   1. Allegro con brio—Sonata form   3:30

                      2. Larghetto—Rondo form, five parts   3:30

                      3. Gavotte: Non troppo allegro—Ternary   1:30

                      4. Finale: Molto vivace—Sonata form   4:10

Those who think of a symphony as something ponderous and formidable will be surprised by the sprightly character of this one. Though adhering to classic form, as the title indicates, this work is not without its 20th-century flavor. The gavotte is substituted for the more usual minuet or scherzo, but otherwise the structural concept is very close to that of Mozart or Haydn.

BELA BARTOK: *Piano Concerto No. 3* (1945)

(1881–1945)   1. Allegretto—Sonata form   6:10

                    2. Adagio religioso—Compound ternary form   8:05

                    3. Allegro vivace—Rondo form, five parts   6:30

The three-movement plan is usual in concertos. The first movement sonata form of this one has but a single exposition, and thus adheres more closely to the structural plan of a classic symphony than a classic concerto. The third movement follows the second immediately without any pause, which is not unusual in concertos.

Cyclic Form

The movements of a complete sonata form have a certain underlying unity of style as a natural consequence of having been written by the same composer, but the only organic unifying element consistently present between movements of classic complete sonatas is that of key. The first movement is in the tonic key, the key indicated in the title, as are the third and fourth movements. The second (slow) movement normally is in a different but closely related key. Some composers have felt the need for stronger bonds between movements, for integrating devices beyond a plan of tempos, forms, and keys. This motivation led to the use of common material in the various

ANTONIN DVORAK

movements. The shared material may be only a motive which appears in more than one movement, or a common body of themes and motives may permeate all of the movements. The purpose is to achieve a higher degree of unification in multimovement compositions. Works in which the same material is used in more than one movement are *cyclic*. Cyclic form is not a plan of organization but a principle that is used in conjunction with other forms. Dvorak employs the cyclic principle effectively in the complete sonata form of his *New World Symphony*, traditionally known as No. 5 but listed as No. 9 in his complete works.

ANTONIN DVORAK: *Symphony No. 5 (9) in E minor, Op. 95* (1893)
(1841–1904)   1. Adagio, Allegro molto—Sonata form   9:35
                  2. Largo—Compound ternary form   10:20
                  3. Scherzo: Molto Vivace—Rondo form,
                       seven parts   7:20
                  4. Allegro con fuoco—Sonata form   10:40

The structures of the individual movements are fairly regular. Common material shared by the movements is in addition to the normal complement of distinctive themes. A *motto theme,* which occurs in each of the four movements, is first heard in the opening adagio played by the low strings. Its contour and rhythm are easily recognized and remembered. The melodic line ascends by leaps in notes of unequal value to a high point, then abruptly descends to or near the starting pitch. (Motto theme p. 312)

The motto theme, faster and somewhat modified from the version in the introduction, becomes the principal theme of the first movement proper and as such figures prominently in the movement.

In the second movement the motto theme is sounded by the trumpets and trombones in an episode which functions as a transition leading to the return of the opening material of the compound ternary form and a partial restatement of the famous "Going Home" melody by the English horn.

The form of the third movement borrows features from rondo and compound ternary forms. It has an A B A C A B A design like a seven-part rondo, but the A B A at the end is written as a *da capo* like a scherzo-trio-scherzo. The motto theme makes fleeting entrances in two of the transitions and appears again in the coda, principally in the French horns.

Thematic elements from all three preceding movements are recalled in the fourth movement, both in the development section and in the coda. The themes of all four movements are combined in a sort of recapitulation of the entire symphony. In addition to the obvious recurrences of the motto theme and the general summing up at the end, similarities of rhythm and contour can be traced between several of the thematic ideas in the four movements. All of this adds up to a highly integrated multimovement work and a convincing argument for the values of cyclic form.

Suite

The *suite* as it crystallized during the baroque period was an important instrumental form consisting of a series of movements, all in the same key. Each movement bears the name of a dance, which gives it a characteristic style and rhythm. The number and order of the dances vary, but one pattern is more prevalent than any other. It consists of the four following dances in order:

Allemande—A dance of German origin with four-beat measures in a moderate tempo, running figures and short upbeats typical, style serious but not ponderous.

Courante—A quick dance frequently paired with an allemande even before both were incorporated in suites, basic three-beat rhythmic pattern sometimes obscured by shifting accents, differing French and Italian versions produce a variety of styles.

Sarabande—A dignified dance in a slow triple meter in which the second beat may be stressed, spread from Spain across Europe but may have originated in the Orient or the New World.

Gigue—A lively dance which originated in the British Isles, six (or a multiple of three) beats in measures often containing long-short rhythmic patterns.

These four dances are standard in baroque suites. Between the sarabande and the gigue one or more optional dances is usually inserted. A prelude or overture may precede the dances, and a nondance movement occasionally is included in the optional group. The form of all the dances typically is binary. The following suite contains the standard dances in their normal order and a typical selection of optional dances.

J. S. BACH: *French Suite No. 6 in E, S.817* (1723)

(1685–1750)			
	1. Allemande		3:00
	2. Courante		1:45
	3. Sarabande		3:45
	4. Gavotte		1:25
	5. Polonaise	Optional group	1:40
	6. Bourrée		1:55
	7. Menuet		1:30
	8. Gigue		2:30

The dances of baroque suites were of international origin. The spelling of the names varied from country to country, and even within a country the spellings were not consistent. Minor discrepancies in spelling and style aside, the same dances were known and accepted throughout England and the Continent.

The obsolescence of the baroque dances brought an end to the suite as conceived by composers of that period, but the name continued as a designation for any collection of movements not classified as a symphony or a complete sonata. Suites often are drawn from stage and dramatic works. Tchaikovsky's *Nutcracker Suite*, arranged from the music of the ballet, is typical.

P. I. TCHAIKOVSKY: *Nutcracker Suite, Op. 71a* (1892)

(1840–1893)		
	1. Overture Miniature	3:10
	2. Characteristic Dances	
	a. March	2:40
	b. Dance of the Sugarplum Fairy	1:45
	c. Russian Dance (Trepak)	1:05
	d. Arabian Dance	3:50
	e. Chinese Dance	1:00
	f. Dance of the Toy Flutes	2:10
	3. Waltz of the Flowers	6:25

The following 20th-century suite is excerpted from an opera.

ZOLTAN KODALY: *Hary Janos Suite* (1926)
(1882–1967)   1. Prelude: The Fairy Tale Begins   3:10
                             2. Viennese Musical Clock   2:10
                             3. Song   5:10
                             4. The Battle and Defeat of Napoleon   3:45
                             5. Intermezzo (Czardas)   4:25
                             6. Entrance of the Emperor and his Court   2:55

Suites of this sort do not have any fixed plan. They customarily are arranged by the composer with due consideration for the requirements of balance and variety in style and tempo. Modern suites, unlike those of the baroque era, have changes of tonality between movements. Movements derived from more inclusive works, such as ballets and operas, are assured a certain underlying unity by their common source. Composers are impelled to make excerpts for concert performance and recording, because problems of presenting the original versions relegate them, whatever their merits, to the list of works infrequently performed. *Hary Janos* is a case in point. The suite is one of Kodaly's most popular works, yet the opera is rarely staged outside of Hungary. Language, casting, and staging, formidable barriers to the performance of the opera, are no problem in the suite.

Autogenous suites are also written. Like complete sonatas, they are independent multimovement works, but they are inclined to differ from the sonata type in several respects. They generally are less profound in character, depart from the prescribed forms and movements in both style and number, and sometimes they have literary or pictorial connotations. Suites, since the time of Bach, have not been sufficiently homogeneous to yield to further generalizing regarding either style or content. Milhaud's *Scaramouche* is an example of a multimovement work specifically conceived as a suite.

DARIUS MILHAUD: *Scaramouche Suite, Op. 165b* (1937)
(1882–   )   1. Vif   2:40
                             2. Modéré   3:15
                             3. Braziliera: Tempo of a Samba   2:10

Several other terms have been applied to suite-like compositions. Terms like *divertimento, partita, serenade,* and *cassation* are sometimes almost synonymous with suite, but sometimes have special implications. Divertimentos usually consist of several short movements and are written for instrumental combinations smaller than full orchestra. A partita originally was a set of variations, but in the 17th and 18th century the term came to be used interchangeably with suite. Serenade and cassation are names which suggest performance out-of-doors. Many works besides those with suite or one of the alternate terms in the title fall in this general category. Most multimovement instrumental compositions which are not complete sonatas can be called suites according to current usage.

Additional Examples
Complete Sonata

BEETHOVEN: *Symphony No. 8 in F, Op. 93*

FRANCK: *Symphony in D minor* (Cyclic)
Violin Sonata in A (Cyclic)

Suite

MILHAUD: *Suite Française* (Band)
Suite Provençale (Orchestra)

SESSIONS: *Black Maskers* (Suite from incidental music for the play)

MOZART: *Serenade in G, K.525, "Eine Kleine Nachtmusik"*
Divertimento No. 11 in D, K.251
Cassation No. 1 in G, K.63

free and
miscellaneous forms

The homophonic, polyphonic, variation, and multimovement forms considered thus far encompass the most prevalent plans of organization in instrumental music. There remain, however, a few additional instrumental forms sufficiently common and standard to warrant attention. Terms which are more properly designations of style and medium but which are used to denote works of special types also are considered in this chapter.

Overture

The term *overture* originally was applied to the instrumental introductions to operas, oratorios, ballets, plays, and the like. Such overtures often are included on concert programs detached from the complete work. The meaning of the term has been extended to include the first movement of suite-type compositions and independent, one-movement compositions for both orchestra and band.

The earliest overtures consisted of two or three sections in contrasting tempos. The sectional concept with changes of tempo persists only in the concert overtures (i.e., independent) written for high school bands. Few of this type remain in the orchestral repertory. They were superceded by two types reflecting subsequent developments. The first embodied the structural principles of sonata form, and the second joined together in a medley tunes selected from the ensuing work.

Overtures in sonata form have the advantage of a highly developed plan of organization, especially important in concert performances. The form does not preclude the possibility of using thematic ideas from the body of the work or of foreshadowing the mood and action of the subsequent drama. The overture to Mozart's opera *The Magic Flute* incorporates these features in its sonata form and is equally effective as a prelude to the opera and as a concert piece.

W. A. MOZART: *The Magic Flute, K.620* (1791)
   (1756–1791)   Overture   8:00

   Composers of the Mozart-Beethoven period were partial to sonata form in their overtures.

   In the 19th century the other type of overture, which is simply a potpourri of melodies from an opera or similar work, emerged. A potpourri overture affords the opera-goer a preview of the tunes which are to follow and gives the concert-goer an abridged version of the opera's thematic content. An overture of this type is essentially lacking in unity, because it consists of a series of unrelated melodies isolated from their dramatic context and loosely held together by transitional passages. Its melodies, culled from the best of the complete work, are the source of its strength. Medleys serve as overtures for many French and Italian operas and for most Broadway musicals. The overture to *My Fair Lady* is representative of the type.

FREDERICK LOEWE: *My Fair Lady* (1956)
   (1904–   )   Overture   3:10
      This overture is made up from the melodies of three songs plus a
      motive from a fourth. A brief introduction captures the listener's
      attention before the theme of *You Did It* is heard. *On the Street
      Where You Live*, and *I Could Have Danced All Night* follow, with
      only a perfunctory transition between them. A motive from *Show
      Me* serves as a coda to the overture and leads directly into the open-
      ing song, *Why Can't The English*, sung by Professor Henry Higgins.

   Concert overtures for orchestra generally follow the plan of sonata form. They provide composers with a substantial vehicle less extensive than the symphony, and on concert programs they serve a very practical purpose. Interruptions between movements of major works while late comers are being seated can be avoided by opening the program with a shorter number. Overtures are ideal in this capacity. They become, in a sense, overtures to the concert. It is customary to provide concert overtures with names, often with pictorial or literary implications as in Mendelssohn's *Fingal's Cave Overture*.

FELIX MENDELSSOHN: *Fingal's Cave Overture, Op. 26* (1832)   9:15
   (1809–1847)
      Mendelssohn conceived the opening of this overture while visiting
      Fingal's Cave, the largest cave on Staffa, a small uninhabited island

of the Hebrides archipelago off the coast of Scotland. The overture is also known as *Hebrides Overture*. Its sonata form did not inhibit the composer's romantic tone painting vividly conveying his impression of the surging sea, the barren coastline with its precipitous basaltic cliffs, and the yawning mouth of the mammoth cave.

Ritornello Form

Ritornello is a form peculiar to the baroque era when texture and tonality were paramount considerations in musical organization. A ritornello form ordinarily has a solo voice, instrument, or combination of instruments that are assigned certain responsibilities in the musical design, the other responsibilities being assigned to the accompanying group. A ritornello form starts with an incisive *ritornello theme* played by the whole ensemble. The solo, voice or instrument(s), enters at the close of the ritornello theme and participates in a passage which ultimately modulates to a new key. The ritornello theme, or a fragment of it, is then stated in the new key. Modulatory passages, called *episodes*, alternate with statements of the ritornello theme in various keys until the last episode modulates back to the tonic key, and a final (usually complete) statement of the ritornello theme in the tonic key completes the form. The number of episodes and keys is flexible, and the basic plan is subjected to many modifications. The last movement of Vivaldi's *Violin Concerto in A minor* is one of the clearer examples of ritornello form.

ANTONIO VIVALDI: *Violin Concerto in A minor, Op. 3 No. 6* (1712)
    (1669–1741)   3. Presto   2:40
        Ritornello form:

> Ritornello theme
>   Tonic key (A minor), orchestra.
> Episode
>   Solo prominent, starts with embellishment of motive from ritornello theme, modulates to dominant key.   :30
> Ritornello theme
>   Starts in dominant key (E minor), orchestra with solo interspersed.   :55
> Episode
>   Solo prominent, modulates to relative major key.   1:15
> Ritornello theme
>   Fragment in relative major key (C) followed by same fragment in dominant key (E minor), orchestra.   1:40
> Episode
>   Solo prominent, modulates back to tonic key.   2:00
> Ritornello theme
>   Tonic key (A minor), solo and orchestra.   2:05
> Coda
>   Solo and orchestra.   2:30
>   (Ritornello theme p. 313)

This concerto, one of twelve known collectively as *L'Estro Armonico* (Harmonic Whim), is scored for one solo violin, string orchestra, and cembalo (harpsichord). When the solo violinist is not playing an independent part, he joins in with the violins of the orchestra. Though written for one solo instrument, this work is conceived along the lines of a concerto grosso (see next), not those of a classic concerto.

Concerto Grosso

The distinguishing characteristic of the *concerto grosso* is the medium. A concerto grosso is written for a small group of solo instruments—usually two violins, cello, and a keyboard instrument—and string orchestra. The solo group may be differently constituted, and wind instruments are occasionally included in both the solo group and the orchestra. Contrasting the full sonority of the orchestra with the lighter sound of the solo group is the essential feature of the form.

A concerto grosso normally has at least three movements, usually more. The individual movements may be simple part forms, ritornello form, or fugal. The concerto grosso flourished from the end of the 17th century to the middle of the 18th century, and it has been revived in the 20th century. Corelli was one of its leading exponents, perhaps its originator.

ARCANGELO CORELLI: *Concerto Grosso, Op. 6 No. 8 "Christmas"*
(1653–1713)

1.	Vivace—Grave	1:30
2.	Allegro	2:00
3.	Adagio—Allegro—Adagio	3:50
4.	Vivace	1:10
5.	Allegro	2:45
6.	Pastorale: Largo	3:45

This concerto grosso bearing the inscription, "Composed for the night of the Nativity," was published posthumously in 1714. The date of composition is not known. It is for the standard solo group (two violins, cello, and a keyboard instrument) and string orchestra. The contrast between the solo group and the larger body of strings is exploited with special effect in the first and last *allegro* sections and in the *vivace* following the *adagio*.

Prelude

Composers seem to have ignored the literal meaning of the term as often as they have observed it in naming compositions *prelude*. Some have used it literally for the first of two pieces in *preludes and fugues* and for the first movement of suites, while others have written collections of piano pieces all of which are called preludes. The most famous of the former category are the

48 Preludes and Fugues of Bach's *Well-Tempered Clavier*. Notable collections in the latter have been written by Chopin, Shostakovich, Debussy, and Gershwin.

Introductory preludes are apt to be based on a single motive or figure and often make extensive use of scale and arpeggio figures. Bach's *C Major Prelude*, the first of the 48 and probably the best known, utilizes one pattern and a constant rhythm throughout.

J. S. Bach: *The Well-Tempered Clavier, Vol. I, S.846* (1722)
    (1685–1750)   1. Prelude in C   2:10

Not much can be said about independent preludes except that they are brief character pieces. They may be in any of the smaller forms, and some are descriptive. Preludes by Chopin and Debussy have been cited previously, so the following are drawn from Shostakovich and Gershwin.

Dmitri Shostakovich: *Preludes for Piano, Op. 34* (1933)
    (1906–   )   No. 24 in D minor   1:30

George Gershwin: *Preludes for Piano* (1926)
    (1898–1937)   No. 1 in B-flat   1:25

Prelude is also used instead of overture to designate the instrumental introduction to an opera, especially when the form is other than sonata or potpourri. Wagner used the term, or at least its German equivalent (*Vorspiel*), for instrumental introductions that lead directly into the first and sometimes subsequent acts of his music dramas. Special endings are provided for concert performances.

Richard Wagner: *Lohengrin* (1850)
    (1813–1883)   Act I. Prelude   7:40
                         Act III. Prelude   2:40

The *chorale prelude* is a special type of composition for organ which developed as an introduction to the singing of the chorale by the congregation in Protestant churches. The form, originally intended for a specific function, has since been used detached from religious services. A chorale prelude is basically an elaboration of the chorale melody, a kind of variation before the theme. In concert performances organists sometimes play the chorale before the prelude, reversing the normal order and placing the prelude in a curious position. This arrangement has the advantage of announcing the theme, which otherwise might be unfamiliar, before the variation.

Several methods of elaboration are employed in chorale preludes. Some are merely enriched settings of the chorale melody, which may be in any voice, and which usually moves slowly against a more animated background. In others the melody itself is embellished. A third procedure is to derive fugue subjects from the chorale, usually one from each phrase, and to use them in a succession of fughettas. Overlapping of methods is not unusual.

J. S. BACH: *Schübler Chorale Prelude No. 1, S.645* (1746)
(1685–1750)   Wachet auf, ruft uns die Stimme (Sleepers Awake)   3:40

> This chorale prelude, the first of a group of six published by Schübler in 1746, is based on a chorale melody by Philipp Nicolai (1556–1608). In this prelude an independent, flowing melody is announced against which the chorale tune is projected a phrase at a time. (Chorale melody p. 313)

Though it is unique rather than one of a type, no discussion of preludes is complete without mentioning Debussy's incomparable *Prelude to the Afternoon of a Faun*. Being an independent, descriptive work for orchestra, it neither fits the literal meaning of the word nor bears any direct resemblance to traditional prelude types, but it illustrates the latitude with which the term has been used by composers.

CLAUDE DEBUSSY: *Prelude to the Afternoon of a Faun* (1894)   9:00
(1862–1918)

> This work was inspired by the poem of the impressionist poet, Stephane Mallarmé. Its content may be summarized: "A faun is lying on the borderland of waking and sleeping in a grove. The atmosphere is palpitating with the golden midday heat. He has seen some slender-limbed, light-footed nymphs flit by; he would perpetuate the lovely vision. But he asks himself, am I in love with a dream? Fully awake, he begins to reflect and analyze, to dissect his sensations and emotions. His thoughts become exaggerated, distorted; his senses predominate. Delicate imagery takes shape in his mind. Had he seen a flight of swans? The current of his ideas becomes more realistic, and he imagines himself under the shadow of Etna with Venus in his arms. While anticipating punishment for such desecration, sleep visits his eyelids once more; he bids adieu to facts and reality and in the shades of oblivion goes in quest of the shadowy, vanished dream."

Rhapsody and Fantasia

Rhapsody and *fantasia* are terms generally applied to freely and often loosely constructed works which follow no prescribed plan of organization. Often they are improvisatory in style, and composers writing them indulge in flights of fancy without the usual regard for conventions of form and style. These procedures are illustrated in the following examples.

FRANZ LISZT: *Hungarian Rhapsody No. 2 in C-sharp minor* (1851)   9:20
(1811–1886)

> Liszt's *Hungarian Rhapsodies*, which served to popularize the form, incorporate Hungarian and gypsy elements in several vividly contrasted, tenuously connected sections. Of the nineteen he composed for piano, the second is most famous. It is included as the fourth of the six Liszt arranged for orchestra.

RALPH VAUGHAN WILLIAMS: *Fantasia on a Theme by Tallis* (1910) 15:45
(1872–1958)

> This fantasia is based on a theme of the early English composer, Thomas Tallis (1505–1585), but the theme serves only as a point of departure. It is freely molded and expanded without obeisance to preconceived notions of structure, unlike the composer's similarly titled and better known *Fantasia on Greensleeves*, which has a broad ternary design.

There are, of course, many other terms, such as *toccata, impromptu, pastorale, song without words, ballade, nocturne*, dance-inspired names, and a host of others too numerous to mention, which are used as designations for musical works. Toccatas are brilliant, idiomatic works for keyboard instruments and, by extension, for other mediums as well. The other appellations are used for brief character pieces reflecting the mood or style indicated by the title but otherwise without special distinctions.

In addition, there are compositions, especially from the romantic and contemporary periods, which do not follow any prescribed plan of organization. This is true, in a sense, of rhapsodies and fantasias, but works in these categories have enough in common to create a type, if not a pattern. Unique design is relatively rare, but not impossible or undesirable. Setting a text or depicting a story may provide the impulse for an unusual sequence of musical ideas. Contemporary composers sometimes revolt against conventions of form as well as those of harmony and line, and, at times, their new musical language demands a new syntax. Composers on the current scene are not adverse to creating new forms, but more often their innovations take the direction of modifying and adapting traditional principles to their distinctive materials. Free or unique form is not to be confused with lack of form. On the contrary, the most skillfully integrated musical expression may defy classification. Works in which ties with traditional patterns are absent or stretched beyond recognition are grouped together as free forms. Their eccentric nature renders impossible generalization and illustration.

Additional Examples

Overture

> Rossini: *William Tell Overture* (Opera)
>
> Rodgers: *The King and I Overture* (Musical show)
>
> Beethoven: *Egmont Overture, Op. 84* (Drama)
>
> Barber: *Overture to the School for Scandal* (Drama)
>
> Brahms: *Academic Festival Overture, Op. 80* (Concert)
> *Tragic Overture, Op. 81* (Concert)
>
> Berlioz: *The Corsair, Overture for Orchestra. Op. 21* (Concert overture inspired by Byron's narrative poem)

Ritornello Form

> Handel: *The Messiah*
> 9. O Thou that tellest good tidings to Zion

Concerto Grosso

> Vivaldi: *L'Estro Armonico, Op. 3 No. 11 in D minor*

Prelude

> Wagner: *Prelude to Tristan and Isolde* (Opera)
>
> Bach: *Orgelbüchlein Chorale Prelude No. 10, S.608*
> In Dulci Jubilo (In Sweet Jubilation)

Rhapsody and Fantasia

> Enesco: *Roumanian Rhapsody No. 1, Op. 11*
>
> Bruch: *Scottish Fantasy for Violin and Orchestra, Op. 46*

program music

Program music is a general classification for music which depicts or is inspired by extramusical ideas, in contradistinction to *absolute music* which is pure music, free of any such influences. Though all music with a text or used in dramatic productions is programmatic in a sense, the designation is commonly used only for instrumental works with literary or pictorial connotations or which imitate the sounds of nature.

The influence of the program on the music ranges from the merest suggestion of a mood to the graphic depiction of specific incidents and scenic details. The crudest examples of program music attempt to generate interest by the realistic portrayal of natural sounds, events, and things. Such exercises may prove that a composer is clever or ingenious, but they rarely transcend the level of short-lived novelties. In contrast with these are the works which pay homage to the programmatic concept with descriptive titles or suggestions of a story but which have their foundations firmly anchored in purely musical values. Form would seem to be the aspect of music most seriously undermined by the requirements of a predetermined program, but this is not necessarily so. Many pieces of program music are in perfectly regular, conventional forms.

The sounds of music are not well suited to conveying concrete visual or dramatic impressions. Not a single idea can be expressed effectively by means of musical sounds alone. The perception of the program underlying a piece of music is dependent in large measure, if not entirely, upon providing the listener with sufficient clues in advance. When descriptive titles are inadequate for the purpose, composers resort to verbal descriptions of what the music is about. Pertinent sections or résumés of literary works are sometimes quoted in scores and reprinted in program notes and on record jackets as an aid to comprehending program music.

The validity of the fundamental precepts of program music is open to question. It is argued that music is incapable of expressing ideas, or at least that it is a poor substitute for words. Proponents of absolute music feel that attaching a program to music robs it of the abstraction which makes it unique among the arts. For this philosophy's adherents music ideally is pure sound stimulating the senses and triggering the emotions directly, and it is most effective when extramusical associations do not intrude.

On the other hand, there is no denying the existence of programmatic musical masterpieces or the popularity of works which tell a story. For many listeners the program serves as a bridge to the realm of music. Its mysteries seem somehow less formidable when a link with tangible reality is provided. There can be no objection to the composer's sharing the source of his inspiration with the listener. However, the practice of inventing stories to go with music when none is intended by the composer is undesirable, even as sugar-coating for music presented to the very young. False values thus established, eventually if not immediately, defeat the avowed purpose of making abstract music more palatable.

The most defensible position with reference to program music is that a program neither assures nor denies the creation and appreciation of admirable music. Descriptive music is not per se either good or bad. A program is no substitute for solid musical value, but the two may exist side by side, as they do in all the best examples of program music.

An undeniable advantage of program music is that its fanciful titles are more easily remembered, even by musicians, than the numbers and keys used to identify absolute music. One wonders if it is coincidental that of Beethoven's 32 piano sonatas, all of the most famous are included in the half-dozen or so associated with names.

The beginnings of tone painting can be traced back to 14th-century vocal music, but in these early examples the music merely illustrates words or ideas occurring more or less simultaneously in the text. One of the first examples of instrumental program music is a fantasia in the *Fitzwilliam Virginal Book* by John Mundy (*d*. 1630). It depicts thunder, lightning, and fair weather. Kuhnau's six *Biblical Sonatas* are somewhat later and more sophisticated examples of program music for a keyboard instrument. The meaning of each movement is described explicitly in the score. Kuhnau must have anticipated opposition to his ideas, for he explained and defended his approach in a preface to the sonatas.

JOHANN KUHNAU: *Biblical Sonata No. 1, David and Goliath* (1700)
(1660–1722) 1. Goliath's stamping and ranting.   1:30
             2. The trembling of the Israelites, and their prayer
                 to God at the sight of this terrible enemy.   2:00

3. The steadfastness of David, his urge to crush
the giant's pride.   1:00
4. The challenge exchanged between David and
Goliath, and the fight—and David took a stone
and threw it and smote the giant in his forehead
—and the stone sank into his forehead and he
fell upon his face to the ground.   1:15
5. The flight of the Philistines, and how the Israel-
ites chase after them and slay them by the
sword.   :45
6. The rejoicing of the Israelites at their victory.   1:15
7. The concert performed by the choirs of women
to the glory of David.   1:05
8. And finally, the general rejoicing which shows
itself in an abundance of dancing and frolicking. 1:15

Couperin carried the programmatic concept a step further and corre-
lated his musical ideas with both human attributes and colors.

FRANÇOIS COUPERIN: *Les Folies Françaises* (1772)   10:20
(1668–1733)   (Follies of the French)
    1. Virginity—Invisible   :00
    2. Modesty—Red   :40
    3. Ardor—Scarlet   1:20
    4. Hope—Green   2:10
    5. Loyalty—Blue   2:55
    6. Perseverance—Flaxen gray   4:10
    7. Languor—Violet   4:50
    8. Coquetry—Various colors   6:05
    9. Aged gallants—Purple   6:35
   10. Benevolent cuckoos—Yellow   7:30
   11. Jealousy—Dark gray   8:20
   12. Frenzy or despair—Black   9:35

Title and color designations notwithstanding, this is a series of variations on a harmonic-bass theme. Virginity is the theme, and each
following attribute is a variation. The similarity of the variations
to each other and to the theme is especially apparent in the cadences
which separate them. The variation form and the program are not
only compatible, but complementary.

Program music occupied an insignificant place in the music of the
classic era, but with the rise of romanticism in the 19th century it assumed

a position of importance and for a time challenged the supremacy of absolute music. Music of every dimension from miniatures to immensities and for every medium from one instrument to full orchestra would be embraced by a catalog of romantic program music. The suggested listening barely hints at its magnitude and scope. Mussorgsky's *Pictures at an Exhibition* is a piece of 19th-century program music in the tradition of Kuhnau and Couperin, but with some added touches.

MODEST MUSSORGSKY: *Pictures at an Exhibition* (1874)   29:30
(1839–1881)

Promenade (Theme p. 313)
    Depicts the viewer (Mussorgsky) as he moves between pictures in the art gallery, serves as a connecting and unifying device between sections, and figures in the finale.

The Gnome 1:30
    A misshapen, comical figure supposedly fashioned as a Christmas tree ornament.

Promenade 4:00

The Old Castle 4:50
    A troubadour sings his lay before a medieval castle.

Promenade 8:30

Tuileries 9:00
    The famous gardens with children and their nurses.

Bydlo 10:10
    A two-wheeled ox-drawn cart lumbering across the fields.

Promenade 12:50

Ballet of the Unhatched Chicks 13:25
    Dancers costumed as chicks emerging from their shells.

Samuel Goldberg and Schmyle 14:45
    A dialogue between a rich Jew and a poor one.

The Market Place at Limoges 17:00
    Women wrangling furiously.

The Catacombs 18:20
    The artist exploring the catacombs of Paris by lantern light.

Baba-Yaga 21:55
    A grotesque clock representing the house of Baba-Yaga, a witch character of Russian folklore.

The Great Gate of Kiev 25:20
    Hartmann's design for a triumphal arch through which passes a pageant of Russian history.

A posthumous exhibition of paintings by Mussorgsky's friend, Victor Hartmann, included the ten canvasses which inspired this composition. It was composed for piano but is better known in transcriptions for orchestra. The recurrent promenade theme serves as an overall unifying element. The other parts have independent themes and their own internal structures.

The sounds of nature are still heard—sometimes subtly, sometimes humorously—in 19th-century program music. Animal and bird sounds are imitated by instruments in *The Carnival of the Animals*. These are served up with parodies of borrowed melodies and engaging original tunes to make musical fare which is certain to entertain children and amuse adults, the latter especially when heard in the version with the Ogden Nash verses interspersed between the musical numbers (Columbia ML–4355). Ironically, Saint-Saens regarded this, his most popular work, as such a trifle that he did not allow it to be published or publicly performed during his lifetime.

C. SAINT-SAENS: *The Carnival of the Animals* (1886)   21:00
   (1835–1921)   1. Introduction and Royal March of the Lion
                 2. Hens and Cocks   1:55
                 3. Fleet-footed Animals (Hemiones)   2:40
                 4. Tortoises   3:20
                 5. The Elephant   5:00
                 6. Kangaroos   6:30
                 7. Aquarium   7:20
                 8. Personages with Long Ears   9:40
                 9. Cuckoo in the Woods   10:15
               10. Aviary   12:30
               11. Pianists   13:45
               12. Fossils   14:55
               13. The Swan   16:10
               14. Finale   19:00

Borrowed melodies are heard in Sections 4, 5, 11, and 12. "Tortoises" begins with the cancan melody from Offenbach's *Orpheus in Hades* and ends with a few measures from Act I of the same opera. "The Elephant" has a parody of the "Dance of the Sylphs" from *The Damnation of Faust* by Berlioz and a hint of the *Midsummer Night's Dream* "Scherzo" by Mendelssohn. Exercises à la Czerny are practiced in "Pianists." The themes of "Fossils" are from Saint-Saens' *Danse Macabre* and Rossini's *Barber of Seville*, with added bits from the French folk songs *J'ai du bon Tabac, Ah! Vous dirai-je Maman*, and *Partant pour la Syrie*. Material from previous sections is recalled in the finale.

The *symphonic poem* or *tone poem* is an important type of 19th-century program music. A symphonic or tone poem is a large-scale, single-movement, programmatic work for orchestra. The concept is attributed to Franz Liszt (1811–1886), who composed twelve works in the form (see page 253).

His innovation was enthusiastically received and widely imitated. The symphonic poem ranks as the most characteristic expression of the romantic impulse in instrumental music.

Goethe's ballad, *The Sorcerer's Apprentice*, is such a natural subject for a symphonic poem that someone was bound to use it. Dukas did, and it is difficult to decide whether the music or the story contributes most to the success of the piece, not that it matters. The details of the story are graphically portrayed without sacrificing musical values in this inimitable tone painting.

PAUL DUKAS: *The Sorcerer's Apprentice* (1897)   8:45
  (1865–1935)

> This work tells in tones the story of an apprentice sorcerer who, in his master's absence, repeats a magic formula he has overheard which enables him to bring a broomstick to life. He commands it to carry water from the well, and it obeys perfectly until the task is completed. Then the apprentice discovers that he does not know the formula to stop it. The broomstick carries bucket after bucket of water until the room is overflowing. In desperation the apprentice chops it in two, and to his dismay both halves carry water faster than ever. At last the sorcerer returns, pronounces the magic words, and restores order.

Multimovement counterparts of the symphonic poem are the *program symphony* and the *program suite*. Because of the less rigid application of structural principles in program music generally, distinctions between program symphonies and suites are not so well defined as between absolute symphonies and suites. Evidence of the closer relationship between program symphonies and suites is manifest by the addition of movements beyond the normal four in some program symphonies. Berlioz' *Symphonie Fantastique*, with five movements, is deservedly one of the most celebrated.

HECTOR BERLIOZ: *Symphonie Fantastique, Op. 14* (1831)
  (1803–1869)   1. Dreams and Passions: Largo—allegro
                          agitato e appasionata assai   12:50
                     2. A Ball (Waltz): Allegro non troppo   5:40
                     3. Scenes in the Country: Adagio   15:30
                     4. March to the Scaffold: Allegretto non
                          troppo   5:00
                     5. A Witches' Sabbath: Larghetto—Allegro   9:10
  Berlioz himself outlined the story of the symphony in a preface
  to the work:

A young, morbid, ardent musician in a state of amorous despair poisons himself with opium. The dose, insufficient to kill him, plunges him into a delirious sleep during which his sensations take the form of musical ideas in his sick brain. His beloved becomes a melody, an *Idée Fixe* (fixed idea) which he hears everywhere. (Idée Fixe p. 314)

Dreams and Passions. He at first recalls the vague melancholy and joy which alternated without apparent reason before he met his beloved; then the volcanic passion with which she inspired him, his jealous fury, his return to tenderness and religious consolation.

A Ball. He finds his beloved waltzing in the tumult of a brilliant fete.

Scenes in the Country. On a summer evening in the country he listens to two shepherds playing a pastoral duet to summon their flocks. The rustic scene, the gentle rustling of the trees in the breeze, hopeful prospects he has recently entertained, all combine to produce an unaccustomed calm but with a bitter tinge. The beloved returns again . . . his heart throbs . . . he is disturbed by forebodings that she might deceive him . . . one of the shepherds resumes his naive melody . . . the other no longer answers . . . the sun sets . . . in the distance thunder rumbles . . . solitude . . . silence . . .

March to the Scaffold. He dreams he has killed his beloved, that he has been condemned to death and is being led to the scaffold. The procession advances to the sound of a march now sombre, now wild, now brilliant, now solemn. Loud outbursts are followed without pause by the plodding sounds of marching feet. The *Idée Fixe* appears for a moment like a last thought of love cut short by the fatal blow of the guillotine.

Witches' Sabbath. He finds himself at a witches' revel in the midst of a horrible group of spectres who have come to attend his funeral. Strange noises are heard—groans, bursts of laughter, distant shrieks to which other shrieks seem to reply. The melody of the beloved appears once more but transformed from its character of nobility and gentleness to a common, grotesque dance tune. Howls of joy accompany her arrival and participation in the diabolic orgy . . . funeral bells . . . parody on the *Dies Irae* . . . witches' dance . . . witches' dance and the *Dies Irae* together.

Berlioz departs from the traditional sequence of movements in this symphony, but his procedures are not unrelated to convention. He substitutes a waltz and a march for a minuet or scherzo, but this is a logical extension of the basic concept. A minuet or corresponding movement usually follows the slow movement, but sometimes preceeds it. Berlioz places the one before and the other after. This provides an ideal balance with the slow movement, longest of the five, flanked on each side by a shorter movement in a relatively moderate tempo. The first and last movements correspond both in tempo and duration. In spite of the program, Berlioz abandons typical structural patterns only in the last movement. The first movement is a sonata form. The second, third, and fourth movements have compound ternary designs. The final movement has a free sectional structure of four large parts.

The appearance of the *Idée Fixe* in each movement provides a cyclic element. It is announced after the slow introduction of the first movement by the violins and flutes in the prevailing fast tempo of the movement. It is the principal theme of the sonata form. In the second movement this theme appears, rhythmically transformed, in the middle section of the waltz played first by flute and oboe and then by flute and clarinet. The *Idée Fixe* in a different rhythmic transformation serves as an answering phrase in flute and oboe in the middle section of the third movement and enters briefly at the end. The hero's memory of his beloved is recalled by her theme just before the end of the fourth movement. The *Idée Fixe* completely transformed into a derisive and sarcastic dance tune by grace notes and trills immediately follows the opening Larghetto section in the final movement. Thus the *Idée Fixe* provides a cyclic as well as a programmatic element.

With the decline of romanticism the appeal of program music waned for composers but not for listeners. Many of the staple items in the current repertoire and some of the most widely accepted and appreciated compositions of all time were products of program music's heyday during the last century.

Additional Examples
Program Music

> DEBUSSY: *Nocturne No. 1, Nuages (Clouds)*
>
> STRAUSS: *Till Eulenspiegel's Merry Pranks, Op. 28* (see page 258)
>
> SMETANA: *Ma Vlast (My Fatherland)*
> 2. The Moldau
>
> BEETHOVEN: *Symphony No. 6 in F, Op. 68, "Pastoral"*
>
> RIMSKY-KORSAKOV: *Scheherazade, Op. 35, Symphonic Suite* after *The Thousand and One Nights*
>
> HONEGGER: *Pacific 231*
> (Also available on a Young America Film showing the locomotive from which the work takes its name and giving a visual interpretation of the music on the sound track.)

CHAPTER 14

dramatic music

Dramatic music is the general classification for music associated with stage presentations and their more recent counterparts, motion pictures and television. Dramatic music is the type least successfully captured in recordings. The visual aspect of a dramatic presentation vies with the aural in actual performance, and a serious void is created by its absence. The full impact of a live production can never be matched by the pale image of the sound alone. The appreciation of dramatic music is immensely stimulated by the experience of seeing and hearing an actual performance. The appeal of the theatre is age old and universal. The combined attraction of beauty in sound, line, color, and motion is irresistible. Of these elements, which are real and abundant on the stage, all but the sound must be supplied by the imagination in recorded performances.

Opera

Broadly defined, *opera* is sung drama, with all the adjuncts of staging, accompanied by orchestra. An opera is a play set to music. Many are based on successful plays. The definition of opera attributed to Saint-Evremonde as "a bizarre affair of poetry and music in which the poet and the musician, each equally obstructed by the other, give themselves no end of trouble to produce a wretched result" probably would find some support even today. Actually, a musical setting endows a drama with special qualities and imposes on it certain limitations. The amalgamation of music and drama is not accomplished without compromises. The success of the union depends somewhat upon the skill of the practitioners and somewhat upon the point of view. If an undue portion of the American public reacts negatively to opera,

misunderstanding of what opera is must share the blame with the poor
rapport between typical opera and current taste. A survey of the operatic
scene should allay misconceptions about its aims and purposes. Recent endeavors both in the creation and production of opera have progressed
toward bringing it in line with the requirements of present-day entertainment.

Enjoyment is contingent upon accepting opera as a highly artificial art
form. It is not natural to burst into song under the impact of emotional
stress or to hit a high C with one's dying breath, but these are conventions
the opera-goer must be prepared to accept. Opera is remote from reality,
but realism in any art is only relative. Though opera is one of the least realistic, this is not a debilitating admission. Frames around landscape paintings
and rhymes in play dialogue are equally artificial but widely accepted conventions.

The particular conventions of opera have a long history. The association
of music with drama dates back to the ancient Greeks. Their musical achievements were not handed down, but in attempting to revive Greek tragedy,
a group of Florentine noblemen known as the *Camerata* laid the foundations
of modern opera just before 1600. This group, conforming to their concept
of Greek drama, evolved a musical style which consisted of vocal declamation with careful attention to the natural rhythm, accent, and inflection of the
text. This vocal declamation, a sort of intensified speech, was carried out over
a simple, instrumental harmonic background. The concept was revolutionary
in its time, and though its influence on the course of music was immense,
the limitations of melodies inseparably bound to natural speech were apparent as soon as the novelty wore off. The advantages of this style were that the
text could be understood and that the action progressed almost as fast as in
spoken drama. Subsequent attempts to enhance the musical value with more
appealing melodies and more expressive harmonies invariably sacrificed
these virtues.

From the beginning of opera, scenes occasionally closed with metric
songs and choruses and with dancing. These features became increasingly
prominent as opera developed. Soon there were distinct sections. *Recitatives*
in declamatory style were followed by lyric and metric *arias*. Meanwhile the
size and importance of the orchestra was expanded to provide overtures and
interludes in addition to accompaniments. The relative emphasis on the
various aspects of opera differed widely with the region and the period.

Arias, ballets, choruses, and instrumental interludes contributed musical interest to the spectacle at the expense of the drama. The plot, often
reduced to the barest thread, was stationary during these episodes and
progressed only in the recitatives. The portions between recitatives, uninhibited by dramatic requirements, developed into closed forms structurally
complete in and of themselves. This facilitated not only detaching the num-

bers from the opera but also exchanging them between operas. In the absence of copyright restrictions, unauthorized borrowing of whole sections was a flagrant practice which reached its ridiculous conclusion in the *pasticcio* (Italian for pie or pastry). These entertainments consisted simply of an uninterrupted succession of favorite operatic selections without regard for the source or sequence.

The demand by singers and audiences alike for vocal display vehicles also detracted from the dramatic possibilities of opera. Star singers demanded roles exploiting their capacity for vocal pyrotechnics and stopped the show to acknowledge applause after each brilliant number. A succession of reformers raised their voices and pens against the forces inimical to the dramatic element in opera, but abuses persist in varying degrees throughout most of the operatic literature. In spite of certain inherent limitations, genuine masterpieces were conceived within the framework of the *numbers opera*, that is, an opera consisting of a series of numbers—recitatives, arias, ensembles, choruses, ballets, and instrumental interludes. As a composer of numbers operas Mozart has no peer, and *The Marriage of Figaro* is an attractive introduction to the type, especially if it can be heard in the new English translation.

Richard Wagner (1813–1883) revolted against traditional opera and fused music and drama in a new relationship which he called *music drama*. The Wagnerian concept of music drama as a transcendental art form required the subjugation of the constituent arts and some negation of their special properties. He composed the music to his own librettos and regarded them as complementary equals in the finished product. There are no divisions or interruptions within scenes of his music dramas. Melodies are continuous and, in a conventional sense, formless. The orchestra participates, almost competes, in the drama, underlining not only the vocal melodies but the emotions and actions as well. Musical motives, called *leitmotivs* in music drama, are associated with particular characters, objects, emotions, or ideas. Leitmotivs, varied and transformed in response to changing dramatic situations on stage, often explain and reinforce the mood and action of the drama in addition to serving as unifying elements. The leitmotiv concept was one of Wagner's outstanding contributions to music, and he was an innovator in the realms of harmony and orchestration as well. Wagner's ideas are most fully realized in the four monumental music dramas comprising *The Ring of the Nibelung*, but as an initiation to his dramatic music *Die Meistersinger von Nürnberg* is recommended.

In Wagner's music dramas there are no interruptions between numbers or musically sterile recitatives as there were in earlier operas, but his approach left many of the problems of opera as an art form unsolved for those not completely sold on the idea of music drama as the successor to traditional opera. For many opera buffs the separate numbers in which musical interest is concentrated are the reason for an opera's existence, and music dramas do not have them. The plot of Wagner's music dramas unfolds continuously, but at a snail's pace, and his preoccupation with mythical subjects, which he regarded as the proper province of music drama, is out of vogue. Though Wagner's music dramas are performed regularly in the major opera houses of the world, no other composer has wholeheartedly adopted his philosophy, and no other work conceived along similar lines has achieved notable success. Richard Strauss (1864–1949) perpetuated and developed a style and technique inherited from Wagner but without subscribing to all tenets of Wagner's artistic credo.

During the time Wagner was formulating the principles of music drama, Giuseppe Verdi (1813–1901) was composing more conventional operas with melodramatic plots and separate numbers but at the same time striving for unity between the music and drama, elimination of extraneous elements, vivid characterization, and effective dramatization. His success in achieving these aims and his apparently inexhaustible supply of captivating melodies have established his operas as international favorites. Of the thirteen that can be heard on recordings, *Aida* and *Rigoletto* are perhaps the best known, with *La Traviata* and *Il Trovatore* not far behind.

Verdi's successor and the composer in whose operas many find the ideal fusion of music and drama is Giacomo Puccini (1858–1924). His operas, in relation to those of Verdi, are characterized by greater continuity and more emphasis upon the realistic treatment of contemporary subjects. *Madame Butterfly*, *La Bohème*, and *Tosca* are representative of his stellar achievements as a composer of operas.

Georges Bizet (1838–1875), by virtue of one fantastically successful work, *Carmen*, must also be listed with the opera composers of first rank. Ruggero Leoncavallo (1858–1919) and Pietro Mascagni (1863–1945) likewise achieved fame on the basis of one operatic work, *Pagliacci* and *Cavalleria Rusticana* respectively. Omitting a host of less distinguished opera composers, this brings us to the present century.

Since opera combines the most attractive elements of stage entertainment —music, drama, and dancing—why is it not the most appealing form of art? An important reason is that each of the arts sacrifices something when combined with the others. Music tied to a text and the human voice lacks the freedom of absolute instrumental music, and an orchestra supporting singers from the pit lacks the power and eloquence of an unencumbered symphony. The slow pace of singing as compared to speaking causes the drama to suffer as does the difficulty of understanding words in song. Dancing in opera adds

RICHARD WAGNER

color and variety but does so at the expense of the drama except when carefully integrated. Anyone expecting to find in full measure all the attributes of a concert, a play, and a ballet in an opera is certain to be disappointed. Opera, to be properly enjoyed, must be accepted as a distinct medium separate and apart from its components.

Accepting opera on its own terms still leaves several unsolved problems. Opera is expensive to produce, and opera companies must be subsidized or charge exorbitant prices for admission. Government subsidy is the usual solution in Europe. The absence of official public support restricts full-fledged professional opera in the United States to a few metropolitan areas and severely limits the number of people who have regular access to live opera. This lends a certain snob appeal but in the long run augurs against true popularity.

The biggest barrier to the widespread popularity of opera, however, is language. This country, more than most, is monolingual, yet the custom of singing opera in other languages is general. Only a dedicated music lover finds satisfaction in an opera without understanding its language, and a school-book knowledge is insufficient for comprehension of a text sung in a foreign tongue.

The present status and outlook for opera in this country is by no means as dismal as a survey of its problems suggests. Securing for opera its rightful place in the hierarchy of the arts is a formidable but not an insurmountable task. The omens are all favorable for a brighter future for opera in America.

In the first place there is a growing tendency to perform opera in English. Excellent translations of several standard works issued recently reflect this trend. Translation is perhaps a makeshift, but it cannot fail to attract new devotees. Opera in English is suitable fare for radio and television,

GIUSEPPE VERDI

GIACOMO PUCCINI

GEORGES BIZET

and the sparse but laudable offerings of opera on television have attracted favorable attention. Television also solves the problem of cost, at least for the individual viewer.

The most significant new development in the field of opera, however, is the surge of interest by college and university music departments. Areas which never could support a professional company now are offered high calibre collegiate performances while increasing numbers of talented students are gaining invaluable training and experience. Grass roots opera played before relatively unsophisticated audiences by young performers has special requirements. In response to this demand a virtually new concept of opera is emerging.

Operas are being composed to English texts with plots designed to appeal to contemporary audiences. Extraneous elements are eliminated and the dimensions scaled down to practical limits. Composers are writing chamber operas requiring few principals, small choruses or none, small orchestras, and a modest staging budget. Far from suffering from these limitations, operas in this new style are thriving. Making opera a believable and exciting dramatic experience is part of the movement, and in this too it is achieving striking success. With these developments a more general acceptance of opera as a form of entertainment seems assured.

A pioneer librettist-composer in this field who has several successful operas to his credit is the Italian-born American-trained Gian-Carlo Menotti. He has combined his dramatic and melodic gifts with a real flare for the theatre to produce a series of flourishing operas. His works have been produced by the Metropolitan Opera Company and innumerable college opera workshops, broadcast on radio and television, and filmed. Perhaps his most spectacular success and the opera probably seen by more people than any other in a comparable span of time is his *Amahl and the Night Visitors*. The National Broadcasting Company telecasts of *Amahl* have been annual Christmas events since its first performance in 1951. It certainly is one of the most appealing operas of the new type.

GIAN-CARLO MENOTTI: *Amahl and the Night Visitors* (1951)   45:45
  (1911–   )

> The full worth of this small masterpiece is perceived only when it can be seen as well as heard. Menotti displays rare skill in creating a setting, developing a plot, delineating character, working up emotional intensity, and bringing off a stunning climax. The music and text contribute in equal measure to the unfolding of this simple yet powerful drama.
>
> The opera is extremely concise, but it has all the ingredients of traditional opera including chorus and dancing. For performance it

requires only a modest number of principals, a small chorus and orchestra, a few dancers, and one stage setting. The scene is the interior of a humble dwelling on the road to Jerusalem on the night of the Nativity. Amahl, a crippled shepherd boy, and his widowed mother are visited by the Three Kings. The memorable events of that night in the lives of Amahl and his mother provide the material of the story. The English text and the fine diction of the singers on the recording render further comment unnecessary.

Broadway *musical shows* represent America's best claim to an indigenous tradition of drama with music. Except for the use of spoken dialogue in place of recitative, they preserve the pattern originated centuries ago in Italian opera. While continuing a venerable form, their style and content are strictly current-popular and change with the season. Irving Berlin, George Gershwin, Jerome Kern, Cole Porter, Richard Rodgers, Meredith Willson, and Frederick Loewe are illustrious names in the annals of the Broadway stage. The impressive list of smash hits they composed over the years prove that musical drama can be tremendously popular and financially rewarding. That which prospers in this country thrives, so the Broadway musical tradition can look forward to a glorious future. There will be no shortage of composers and librettists searching for the magic formula to produce a hit. Whether any of the hits will have enough substance and value to survive as works of art is another question. Gershwin's folk opera *Porgy and Bess* is one descendant of the Broadway tradition which as yet shows no sign of succumbing to the fate of most musicals. Perhaps it will escape the early oblivion which seems inevitably to be the price of immediate popularity. Leonard Bernstein's *West Side Story* is another work that may presage a more significant future for American music theatre. Until the styles become more stabilized, one hesitates to suggest a specific example for listening. An original cast recording of any show now on Broadway will illustrate the latest trends in musical shows.

Light operas and *operettas* are in a style somewhere between that of grand operas (or music dramas) and that of musical shows and comedies. Light operas and operettas usually have spoken dialogue and music in a light but not a popular vein. They are staple fare in amateur and outdoor summer productions.

Ballet

A performance by a troupe of dancers in costume to the accompaniment of music is a *ballet*. Ballet exists in four more or less distinct types: *classic ballet*, *modern ballet*, *modern dance*, and *incidental ballet* connected with other types of entertainment, especially opera and recently, motion pictures.

GEORGE GERSHWIN

Classic ballet often is adapted to existing absolute music. It is done in attire without special significance but which by color or design may contribute indirectly to the general mood of the dance. The stage customarily is bare except for a plain backdrop. The highly stylized steps, gestures, and movements of the ballet are executed with absolute precision. Episodes featuring individual dancers and small groups alternate with those involving the entire company. The motions are graceful and restrained. Evidence of effort is carefully concealed. The ballerinas wear special slippers which permit them to dance on the very tips of their toes, and steps executed thus are a characistic feature of ballet. Classic ballet is abstract. It tells no story and conveys no message. Aesthetic satisfaction derives from the beauty of line and movement of the individuals, from fluid patterns and designs created by the movement and disposition of groups, and from the music. The music itself has no special properties. The choreographer who conceives the dance selects a composition and adapts appropriate movements to it.

The most obvious difference between classic and modern ballet is that modern ballet dramatizes a story in pantomime. Costumes are used to delineate characters, but they are often more fanciful and suggestive than realistic. Ballerinas wear the same shoes as for classic ballet, and all the classic steps are employed, plus any others required by the story. Because of the limitations of pantomime, plots are relatively uncomplicated. Even so, audiences usually are provided an outline of the story in the program. The stage is kept relatively unobstructed, but scenery, stage properties, and lighting contribute to the total effect. Colorful stories suggestive of varied actions and providing for solo, small group, and full company scenes are most likely to be used. Music for modern ballets ideally is specifically composed for a given story with the composer and choreographer working in close collaboration. Several of the most celebrated works of the 20th century were created in this way on commissions from Sergei Diaghilev (1872–1929), impresario of the renowned Russian Ballet. Among them is *The Firebird* with music by Igor Stravinsky and choreography by Michel Fokine. This is the work which first brought Stravinsky international acclaim. It was followed by a series of ballets in the same genre which solidly established his reputation as the leading composer of his time.

IGOR STRAVINSKY: *The Firebird* (1910)   21:00
  (1882–   )   Introduction and Dance of the Firebird
                 Dance of the Princesses
                 Dance of Kastchei
                 Berceuse
                 Finale

In the ballet, based on Russian legend, young Prince Ivan wanders at night through the enchanted forest and captures the radiant Firebird. In return for her release the Firebird rewards him with one of her feathers. The darkness dissipates and twelve beautiful princesses are seen playing with the golden fruit of a silver tree in front of an imposing castle. The princesses warn Ivan that the castle is the abode of the infernal monster, Kastchei, who casts spells over intruders in his domain. Ivan is saved from destruction by the magic feather. The Firebird lulls the demons to sleep and reveals to the Prince the source of the monster's evil power, an egg hidden in the trunk of the silver tree. Ivan smashes the egg, vanquishing the monster and freeing his captives. The most beautiful of the princesses becomes his bride.

There are three different concert versions of this ballet music. The most familiar consists of the sections listed above as rescored by the composer in 1919.

Music from preexisting scores is sometimes used for modern ballets. This is feasible especially when the music itself suggests a story. Ballets using the music of Debussy's *Afternoon of a Faune* and Rimsky-Korsakov's *Scheherazade* are in this category. There are instances, too, in which music from various sources is arranged and adapted to accompany the intended story and action.

The distinctions between modern ballet and modern dance are by no means clearly defined. In general, modern dance has in common with modern ballet a pantomimed story, specially composed and arranged music, stage effects, and costumes. Differences lie in the types of movements and gestures used by the dancers. Modern dance places more emphasis on realism and less on stylized motions. Ballet dancers are thoroughly schooled in the traditions of classic ballet, whereas modern dancers stress individual expression through bodily movement. The subject matter of modern dance tends to be more earthy and the action more violent, but tender and sentimental moods are not excluded. Ballet slippers are an artifice usually discarded by modern dancers, and bare feet are common. Precision of group movement is less in evidence in modern dance, as rigid order yields to spontaneity. Martha Graham is a leading exponent of modern dance. Her *Appalachian Spring* with music by Aaron Copland is a magnificent example both musically and choreographically. Modern dance is not, of course, a separate art but an aspect of ballet, and no distinction between types can be detected in the music.

AARON COPLAND: *Appalachian Spring* (1944)   20:00
  (1900–   )

> *Appalachian Spring* was commissioned by the Elizabeth Sprague Coolidge Foundation for Martha Graham. It received the 1945 Pulitzer Prize for music and the Music Critics Circle award for the outstanding theatrical work of the 1944–45 season. Originally scored for a chamber ensemble of thirteen instruments, the music was subsequently arranged by the composer for full orchestra. This version, heard in concerts and on recordings, contains the essence of the ballet music but omits sections in which the interest is primarily choreographic. The music has no formal divisions and is played without pause. The action of the ballet is summarized in the Boosey & Hawkes score of the music as follows:
>
>> A pioneer celebration in spring around a newly-built farmhouse in the Pennsylvania hills in the early part of the last century. The bride-to-be and the young farmer-husband enact the emotions, joyful and apprehensive, their new domestic partnership invites. An older neighbor suggests now and then the rocky confidence of experience. A revivalist and his followers remind the new householders of the strange and terrible aspects of human fate. At the end the couple is left quiet and strong in their new house.

Until recently ballet was rarely seen in the provinces, but this rapidly is changing. Now dance troupes are regularly included on civic and community concert series, albeit often small companies with piano accompaniment in place of orchestra. Even under these less-than-perfect circumstances, packed houses attest to the popularity of these events and portend a growing market for ballet. Motion pictures and television, too, have discovered the magic of music and the dance. Music and dance production numbers are thoroughly exploited in Hollywood extravaganzas. More significant was the spectacular success a few years ago of *The Red Shoes*, a British motion picture with a ballet milieu and a cast of renowned dancers in which complete scenes from several ballets were shown. Television, besides showing motion pictures containing ballet scenes, occasionally programs live broadcasts of ballet. Through these mediums, ballet undoubtedly is reaching and pleasing a wider audience than ever before. The producers and sponsors of these shows are to be applauded for providing brief respites from the tedium of participation shows and westerns and for their contribution to the progress of art.

Dancing incorporated in other forms of entertainment such as operas and motion pictures is not a distinct type. Most often it is of the modern dance variety loosely connected to the main action by some specious pretext. Only rarely does it become an integral part of the story line and advance the plot, though it is most effective in this role. Obviously not all dancing in motion pictures bears a resemblance to ballet. Tap, acrobatic, ballroom, soft shoe, and the like occupy a secure if lowly niche in the realm of the dance similar to that of pop tunes in the realm of music.

Incidental Music

Incidental music is a classification for music which is subservient to drama. Though sometimes extended to include music played before and between acts, its particular function is to heighten the effect of the drama during the course of the action.

The use of incidental music can be traced throughout the history of drama. It figured prominently in Greek drama, in the Mystery and Miracle plays of the middle ages, and in the Elizabethan theatre. If practical limitations restrict its use currently on the legitimate stage, its expanded role in motion pictures and television more than compensates. Sound motion pictures and tape recording have revolutionized concepts of incidental music and have added a fascinating new tangent to the art of music. Most dramatic television shows are filmed or video-taped, so their processes are identical with those of the movies. The functions of incidental music are the same regardless of medium.

A paramount function of incidental music is to intensify the emotional impact of important scenes. Whether the emotion conveyed is one of joy or sorrow, elation or dejection, appropriate music has an uncanny power to evoke greater audience response. Used in this manner, incidental music supplements and augments the effect of words and actions. It underlines turning points and heightens climaxes in the story line.

Closely related to this is music with psychological significance. Music in this category is used to suggest subconscious thoughts and emotions and the presence of the unseen. Also included is music employed to create moods, to develop suspense, and to foreshadow impending action.

Music has utilitarian functions, too. It serves to indicate the passage of time. It fills voids created by the suspension of dialogue and sound effects.

It smooths transitions between contrasting scenes. It aids in establishing the locale by exploiting indigenous musical devices, for example, native drums for Africa, Spanish rhythms for the Iberian peninsula, and oriental scales for the far East. In these capacities incidental music helps to maintain the pace and continuity of the drama and to place it in the proper time and setting.

Actions sometimes are portrayed musically in an exaggerated and ludicrous manner for humorous effect. In this case the music has no psychological implications but simply mimics in an obvious fashion the visual elements. This procedure, called "Mickey Mousing" the action, is the stock approach to scoring cartoons and certain types of comic situations.

Incidental music occasionally is introduced realistically, that is, showing the musicians playing, and stories sometimes require a character to sing or to play an instrument on camera. Music in such cases may be an essential part of the plot, a diversion from the main argument, or a contrived device to display special talents of a star. Incidental music of this type is of necessity confined to situations where it is not inconsistent with the requirements of the story.

And finally, *title music* occupies the two spots where film music is most likely to command the listeners' attention, during the credits at the beginning of a picture and during the notice of completion at the end. *Opening title* music provides background for the studio trademark, the title of the picture, the list of characters and actors, credit lines, and notices. It is interesting to observe the location of the musical climax in this section, whether it coincides with the name of the star, the producer, the director, or perhaps with that of the composer himself! Besides providing background for the preliminaries, the opening title music establishes the tenor of the drama or the mood of the opening scene. *End title* music rarely is more than a cadence swelling up under the fadeout of the last scene and reinforcing the sense of finality at the end. It would be revolutionary for a film score to end quietly.

Recording the sound track of a motion picture is an intricate and demanding process. The casual viewer rarely is aware of the care and effort devoted to it. The composer's work really begins after the final editing of the film is completed. A product sometimes costing in the millions awaits his crowning touch before it can be marketed. This puts considerable pressure on the composer to work fast and jeopardizes the artistic quality of the music. The first step is to decide where music is to be used. This is done by production executives in collaboration with the music staff. The amount of music averages about half the total running time of the picture, but it may be much more or less. The location and extent of the music is largely a matter of personal taste, but in general it appears wherever it can provide one of the functions outlined above.

The film composer is furnished a *cue sheet* giving a synopsis of the action and the dialogue with timing to a fraction of a second for scenes involving music. From this he knows whether the music is to be under voices, with sound effects, or *in the clear*. He has unlimited access to the film and views repeatedly on a Moviola machine the scenes he is to underscore. Though he may have done some preliminary sketching of thematic ideas, only now is he ready to start composing music for specific scenes.

Music cues vary in duration from a few seconds to a few minutes. Composing within rigid time limits poses a problem, but those with experience working in the medium do not find this restriction burdensome. The episodes are brief, and the predetermined mood and function of the music stimulates the composer's imagination. Music's mission in relation to drama is achieved more readily than innate artistic merit, and it is not subjected to the same scrutiny as concert music. On the whole, dramatic music is written faster and less laboriously than nondramatic music.

Film music is turned out on a sort of assembly line by a small group of specialists. The composer's draft is handed to an orchestrator who arranges it for orchestra. A copyist then prepares parts for the individual players. Before the ink is dry on the last page, a recording time is set.

The orchestra is assembled on a sound stage equipped with the most advanced recording facilities. The conductor, usually the composer or the music director of the studio, faces a screen on which the picture is projected during the recording. The picture is started a bit before the music entrance, and preparatory signals are flashed on the screen. The conductor starts on cue and synchronizes the music with the action. He is assisted by a battery of timing devices including, when necessary, a *clicktrack* which produces clicks in an earphone at a preset rate. A run-through just before recording is the only rehearsal, so superb players are essential. Each scene is recorded as many times as necessary to achieve a "perfect take." Then the sound technicians take over.

Each facet of the sound—music, dialogue, sound effects, and background noise—is recorded on a separate sound track. These are synchronized with the picture and combined on a master sound track with strict attention to balancing the dynamic levels of the various components. The recording up to this point is done on magnetic tape. The completed master sound track is transferred to film where it appears as a narrow line of variable area and/or density running along the side of the picture. This line is scanned by a light focused on a photoelectric cell in the projector which reproduces it as sound in the theatre sound system.

The procedures are different when singing, playing, or dancing is shown on the screen. Music for these scenes is prerecorded. The recording then is played back while the action is being filmed, and the action is synchronized with the music. Performances of professional musicians are *dubbed in* when the musical ability of the actors is inadequate.

Except in musicals, incidental music is a subsidiary of the drama. How conscious should the audience be of its presence? Ideally, the viewer should not be aware of the music as such, but should miss it if it were stopped. Incidental music which intrudes or detracts from the drama is objectionable. The task of film composers is rather menial, but in comparison with composers of symphonies and string quartets remuneration, if not their satisfaction, is greater. They are accused of writing in imitative and derivative styles, but their contribution to the success of the total production is significant.

Recently cinema composers have followed the precedent of ballet and opera composers and have arranged excerpts from film scores for concert performance. Songs from movies are prominent on the popular hit parades. Incidental music is best appreciated, however, in context. Next time you see a motion picture, concentrate on the music. If you are among the many who have always taken it for granted, its scope and importance probably will come as a revelation.

Additional Examples

Opera

> GERSHWIN: *Porgy and Bess*
> MENOTTI: *The Telephone*
> WEILL: *Down in the Valley*
> BRITTEN: *Peter Grimes*
> WARD: *The Crucible*

Musical Show

> LOEWE: *My Fair Lady*
> RODGERS: *South Pacific*
> LEIGH: *Man of La Mancha*

Operetta

> LEHAR: *The Merry Widow*
> ROMBERG: *The Desert Song*
> HERBERT: *Naughty Marietta*
> STRAUSS: *Die Fledermaus (The Bat)*

Ballet

> FALLA: *El Amor Brujo (Love, the Sorcerer)*
> PROKOFIEV: *Cinderella, Op. 87*

BERNSTEIN: *Fancy Free*

KHACHATURIAN: *Gayne*

Incidental Music

MENDELSSOHN: Music for *A Midsummer Night's Dream* (Shakespeare's complete play with Mendelssohn's incidental music is recorded in RCA Victor album LVT–3002)

WALTON: *Henry V Suite* (from the film score)

PROKOFIEV: *Lieutenant Kijé Suite, Op. 60* (from the film score)

song forms

The forms used for instrumental music are also used in music for voices, and the small forms, even in instrumental music, are sometimes called song forms. The song form classification as used in this book, however, encompasses only the three plans of musical organization peculiar to music with words and found in song literature.

Strophic Form

When each stanza, or strophe, of a poem is set to the same music, the form of the resulting song is *strophic*. Strophic form is common in folk and familiar songs, children's songs, patriotic songs, hymns, and chorales, as well as in art songs. In art music this type of setting is appropriate only for simple, lyric poems with a limited number of uniform stanzas. From a musical point of view strophic form has several limitations, consisting as it does of an uninterrupted series of literal repetitions. There is no provision in the form for departure, return, variation, or development. The emotional range of the music, and consequently of the text, cannot be great. Musical interest must be concentrated in a single, cogent statement which fits all of the stanzas of the poem. Within the relatively narrow confines of strophic form many gems of the song literature, both traditional and art, have been conceived. One such gem, *Who Is Sylvia*, is a perfect example of the form, with identical music for each of its three verses.

FRANZ SCHUBERT: *Who Is Sylvia, Op. 106 No. 4* (1826)   2:47
   (1797–1828)

Strophic form:

A   Who is Silvia, what is she,
        That all our swains commend her?
    Holy, fair, and wise is she;
        The heaven such grace did lend her,
    That she might admired be.

A   Is she kind as she is fair?
        For beauty lives with kindness.
    Love doth to her eyes repair
        To help him of his blindness,
    And, being helped, inhabits there.

A   Then to Silvia let us sing,
        That Silvia is excelling;
    She excels each mortal thing
        Upon the dull earth dwelling;
    To her let us garlands bring.
        ——William Shakespeare: Two Gentlemen of Verona

In the song the last line of each stanza is repeated. Schubert's spelling of the name does not agree with Shakespeare's.

Through-Composed Form

The procedures in a *through-composed form* are just the reverse of those in a strophic form. For each part of the text a distinctive musical setting is created which is uniquely suited to the rhythm and sentiment of the words. Unifying elements may appear more than once, but there is no systematic repetition of sections. The sequence of musical ideas is dictated by the logic of the words rather than by the requirements of abstract musical design. This type of setting is appropriate for dramatic and narrative poems and those expressing a wide range of emotions. It is the only feasible way of setting blank verse and poems in which the rhythms are inconsistent or the stanzas irregular.

The fact that a through-composed song is organized around the text does not mean that unifying elements are lacking in the music. Tonality, style, and tempo give a sense of direction and purpose to musical events, even in the absence of a preconceived structural design. Melodic, motivic, rhythmic, and harmonic elements may be repeated, modified, and adapted in the process of illuminating the text. Literal repetitions inspired by textual rather than musical considerations do not violate the concepts of through-composition.

Goethe's *Erlkönig* is a poem that demands a through-composed setting, and Schubert masterfully delineates every feature of the dramatic text in his music. The musical style changes with each shift from narration to dialogue and for each character—the father, the son, and the Erl-King, a symbol of death. The first stanza is preceded by an introduction in which the piano establishes the mood and states the leading motive four times. This motive is heard throughout the song, but always in the accompaniment, never in the voice part. The complete fusion of poetic and musical ideas produces a spectacular example of through-composed form.

FRANZ SCHUBERT: *Erlkönig (The Erl-King), Op. 1* (1815)   4:00
   (1797–1828)

    Through-composed form:

      Introduction

      A   Who rides there so late through night so wild?
                A loving father with his young child;
                He clasped his boy close with his fond arm,
                And closer, closer to keep him warm.

      B   "Dear son, what makes thy sweet face grow so white?"
                "See, father, 'tis the Erl-King in sight!
                The Erl-King stands there with crown and shroud!"
                "Dear son, it is some misty cloud."

      C   "Thou dearest boy, wilt come with me?
                And many games I'll play with thee;
                Where varied blossoms grow on the wold,
                And my mother hath many a robe of gold."

      D   "Dear father, my father, say did'st thou not hear,
                The Erl-King whisper so low in mine ear?"
                "Be tranquil, then be tranquil, my child,
                Among withered leaves the wind bloweth wild."

      E   "Wilt come, proud boy, wilt thou come with me?
                Where my beauteous daughter doth wait for thee;
                With my daughter thou wilt join in the dance every night,
                She'll lull thee with sweet songs to give thee delight,
                And lull thee with sweet songs to give thee delight."

      D′   "Dear father, my father, and can'st thou not trace
                The Erl-King's daughter in yon dark place?"
                "Dear son, dear son, the form you there see
                Is only the hollow gray willow tree."

     F(D) "I love thee well, with me thou shalt ride on my course,
                And if thou art unwilling, I'll seize thee by force!"
                "Oh father, my father, thy child closer clasp,
                Erl-King hath seized me with icy grasp!"

      G   The father shuddered, his pace grew more wild,
                He held to his bosom his poor swooning child,
                He reached that house with toil and dread,
                But in his arms, lo, his child lay dead!

                                 ——J. W. von Goethe
                          (Translation by Theodore Baker)

Song Cycle

A *song cycle* is a group of songs related by text, thought, medium, or style which collectively constitute a musical entity. Songs joined together in a unified group expand the scope and dimensions of the art song concept. The texts for a song cycle are usually the work of one poet, but they may be selected by the composer from random sources. The number of songs in a cycle varies considerably. There are three in Hugo Wolf's *Michelangelo Songs* and twenty-four in Franz Schubert's *Winterreise* (Winter Journey). In other respects song cycles are similarly lacking in uniformity, so to attempt to generalize about them is futile.

The number of existing song cycles is not large as compared with, for instance, the number of symphonies. Each one tends to be a law unto itself and unlike any other. If any cycle can be regarded as typical, it is Schumann's *Frauenliebe und Leben* (Woman's Love and Life). Its eight songs collectively constitute a model song cycle and individually illustrate three distinct approaches to setting a text. Two songs are essentially strophic; one is through-composed; and the other five are in forms associated with instrumental music.

ROBERT SCHUMANN: *Frauenliebe und Leben, Op. 42* (1840)   20:15
(1810–1856)

1.	Ever since I saw him	
2.	He of all mankind	2:30
3.	I can't believe it	5:30
4.	O ring upon my finger	7:30
5.	Help me dear sisters	9:45
6.	Dearest man	11:30
7.	Here at my breast	15:35
8.	Now hast thou hurt me first	16:50

Song Cycle:

1. Strophic, tonic key (B-flat).

A   Ever since I saw him,
I seem blind to be,
For whate'er I look at,
Only him I see;
Stays his face before me
As in waking dream,
In the deepest darkness
Brighter, brighter doth it gleam.

A   All the world without him's
    Colorless and bare,
    For my sisters' pastimes
    No more can I care,
    To my little chamber
    I would weeping flee;
    Ever since I saw him,
    I seem blind to be.

2. Rondo, five-part, subdominant key (E-flat).

A   He, of all mankind the noblest,
    And so gentle, and so kind!
    Lips of frankness, eyes of crystal,
    Steadfast courage, flashing mind.

A   As, in those blue heights above us,
    Bright and noble is yon star,
    So is he, in my own heaven,
    Bright and noble, high and far.

B   Forward, forward on thy highway;
    Let me but thy glory see,
    In all humbleness but see it,
    Blessed in my sadness be.

A   Do not hear my silent prayer,
    Thy high fortunes follow free;
    Heed not me, a lowly maiden,
    Lofty star of majesty!

C   None but worthiest of women
    May deserve thy happy choice;
    I will bless high heaven always,
    Thousand times rejoice!

C′   I will joy then in my weeping,
    Blessed, blessed will I sit;
    And if my poor heart be breaking—
    Break, my heart! What matters it?

A′   He, of all mankind the noblest,
    And so gentle, and so kind!
    Lips of frankness, eyes of crystal,
    Steadfast courage, flashing mind.
        And so gentle, and so kind!

3. Free part form, supertonic key (C minor).

A   I can't believe it, conceive it,
    'Tis all a dream and a lie,
    For how could he over others
    Poor me have set happy and high?

B   Methought his voice was speaking:
    "For ever I love thee!"
    Methought—I must have been dreaming,
    It never, never can be!

C   So dreaming, fain would I die now,
       Here cradled upon his breast;
       How welcome were death, by rapture
       Of tears everlasting caressed!

A   I can't believe it, conceive it,
       'Tis all a dream and a lie,
       For how could he over others
       Poor me have set happy and high?

Coda I can't believe it, conceive it,
       'Tis all a dream and a lie!

4. Rondo, five-part, subdominant key (E-flat).

A   O ring upon my finger,
       My little ring of gold,
       Dear jewel, devoutly I kiss thee,
          Devoutly I kiss thee,
       To my heart I hold.

B   I had awaked from dreaming
       My childhood's dream of peace and grace;
       I found me lost and forsaken
       In boundless untenanted space.

A   O ring upon my finger,
       'Twas taught to me first by thee,
       From thee the revelation
       How precious a jewel our life can be.

C   I'll live for him, I will serve him,
       Belonging to him whole,
       Will give him myself, and discover transfigured
       Discover transfigured in him, my soul.

A   O ring upon my finger,
       My little ring of gold,
       Dear jewel, devoutly I kiss thee,
          Devoutly I kiss thee,
       To my heart I hold.

5. Rondo, five-part, all parts begin alike, tonic key (B-flat).

A   Help me, dear sisters,
       Help to adorn me,
       Me, the fortunate, tend me now;
       Busy your fingers,
       Daintily wreathing
       Myrtle flowers about my brow.

B(A) When, with a tranquil
       Heart and a happy,
       Safe in the arms of my love I lay,
       Often he whispered
       All his impatience,
       All his longing to hasten the day.

A   Help me, dear sisters,
       Help me to banish
       Foolish fears that my heart oppress,
       That with unclouded
       Eyes I may greet him,
       Him, the fountain of happiness.

C(A)   When, my beloved,
       Thou art before me,
       When thou, my sun, dost on me shine,
       Let me devoutly,
       Let me all humbly,
       Let me bow down to thee, lover mine.

A′   Strew for him, sisters,
       Strew for him flowers,
       Bring for him beautiful rosebuds too.
       And to you, sisters,
       Love and leave-taking;
       Sadly, gladly I part from you.

6. Ternary, major submediant key (G).

A   Dearest man, thou eyest
       Me with wonder deep;
       Dost not guess the reason
       Why today I weep?
       See the liquid pearl-drops,
       Gems I seldom wear,
       Tremble bright and happy
       On my eyelid there!

A   Why my bosom flutters,
       Why my heart is proud,
       Would my lips were able
       To confess aloud;
       Come and hide thy face here
       On my trembling breast—
       In thine ear I'll whisper
       How our love is blest.

B   Now thou knowest the reason
       Of the tears that ran,
       Though thou canst not see them,
       My beloved, beloved man!
       Stay upon my heart here,
       Feel it beat and thrill,
       So that close and closer
       I may clasp thee still!
           Close and closer!

A   Look, beside my bed here
         Will the cradle bide
         Where the pretty picture
         Of my dream I'll hide;
         Soon will come the morning,
         Waked the dream will be;
         There will lie thine image
         Laughing up at me!

Coda   Thine image!

7. Strophic, modified, parts begin alike, end differently, major mediant key (D).

A   Here at my breast, my beautiful boy,
         Thou art my treasure, thou art my joy.
         O love it is gladness, and gladness is love;
         So have I said, and so it will prove.

A′   I deemed my fortune all too high,
         But still more happy now am I;
         Only the heart, only the breast
         That baby lips have sweetly pressed.

A″   Only a mother knows full well
         What love and happiness may spell.
         Pity on man I must bestow,
         Who mother's joy can never know.

A‴   My darling, darling angel, thou,
         Thou lookest at me and smilest now!
         Here at my breast, my beautiful boy,
         Thou art my treasure, thou art my joy!

8. Through-composed, mediant key (D minor).

A   Now hast thou hurt me first since love began,
           And wounded deep!
         Thou sleepest, O cruel, most unpitiful man,
           Death's endless sleep.

B   The world is empty now for me, a wife
           Left all alone—alone;
         For I have loved and I have lived, but life
           I now have none.

C   I shrink away into my heart's recess,
           The veil doth fall;
         I there find thee and my lost happiness
           My world and all!

Coda The piano part of the first song, complete but without the voice part or the repetition, returns as a coda to the complete cycle; tonic key (B-flat).

——Adelbert von Chamisso
(Translation by Robert Randolph Garran)

Additional Examples

Strophic Form

SCHUBERT: *Haiden-Röslein (Hedge Roses)*
Die Schöne Müllerin (The Maid of the Mill)
1. Das Wandern (Wandering)

BRAHMS: *Volkskinderlieder (Children's Folk Songs)*
4. Sandmännchen (Little Sandman)

Through-Composed Form

SCHUBERT: *Der Tod und das Mädchen (Death and the Maiden)*
Morgenständchen (Hark, Hark! the Lark)

R. STRAUSS: *Cäcilie (Cecilia), Op. 27 No. 2*

Song Cycle

BEETHOVEN: *An die Ferne Geliebte (To the Distant Beloved), Op. 98*

BRAHMS: *Ernste Gesänge (Serious Songs), Op. 121*

DEBUSSY: *Chansons de Bilitis (Songs of Bilitis)*

BRITTEN: *Serenade for Tenor, Horn, and Strings, Op. 31*

CHAPTER 16

choral forms and religious music

Choral music is linked inseparably with religion. The arts have occupied a central position in sacred ceremonies from their beginnings down to the present. Music, painting, architecture, poetry, prose, drama, and the dance all have drawn nurture and sustenance from the font of religion. In turn the arts have given expression to the faith and aspirations of mankind through the ages. Art and religion are almost synonymous in primitive societies. The striving for beauty independent from service to divinity and the cultivation of art for art's sake are characteristics of advanced civilizations. Varying concepts of deity in different places and times have led to the development of appropriate modes of worship with attendant arts. Those displayed only within the confines of a holy edifice are of interest primarily to communicants of a particular faith. Between the sacred and the profane lies a body of art, religiously inspired but universal in appeal, which reaches beyond the place of worship and into the museums and concert halls of the world. What is true of the arts and music in general is especially apropos in regard to choral music. The choral repertory is preponderantly of religious derivation.

Mass and Requiem

The *Mass* is a solemn rite of the Roman Catholic Church commemorating the sacrifice of Christ. The complete ritual has a complex structure of many sections only part of which are sung. Some portions of the text change with the day and the season while others are constant. In recent times composers have set only those items which are sung and which are the same in every Mass. There are five such sections: *Kyrie, Gloria, Credo, Sanctus,* and *Agnus Dei.*

The text of the Mass is drawn from several sources. The Kyrie, a supplication for mercy, is part of an ancient Greek litany, and the words are Greek.[1] The rest of the Mass is in Latin.[1] The Gloria, a hymn in praise of the Trinity, is from Luke 2:14 and Eastern Liturgies. The Credo is a profession of faith from the 4th-century Council of Nicaea. The Sanctus translated begins, "Holy, Holy, Holy, Lord God of Hosts, heaven and earth are full of Thy glory." The phrases of this song of praise are taken from Isaiah 6:3, Psalm 118, Apocalypse 4:8 and Matthew 21:9. The message of the Agnus Dei is, "Lamb of God, Who taketh away the sins of the world, have mercy upon us and grant us peace." These texts have inspired some of the most eloquent pages in the literature of music.

Composers writing for concert rather than liturgical use are inclined to augment the performance resources and expand the dimensions of the Mass. Whereas liturgical Masses originally were for unaccompanied voices, concert Masses may be for chorus, soloists, and orchestra. The original five sections may be subdivided into many. The Sanctus is frequently divided, with the Benedictus becoming a separate part. In the most expansive examples of the Mass the texts, especially the lengthy ones of the Gloria and the Credo, are sectioned, with verses and even sentences being treated musically as distinct units. Masses of this type are too long and demanding for ordinary church services, but they are splendid examples of religiously inspired music.

Bruckner, who was extremely devout, adheres to the five-part division in his *Mass No. 3,* but he exploits the full resources of his expanded medium: four soloists (soprano, alto, tenor, and bass), mixed chorus, and orchestra.

ANTON BRUCKNER: *Mass No. 3 in F minor, "Great"* (1868)   57:10
(1824–1896)   1. Kyrie
                                      2. Gloria
                                      3. Credo
                                      4. Sanctus
                                      5. Agnus Dei

It must have been an extraordinary event, but the first performance of this Mass was given at St. Augustine church in Vienna as part of the regular Sunday morning service.

A *Requiem* is a *Mass for the Dead.* It differs from the usual Mass in that the joyous Gloria and the Credo are omitted, and sections peculiar to

---

[1] The vernacular may now be substituted for the traditional languages.

ANTON BRUCKNER

the Requiem are inserted. The *Requiem Aeternam* (Eternal Rest) from which the service takes its name precedes the Kyrie. A long Latin hymn, *Dies Irae* (Day of Wrath), and an Offertory, *Domine Jesu Christe* (Lord, Jesus Christ), follow the Kyrie. The Requiem concludes with the *Lux Aeterna* (Eternal Light).

Mozart's last work, left unfinished at his death, was his *Requiem in D minor*. The treatment of the text in the Kyrie (*Kyrie eleison* and *Christe eleison* are sung simultaneously as the two subjects of a double fugue) disqualifies it for strict liturgical use, but it is a magnificent example of religiously inspired music.

W. A. MOZART: *Requiem in D minor, K.626* (1791)   57:00
  (1756–1791)   Introit (Requiem aeternam) and Kyrie
                     Dies Irae
                     Offertory (Domine Jesu Christe)
                     Sanctus
                     Benedictus
                     Agnus Dei and Communion (Lux aeterna)

An anonymous stranger under conditions of absolute secrecy commissioned Mozart to compose a Requiem just five months before his death. Mozart became obsessed with the idea that the stranger was an emissary of death and that the Requiem was his own. He was obliged to interrupt his labor on this work, and it was incomplete when he died. The night of his death he gave the score to his friend and pupil, Sussmeyer, who finished it and delivered it to the mysterious stranger. It turned out that he was acting as agent for a nobleman, Count Franz von Walsegg, who wished to pass off the Requiem as his own composition. The Count actually was listed as the composer at the first performance.

The Requiem is scored for a quartet of solo voices (of which the soprano is most prominent), chorus, and orchestra. The Sanctus and Benedictus are treated as separate parts. Complete breaks between sections of the major parts create the effect of distinct movements.

Brahms' *German Requiem* is a noteworthy exception to the usual plan. Its text was selected by the composer from the German Bible without reference to the traditional content of the Roman Rite. It is in every respect a unique work.

Motet and Anthem

The meaning of *motet* has varied considerably during the 700 years that the term has been used, and no single definition covers all of its ramifications. Motets most often are unaccompanied choral compositions with sacred Latin texts and polyphonic texture, but there are many exceptions. Motets were an important adjunct of the Catholic service during the Middle Ages and the Renaissance. These, of which *Super Flumina Babylonis* is representative, and their immediate successors have great historical significance.

G. P. DA PALESTRINA: *Super Flumina Babylonis*   3:15
(1525–1594)

"By the rivers of Babylon we sat down and wept when we remembered thee, O Zion. On the willows in the midst thereof, we hung up our instruments." Both in text (Latin from the Vulgate) and treatment this is a typical motet by the greatest 16th-century composer of church music.

Anthems are the Anglican Church equivalent of the Catholic motet, and the term is also used for a wide variety of selections sung by choirs in Protestant church services. The most obvious difference between anthems and motets is that of language, Latin in motets and English in anthems, though scholars also detect differences of style. In Anglican music *full anthems* follow the plan of motets while *verse anthems* are essentially an English innovation. The characteristic feature of verse anthems is the systematic juxtaposition of instrumental and choral textures. Passages for full chorus unaccompanied alternate with passages for one or more voices accompanied by instruments. In the following example two parts for treble (high) voices continue during the instrumentally accompanied sections. William Byrd is the first of a series of great English composers in the 16th and 17th centuries.

WILLIAM BYRD: *Christ Rising Again*   3:15
   (1543–1623)

> Christ rising again from the dead, now dieth not.
> Death from henceforth hath no power upon Him.
> For in that He died but once to put away sin,
> But in that He liveth, He liveth unto God.
> So likewise count yourselves dead unto sin,
> But living unto our God in Christ Jesus, our Lord.
>
> ——Romans 6:9–11

Instruments provide a short introduction and continue under the singing of the first line. The second line is for full chorus unaccompanied. In line three the first phrase is for high voices with instruments; the second phrase for unaccompanied chorus. The fourth line is for high voices with instruments. Line five is sung by the full chorus alone. Line six is divided like line three. This anthem is in *Music of the Sixteenth Century*, RCA Victor LM 136.

Madrigal

Madrigals are secular vocal works with texts drawn mostly from contemplative and idyllic poetry in the vernacular. Madrigals are the secular counterparts of motets. As with the motet, considerable change in the form occurred between its inception and its flowering two hundred years later in the 16th and 17th centuries. The fully-developed madrigal generally is for unaccompanied voices in four to six parts. The style is predominantly but not exclusively polyphonic.

The high order of Italian and English poetry available as texts gave impetus to the madrigal movement. The music is inspired directly by the words. It portrays the moods and thoughts of the text, and at times programmatic effects are induced by a particularly piquant word or phrase.

Madrigals were intended primarily as a source of entertainment for the participants in their performance. The ability to sing a madrigal part at sight was a social grace expected of every gentleman and lady. The singing of madrigals was one of the most prevalent forms of entertainment at intimate social gatherings of the period. The vocal skills of a vast public must have been unusually well developed, for the intricate music customarily was performed with the singers seated around a table reading from part books with no conductor and with only one on a part.

The madrigal originated in Italy, and Orlandus Lassus (also known as Roland de Lassus and Orlando di Lasso) is generally grouped with the Italian madrigalists, though he was born in the Netherlands and died in Munich. His formative years were spent in Italy, and his first printed work contained 22 madrigals to poems of Petrarch. His *Echo Song*, with its double chorus and homophonic texture, is not exactly a typical madrigal, but it illustrates the typical affinity between the text and the music in a most engaging manner.

ORLANDUS LASSUS: *O là, O che bon'eccho (Echo Song)* (1580)   1:05
(1532–1594)

> A series of questions and invectives are echoed, rather than an-
> swered, by an antiphonal chorus. This novel piece is one of the most
> celebrated of the Italian madrigals. It is included in several collec-
> tions and on the following recordings: Vox DL 380, Columbia ML
> 5373, and RCA Victor LM 136.

Influence of the Italian madrigal was evident in England during the last half of the 16th century. Lassus may have visited there briefly in 1554 or 1555. A collection of Italian madrigals provided with English texts, *Musica Transalpina*, was published in 1588 and widely disseminated. It firmly established the Italian madrigal style in England. The time was ripe for the new form. English poets and composers were of a high order. They adapted the Italian madrigal style to the English language and tastes and produced a large number of indigenous madrigals which are still sung and enjoyed. Thomas Morley was one of the first generation of English madrigalists. The spelling in the title of his madrigal collection gives a clue to its age.

THOMAS MORLEY: *Madrigalls to Foure Voyces* (1594)
(1557–1602)   Ho! who comes here   2:10

> Morley probably wrote both the words and the music of this madri-
> gal, proving that he was a better composer than he was a poet. The
> whole collection is recorded, and this particular madrigal is also
> in *The History of Music in Sound, Volume IV*, RCA Victor LM–
> 6029.

To Shorten Winter's Sadness is by Thomas Weelkes, a second genera-
tion English madrigal composer. It employs, as do many English madrigals, the nonsense syllables "fa la la" as part of the text. These syllables are interspersed between the phrases of the poem.

THOMAS WEELKES: *To Shorten Winter's Sadness*   1:45
(1575–1623)

Cantata

Cantatas are types of vocal compositions for which no precise definition is possible. In general, cantatas are compositions consisting of several sections for one or more voices with instrumental accompaniment. The sections often contrast in style and medium, with recitatives, arias, duets, choruses, and instrumental episodes common ingredients. The texts of the various sections are related parts of a single narrative which may be sacred or secular in subject matter, lyric or dramatic in style.

Bach's cantatas (almost 200 extant out of a much larger production) represent the largest body of relatively consistent works in the form. A typical Bach cantata opens with a polyphonic chorus followed by a series of recitatives and arias and closes with a harmonized chorale. The chorale with which a cantata closes often provides a basic source of material, both textual and musical, for the entire cantata. One practice is to use each stanza of the chorale text or a paraphrase of it as the basis for one section of the cantata. The chorale melody, too, may figure in the various sections. Embellished versions of the chorale tune sometimes are used, and at other times phrases of the chorale melody in long notes are given a florid contrapuntal setting. These procedures are illustrated in Bach's Cantata No. 1, *Wie schön leuchtet der Morgenstern* (How Brightly Shines the Morning Star).

J. S. BACH: *Wie schön leuchtet der Morgenstern* (1736) 24:50
(1685–1750) 1. Chorale fantasia (Chorus and Orchestra)
  2. Recitative (Tenor with continuo)
  3. Aria (Soprano with oboe da caccia and continuo)
  4. Recitative (Bass with continuo)
  5. Aria (Tenor with 2 solo violins, strings and continuo)
  6. Chorale (Chorus and orchestra)
  (Chorale melody p. 314)

The hymn *How Brightly Shines the Morning Star* on which this cantata is based was composed by Philipp Nicolai (1556–1608). In No. 1, after an instrumental introduction, the chorus sopranos sing the words and melody of the hymn doubled by the horns while the other voices and instruments provide an elaborate contrapuntal setting. The tenor recitative text is a paraphrase of the second stanza of the hymn. The next three sections have texts based on successive stanzas. The soprano aria is in effect a duet between the voice and the oboe da caccia, an obsolete instrument resembling an English horn. In the tenor aria, two solo violins form a trio with the solo voice. No. 6 is a straightforward statement of the chorale melody with the words of the sixth stanza. In this section, instruments double the voices except for a brilliant horn countermelody.

The numbers used to identify Bach cantatas are derived from their order in the collected edition of his works and have no chronological significance. This cantata, though numbered 1, is a product of his maturity. It was written for the Feast of Annunciation, March 25, and reflects the joyous mood appropriate to the occasion.

Oratorio

Oratorios in general are dramatic compositions of large dimensions for soloists, chorus, and orchestra based on religious but nonscriptural texts. They are distinguished from operas by the absence of scenery, costumes, and action as well as by subject matter and from sacred cantatas by their size. The chorus is prominent, more so than is customary in either operas or cantatas. An overture or opening orchestral introduction is usual. Recitatives by the soloists carry the burden of the narrative. One of the soloists sometimes is a narrator who explains the action, introduces the characters, and provides continuity between the various numbers, all in recitative. Arias generally follow the recitatives. Choral numbers usually are comments on or reactions to the immediately preceding passage, frequently with the chorus representing a crowd in the dramatic situation.

Not all oratorios conform to this plan. Some have secular subjects, and some are done in costume. These must be regarded as departures from the norm, which is represented perfectly in the most famous of all oratorios, Handel's *Messiah*.

G. F. HANDEL: *The Messiah* (1741)   2:25:00
 (1685–1759)

   Part I
      1. Overture
      2. Recitative (Tenor): Comfort ye
      3. Air (Tenor) Every valley shall be exalted
      4. Chorus: And the glory of the Lord
      5. Recitative (Bass): Thus saith the Lord of hosts
      6. Air (Bass): But who may abide the day of His coming
      7. Chorus: And He shall purify the sons of Levi
      8. Recitative (Alto): Behold, a virgin shall conceive
      9. Air (Alto and chorus): O thou that tellest good tidings to Zion
     10. Recitative (Bass): For, behold, darkness shall cover the earth
     11. Air (Bass): The people that walked in darkness
     12. Chorus: For unto us a child is born
     13. Pastoral Symphony (Orchestra)
     14. Recitative (Soprano): And suddenly there was with the angel
     15. Recitative (Soprano): And the angel said unto them, Fear not
     16. Recitative (Soprano): And suddenly there was with the angel
     17. Chorus: Glory to God in the highest
     18. Air (Soprano): Rejoice greatly O daughter of Zion
     19. Recitative (Alto): Then shall the eyes of the blind be opened

20. Air (Alto): He shall feed His flock
    Air (Soprano): Come unto Him
21. Chorus: His yoke is easy and His burden light

Part II

22. Chorus: Behold the Lamb of God
23. Air (Alto): He was despised and rejected of men
24. Chorus: Surely He hath borne our griefs
25. Chorus: And with His stripes we are healed
26. Chorus: All we like sheep have gone astray
27. Recitative: (Tenor) All they that see Him, laugh Him to scorn
28. Chorus: He trusted in God
29. Recitative (Tenor): Thy rebuke hath broken His heart
30. Air (Tenor): Behold, and see if there be any sorrow
31. Recitative (Tenor): He was cut off out of the land of the living
32. Air (Tenor): But Thou didst not leave His soul in hell
33. Chorus: Lift up your heads
34. Recitative (Tenor): Unto which of the angels said He
35. Chorus: Let all the angels of God worship Him
36. Air (Bass): Thou art gone up on high
37. Chorus: The Lord gave the word
38. Air (Soprano): How beautiful are the feet of them that preach
39. Chorus: Their sound is gone out into all lands
40. Air (Bass): Why do the nations so furiously rage together
41. Chorus: Let us break their bonds asunder
42. Recitative (Tenor): He that dwelleth in heaven
43. Air (Tenor): Thou shalt break them with a rod of iron
44. Chorus: Hallelujah

Part III

45. Air (Soprano): I know that my Redeemer liveth
46. Chorus: Since by man came death
47. Recitative (Bass): Behold, I tell you a mystery
48. Air (Bass): The trumpet shall sound
49. Recitative (Alto): Then shall be brought to pass the saying that is written
50. Duet (Alto and tenor): O death, where is thy sting
51. Chorus: But thanks be to God
52. Air (Soprano): If God be for us
53. Chorus: Worthy is the Lamb
    Amen

The Messiah is practically never given in its entirety. Numbers 34, 35, 36, 49, 50, 51, and 52 customarily are omitted, and they are not included in the timing. More severe cuts are often made, and it is not unusual for the order of the numbers to be rearranged.

The Messiah ranks as one of the great artistic creations of man. It was received enthusiastically at its first performance, and its appeal has continued undiminished through the years. Mozart scored orchestral accompaniments for use where no organ was available, but they are now used almost universally.

Several passages of scripture and liturgy have been used repeatedly in choral compositions. Among them are: the Gospels of Matthew, Mark, Luke, and John which provide the texts for *Passion Music;* the *Te Deum*, a hymn of praise and thanksgiving in the Catholic liturgy which is freely set, often commemorating joyous occasions; the *Magnificat*, canticle of the Virgin in both the Catholic and Anglican rites; and the *Stabat Mater*, a 13th-century addition to the feast of the Seven Dolours. The Jewish *Sacred Service* is represented in one superlative example by Ernest Bloch (1880–1959).

Additional Examples

Mass and Requiem

PALESTRINA: *Missa Brevis* (A cappella, appropriate for liturgical
    use)

STRAVINSKY: *Mass* (Voices and instruments)

SCHUBERT: *Mass No. 2 in G, D.167* (Chorus and Orchestra)

FAURE: *Requiem, Op. 48* (Chorus and Orchestra, not regular)

Motet

BACH: *Motet No. 5, Komm, Jesu, komm, S.229*

BYRD: *Ego sum panis vivus*

Madrigal

GESUALDO: *Tu m'uccidi, o crudele*

BYRD: *I Thought that Love Had Been a Boy*

Cantata

BARTOK: *Cantata Profana*

PROKOFIEV: *Alexander Nevsky, Op. 78* (Cantata arranged from
    the film score)

Oratorio

MENDELSSOHN: *Elijah, Op. 70*

WALTON: *Belshazzar's Feast*

Passion

BACH: *St. Matthew Passion, S.244*

SCHUTZ: *St. Luke Passion*

Te Deum

KODALY: *Te Deum*

Magnificat
> BACH: *Magnificat in D, S.243*
> HOVHANESS: *Magnificat, Op. 157*

Stabat Mater
> PERGOLESI: *Stabat Mater*

Sacred Service (Jewish)
> BLOCH: *Sacred Service, "Avodath Hakodesh"*

The Periods and Styles of Music

Chronology[1]

2000 B.C.	Earliest notation			
700 B.C.	Terpander			
138 B.C.	First surviving composition			
540	Pope Gregory I	604		
850	Beginnings of polyphony			
1100	Troubadours and trouvères			
1200	Minnesingers			
1240	Sumer Is Icumen In			
1300	Machaut	1377		
1450	Des Prez	1521		
1501	First music printing			
1505	Tallis	1585		
1525	Palestrina	1594		
1532	Lassus	1594		
1543	Byrd	1623		
1546	Caccini	1618		
1557	Morley	1602		
1560	Gesualdo	1613		
1571	Praetorius	1621		
1575	Weelkes	1623		

---

[1] Composers and milestones of music mentioned in the text. Some of the dates are approximate.

music before 1600

The origins of music are shrouded in mystery. Its beginnings can only be inferred from indirect evidence supplied by studies in anthropology and archaeology. By the dawn of history music was firmly established as an adjunct of rituals, ceremonies, and festivals. The singing and dancing of the celebrants was accompanied by a variety of percussion, wind, and string instruments.

Music was highly developed and widely practiced in the ancient civilizations of Egypt, Sumer, Babylonia, Assyria, Arabia, China, India, and throughout the Orient. Jewish musical traditions date back to 2000 B.C. Influences of pre-Christian Hebrew chants have survived in the synagogues of isolated Jewish tribes and in Christian chants, though none of the actual music has been preserved.

The earliest known musical notation is on a 4,000 year old clay tablet in the University of Pennsylvania museum. The tablet was one of thousands excavated by a museum archaeological expedition to Mesopotamia around the turn of the century. Its significance was undetected until Dr. M. Duchesne-Guillemin visited the museum in 1967. She identified the inscription as a Sumerian scale. The notation was etched on the clay tablet using the same wedge-shaped cuneiform script employed by the Sumerians in their writing. Their culture was very advanced, and they used music extensively in their festivals, pageants, and religious rites. The death pits of Ur have yielded the remains of court musicians buried with their lyres and harps which were richly ornamented with gold, silver, shell, lapis lazuli, and red stone.

The only written music preserved from antiquity is the single example of Sumerian notation and a few remnants of Greek music. In the Greek culture music occupied an exalted position. Music was included in the quadrivium of liberal arts, along with arithmetic, geometry, and astronomy. Greek philosophers wrote in detail about music theory and the place of music in society. During the 7th century B.C. Terpander established the first music school in Greece. He is credited with being the first to set poetry to music and is regarded as the father of Greek lyric poetry. The poems of Sappho were sung, and music figured prominently in Greek drama. The quantity of Greek music must have been great, but only one brief song and a dozen or so fragments survived the collapse of the Hellenic world. Two of them have been transcribed into modern notation and recorded.

ANONYMOUS: *First Delphic Hymn* (138 B.C.)   3:30

> This is the longest extant example of Greek music. Some reconstruction of the melody is necessary, and transcribed versions are not in complete agreement. A translation of the text and the melody in modern notation are included with the recording in *The History of Music in Sound,* Volume I, RCA Victor LM–6057.

ANONYMOUS: *Epitaph of Seikilos* (before 100 A.D.)   :40

> This is the only piece of Greek music preserved intact. The message cut on the tombstone of Seikilos' wife is still timely: "As long as you live, be cheerful; let nothing grieve you. For life is short, and time claims its tribute." This example follows the *First Delphic Hymn* in *The History of Music in Sound* album, and it is also included in *2000 Years of Music,* Decca DX–106.

Little is known about Roman music beyond the fact that it was influenced by the theories and practices of the Greeks. The separation of music from poetry and drama and the development of brass instruments are attributed to the Romans. Slaves played music in the homes of the rich citizens and in theaters. The *hydraulis,* an organ of Greek origin, was popular at outdoor entertainments such as the exhibitions by gladiators.

Music in the early Christian era was concerned principally with the development of the sacred monody of the Catholic liturgy. Between roughly 200 and 1300 A.D. a supreme body of unaccompanied vocal music was collected under the patronage of the Church. It is known variously as *plainsong, plainchant, Gregorian chant,* or by its Latin name *cantus planus.* The codification of the chant was accomplished during the pontificate of Gregory I (590–604), and it is most often known by his name. The Benedictine monks of Solesmes (a village near Le Mans, France) have dedicated themselves to restoring and performing authentic versions of Gregorian chant. Several London recordings are devoted to their performances, any one of which will serve as an example of Gregorian chant.

Descriptions and examples of polyphonic (multipart) music first appeared in 9th-century treatises, but this new type of music was slow to develop. Examples of 10th- and 11th-century polyphony are discussed on page 107. During the centuries when the early development of polyphonic music was taking place, both sacred and secular music continued to be preponderantly monophonic.

Concurrently with the early attempts at polyphony, secular monophonic songs were being disseminated by traveling minstrels and students in minor church orders who roamed Europe. At first the language was Latin as in the music of the church, but by the 12th century poet-musicians were writing aristocratic poetry in the dialect of southern France and setting it to music. These poet-musicians were the *troubadours*. Raimbaut de Vaqueiras was one of the 400 known troubadours who left a legacy of some 2500 poems and 250 melodies. His *Kalenda Maya* was set to a dance tune played on a vielle an important string instrument of the 12th and 13th centuries.

RAIMBAUT DE VAQUEIRAS: *Kalenda Maya* (1195) :45
  (Died 1207)
> A recording of this troubadour song is included in *2000 Years of Music*, Decca DX–106.

The *trouvères* wrote and sang songs similar to those of the troubadours but using the dialect of northern France. Hundreds of melodies and thousands of poems have been preserved in trouvère manuscripts, some of which are now available in facsimile editions. Richard the Lionhearted (1157–1199) was the most illustrious of the trouveres, but Adam de la Halle (1240–1287) was the author of the most extensive work, *Le Jeu de Robin et Marion* (The Play of Robin and Marion). This pastoral drama is recorded, and Darius Milhaud has made a delightful adaptation of it for contemporary stage presentation.

The practices of the troubadours and trouvères, and even some of their melodies, were taken up about a hundred years later in Germany by the *minnesingers*. The Germans were less influenced by popular dance music than the French, and the style and subject matter of their songs were sometimes of a religious nature. Walter von der Vogelweide's *Palästinalied* (Palestine Song) commemorates the Crusade of 1228.

WALTER VON DER VOGELWEIDE: *Palästinalied* (1228) :50
  (1170–1230)
> The text of this song says, in essence: "Only now, since I have come to the place where God walked as man, do I live a true man's

life." A translation is given in the *2000 Years of Music* album, Decca
DX–106.

The English produced some monophonic songs during this period, but
an insignificant number in comparison with the French and Germans. By
this time the English were already writing multipart music like the monumental *Sumer Is Icumen In* (see page 145).

GUILLAUME DE MACHAUT (1300–1377) was a cleric, courtier, poet,
and the greatest musician of his age. He composed in a wide range of forms
and styles—monophonic, polyphonic, secular, and sacred. He secured a
unique place in the history of music by being the first individual to write a
complete polyphonic setting of the Ordinary of the Mass. The assumption
that this Mass was performed in 1364 at the coronation of Charles V of
France, whom he served, is not well founded. The entire Mass, sometimes
identified as the *Mass of Notre Dame*, is recorded, and excerpts are included
in various anthologies. The technical devices characteristic of Machaut's
style are especially evident in the *Benedictus*, the concluding section of the
Sanctus. The harmonies of Machaut's polyphonic music sound crude to
modern ears, because in his time the principles of chord structure and progression that we have come to accept were not yet formulated.

GUILLAUME DE MACHAUT: *Mass of Notre Dame* (before 1364)
(1300–1377)   Benedictus   1:40

In the century following Machaut the procedures of polyphonic music
were refined and perfected at an accelerated rate facilitated by improvements
in the system of rhythmic notation. Music history books list an array of distinguished names and achievements for this period, but the first composer
whose music is apt to appeal immediately to 20th-century listeners is Josquin
des Prez (spelled a variety of ways and alphabetized under J, D, and P).

DES PREZ (1450–1521) was born in Belgium but studied in Paris and
spent 30 years as a musician in the chapels of Italy before returning to his
homeland where he was provost of a cathedral until his death. He met many
of the notables of his day in his extensive travels. His music was sung everywhere, and his influence was enormous. Some of his compositions still display
the intricate contrapuntal manipulations typical of his predecessors, but the
style for which he is remembered places greater emphasis on harmonic considerations. For the first time chord structures and progressions are consistently governed by principles that later became standard. The horizontal and
vertical aspects of his music give the impression of being in perfect balance

and under complete control. The *Ave Maria* cited on page 59 is typical of the style found in the sacred and serious compositions of Des Prez. The style of the frivolous *El Grillo* is too homophonic to be typical, but it demonstrates clearly his mastery of harmony.

JOSQUIN DES PREZ: *El Grillo (The Cricket)* (1505)   1:20
   (1450–1521)

   Des Prez is represented in Volume III of *The History of Music in Sound* by this and three other examples.

The printing of music was first accomplished during Des Prez's lifetime. A liturgical book containing monophonic music was printed in 1476, just 21 years after Gutenberg's Bible. The first printing of polyphonic music was done by Ottaviano dei Petrucci of Venice in 1501. The publication was a collection of multipart songs, supposedly 100 but actually only 99. Des Prez was amply represented by 8. Subsequent publications by Petrucci contained many works by Des Prez, including *El Grillo*. The printing of their music enhanced the reputations of composers and diffused their musical styles throughout Europe.

Prior developments culminated in the 16th century with a period known as "the golden age of vocal polyphony" which matched the splendor of Renaissance painting and literature. The art of creating beautiful, euphonious texture by interweaving graceful, fluid, melodic lines was developed to the ultimate degree. Sacred music fostered by the Church and secular music fostered by the courts vied for the first time on nearly equal terms. The two composers who contributed the most to vocal polyphony's Golden Age were Giovanni Pierluigi da Palestrina and Orlandus Lassus.

PALESTRINA (1525–1594) for almost 400 years has been universally regarded as the greatest composer of Catholic church music. He was a choirboy from the age of seven until his voice changed. After a period of study he became an organist and choirmaster. In 1551 he was appointed maestro of the Cappella Giulia, the post he held at his death, but between 1555 and 1571 he held appointments in other churches and was for a time music director of a seminary. He and Annibale Zoilo under a decree issued in 1576 by Pope Gregory XIII prepared a revised version of the Gradual, the variable parts of the Mass sung by the choir. Though Palestrina's creative and professional life was inseparably bound with the Church, he was no ascetic. Emperor Maximilian and the court of Mantua sought his services but would not meet his terms. He was married twice, had two sons, and during the last years of his life ran a successful fur business in addition to holding a church post. He was a prolific composer. His complete works fill 33 volumes.

His music and particularly his *Pope Marcellus Mass* have been cited repeatedly as models of the purest religious style. As recently as 1903 Pope Pius X singled out his works for special commendation in the *Motu Proprio* on sacred music. If time permits, one of his Masses should be heard. If not, the *Hodie Christus Natus Est* will serve as a small sample of his magnificent music.

PALESTRINA: *Hodie Christus Natus Est (Today Christ Is Born)*   2:50
   (1525–1594)

ORLANDUS LASSUS (1532–1594) was a most versatile composer. He wrote in the reserved style of the church and in the popular idiom of the day with equal fluency, and he set Italian, French, German, and Latin texts with equal skill. He was born in the Netherlands and, like Palestrina, started in music as a choirboy. By the time he was 12 he was in the service of the viceroy of Sicily. He held posts briefly in Milan, Laterano, and Naples and perhaps visited England and France before settling in Antwerp in 1555, the year his first compositions were published in Venice. The following year he accepted a court appointment in Munich where he remained, except for occasional journeys, until his death. He wrote in all the styles and forms of his day, and his output totals an incredible 2000 compositions. Emperor Maximilian made him a hereditary nobleman, but he may have been even more proud of the title conferred by fellow musicians, "Prince of Music." Two madrigals, *Matona mia cara* written when he was only 18 years old and *Il grave de l'eta* composed 37 years later, give some idea of the range of his style in this one type of composition.

ORLANDUS LASSUS: *Matona mia cara (Matona, my dear)* (1550)   2:50
   (1532–1594)
      This delightful little piece is still a favorite with madrigal singers
      and a cappella choirs. Its text is humorous, and slightly suggestive.

ORLANDUS LASSUS: *Il grave de l'eta (The Burden of Age)* (1587)   2:40
   (1532–1594)
      Lassus dedicated his last volume of madrigals to the physician who
      attended him during his declining years. The words by Gabriele
      Fiamma contain the phrases, "In the war of daily living I weaken.
      In vain do I search for peace or armistice."

When Palestrina and Lassus died, the golden age of vocal polyphony and the Renaissance were drawing to a close. Music was on the threshold of a new era, one that would have to suffer through its growing pains before it could rival the splendor of the past.

References

Curt Sachs, *The Rise of Music in the Ancient World* (New York: W. W. Norton, 1943).

Albert Seay, *Music in the Medieval World* (Englewood Cliffs: Prentice-Hall, Inc., 1965).

Manfred F. Bukofzer, *Studies in Medieval and Renaissance Music* (New York: W. W. Norton, 1950).

Gustave Reese, *Music in the Renaissance*, revised edition (New York: W. W. Norton, 1959).

Chronology

1546	Caccini	1618
1567	Monteverdi	1643
1582	Allegri	1652
1585	Schutz	1672
1588	Musica Transalpina	
1590	Florentine camerata	
1597	First opera	
1600	First use of figured bass	
1602	Nuove Musiche	
1653	Corelli	1713
1659	Purcell	1695
1660	Kuhnau	1722
1668	Couperin	1733
1669	Vivaldi	1741
1681	Teleman	1767
1683	Rameau	1764
1685	J. S. Bach	1750
1685	D. Scarlatti	1757
1685	Handel	1759
1710	Pergolesi	1736

the baroque period
1600-1750

The baroque was a period of bustling activity in science, politics, and the arts. Baroque music trailed a similar movement in painting and architecture by half a century. In keeping with the spirit of the times, it is characterized by luxuriant elaboration, grandiose concepts, and spectacular designs. Theatricalism, heretofore limited to an occasional picturesque passage, became a significant trend. The period saw decisive changes in the materials, styles, forms, and mediums of music and the birth of the first great universal geniuses.

During the baroque era Protestant church music was established on a par with that of the Catholic church. New forms appropriate to the Protestant services evolved. The production of secular music, encouraged by the nobility and upper classes, exceeded that of sacred music. Emphasis on secular music coupled with mechanical and technical improvements in instruments stimulated the writing and performance of instrumental music. For the first time the supremacy of vocal music was challenged by instrumental music. Concurrently an independent instrumental style began to emerge. In this period major and minor tonality supplanted the church modes as a basis of musical organization. It was, indeed, a time of change and innovation.

That the participants were aware of the revolutionary aspects of their musical activities is apparent from the title of a song collection by Giulio Caccini (1546–1618), *Nuove Musiche* (New Music), subsequently applied to the whole period and style. A revolt against the mannered polyphony of the previous age generated the impulse which led to the new music. Three basic innovations stemmed directly or indirectly from this revolt: *recitative*, *figured bass*, and *homophonic texture*.

Recitative was the direct outgrowth of the emphasis placed on the text of vocal music by baroque composers. To quote Claudio Monteverdi

(1567–1643), "The text should be the master of the music, not the servant." This was not possible in the 16th-century polyphonic style, because the imitative entrances and overlapping phrases made the words and syllables of the text occur at different times in the various parts. With each of four or more voices singing different syllables at the same time, comprehension of the text was impossible. The baroque solution to this problem was recitative, a sort of inflected declamation by a solo voice. This style of singing was used almost exclusively in the first operas and throughout the period in operas, oratorios, and cantatas whenever the text was of primary importance.

The recitative style was ideal for enunciating a text, but it was musically uninteresting. However, the declamatory vocal line had only to be made more lyric and continuous to produce the solo song and aria, developments which were not long in the making. Musical values were thus enhanced without reducing the text to the status of "servant." The first objective of the new music was accomplished.

This new style was conducive to a kind of musical shorthand. The accompaniment for the voice part involved no carefully prescribed lines, only a simple harmonic background played by instruments. This could be notated by writing just the bass line with numbers below it to indicate the other chord components. This type of notation is called *figured bass* or *thorough bass.* Except for the bass line, it does not indicate the specific notes to be played but does provide a basis for improvisation. The realization, that is the performance, of the figure bass part was done on a keyboard instrument, ordinarily with the bass line reinforced by one or more melody instruments. The complete realization, which customarily proceeded without interruption throughout a composition, was called *basso continuo* (continuous bass) or just *continuo.* It served both as foundation for the musical edifice and as mortar in the musical texture. Its importance can be deduced from the fact that performances were directed by the player at the harpsichord or organ, who often was the composer, while at the same time realizing the figured bass part. The practice of writing out the melody and the bass, leaving the inner parts to the discretion of the performer, had the effect of polarizing interest in the outer voices. Because the use of figured bass was general in both vocal and instrumental music, the entire period sometimes is known as the *thorough bass period.*

The vertical concept of chords built over bass tones implicit in the figured bass system is diametrically opposed to the horizontal-linear concept of polyphony. Music conceived as a single, predominant melody supported by vertically ordered harmony is homophonic. Homophonic texture is the third basic innovation of the baroque period. The homophonic style did not supersede the polyphonic style. The two flourished side by side. Elements and passages were intermixed. A recitative and aria in the new style might be followed immediately by a fugue in the old. Elaborate polyphonic texture, both instrumental and vocal, often was provided with a figured bass part. After the beginning of the baroque the relative emphasis between homophonic and polyphonic texture varied, but neither disappeared. By 1750 the homophonic style was gaining ascendency, but the baroque era closed with the death of Bach, the greatest contrapuntalist of all time.

Inventiveness in the matter of musical form was also a baroque characteristic. The 17th century probably contributed more than any comparable period to the introduction and crystallization of enduring modes of musical expression. Continuous variation, sectional variation, suite, sonata, rondo, concerto, opera, oratorio, overture, chorale, chorale prelude, and fugue all were either conceived or perfected during the baroque period. While it is true that modern examples of these forms are rather different from those of the baroque, the foundations of musical organization were well defined before the period ended. Present day forms not anticipated before 1750 are few in number.

Opera was the first great achievement of the baroque. Several of the most characteristic features of the period were incorporated in this one composite form. It was well suited to the exploitation of spectacular theatrical effects. Recitatives and arias were conspicuous elements. Figured bass was used consistently. Rather early the accompanying ensembles of opera were expanded to include large numbers of diverse instruments, paving the way for future development of orchestras. Instrumental *sinfonias* before and between operatic scenes and dramatic accompaniments utilized distinctive instrumental effects and contributed to the development of an independent instrumental style. The da capo aria, in which the opening section is repeated at the end, became a standard pattern. Operatic finales were often continuous variations over a ground bass (constantly repeated melodic pattern in the bass.) All in all, baroque opera represented a remarkable artistic achievement which strongly influenced subsequent music, nondramatic and instrumental as well as operatic.

CLAUDIO MONTEVERDI (1567–1643) was easily the most significant of the early opera composers. Before 1600 he was well established in the court of Mantua as a viol player, singer, and composer in the old style. At middle age he turned from aristocratic chamber music to the stage and a wholehearted endorsement of the then revolutionary style of the rising baroque. He composed several operas between his first, *Orfeo* (1607) and his last, *The Coronation of Poppea* (1642). From 1613 until his death he was director of music at St. Mark's Cathedral in Venice, writing much church music. His genius knew no bounds. He was equally adept at writing court, church, and dramatic music, but it was in the field of opera that the striking originality of his genius is most apparent. Though one of the great innovators of music, Monteverdi was astute enough to temper the revolutionary practices of the Florentine Camerata (see page 181) in writing opera with more conventional means. He adopted the new recitative style for the most part in *Orfeo*, but he breathed the breath of melody into his declamation and was not disdainful of polyphony when it served his purpose.

CLAUDIO MONTEVERDI: *Orfeo* (1607)
   (1567–1643)   Overture and Prologue   10:00

> *Orfeo* requires a large and varied orchestra with assorted wind, string, and keyboard instruments. The orchestra contributes to the drama in the accompaniments and supplies many instrumental interludes. The harmonic materials are unusually rich for the period and style. It is a tribute to Monteverdi's creative gifts that so mature an opera could be brought to fruition within a decade after the birth of the form. *Orfeo's* first performance under the auspices of the Duke of Mantua was received enthusiastically. Unlike the first opera which was lost and the other early operas which remained in manuscript, the score of *Orfeo* was published in 1609 and reissued in 1615, spreading the practices of the early baroque.

In music the baroque was born and nurtured in Italy but reached its ultimate maturity and fulfillment in the hands of two composers of German birth, Bach and Handel.

JOHANN SEBASTIAN BACH (1685–1750) was the most imposing member of a prodigious dynasty of musicians who established the name Bach as a synonym for musician. He was exposed to music at an early age, and his training while unsystematic was typical for the times. His first significant position was as court organist and chamber musician at Weimer (1708–1717) during which time he wrote extensively for organ. In 1717 he was appointed director of chamber music by Prince Leopold of Anhalt at Cöthen, a position he held until 1723. This period was especially rich in the production of chamber and orchestral music. From 1723 on he lived in Leipzig as organist and music director (cantor) of the St. Thomas Church and School and eventually also as director of music in the university. These duties did not require him to relinquish the title of chamber music director in the service of Leopold. He enjoyed further honorary appointments from the Duke of Weissenfels and the King of Poland, Elector of Saxony. His most significant church music was written during his tenure at Leipzig.

A cursory review of Bach's appointments and areas of activity gives little clue to the tremendous magnitude and scope of his overwhelming genius. Bach's complete works, which due to many losses are by no means complete, fill 47 massive volumes. Practically every form, medium, and style of his time with the exception of opera and ballet is represented with incomparable masterpieces. He was consummate master of contrapuntal technique and achieved an ideal balance between the horizontal and vertical aspects of musical texture. Coming as he did at the end of an epoch when music was on the verge of another metamorphosis, his music was not appreciated by his immediate successors or even by his own sons, distinguished musicians who continued the family tradition. Felix Mendelssohn (1809–1847) is credited with starting the Bach revival which each succeeding year heaps new tribute on his already lustrous reputation. In a recent poll[1] the members of the American Musicological Society ranked J. S. Bach as the most eminent composer of all time.

There is no single work which summarizes Bach's creative activity. His range was too broad and his approach too varied to be reduced to generalities and isolated monuments. This volume, as any concerned with the history or literature of music must be, is replete with references to Bach and his music. One final example must suffice for here and now, though volumes and courses devoted to a single phase of Bach's creative life leave much unsaid. The *Brandenburg Concerto No. 3* is one of six for various instrumental combinations commissioned by and dedicated to Christian Ludwig, Margraf of Brandenburg.

J. S. BACH: *Brandenburg Concerto No. 3 in G* (1721)
   (1685–1750)   1. Allegro moderato   7:00
                       2. Adagio   :10
                       3. Allegro   6:10

> This concerto, like the others in the group, is of the concerto grosso type but somewhat atypical. It has three parts each for violins, violas, and cellos plus string bass and continuo. There is no solo group as such, but the scoring contrasts the massive sound of the entire ensemble with the lighter sound of small sections. The first movement is a ritornello form. The Adagio consists of just two chords, which may have been intended as a point of departure for the harpsichord (continuo) player to improvise a slow movement. An elaborate binary form concludes the work, a magnificient example of baroque instrumental polyphony and prime example of Bach's incomparable contrapuntal technique.

GEORGE FRIDERIC HANDEL (1685–1759) was born in Halle, Saxony in close proximity to Bach in both time and place. If the two men had been regarded as competitors, Bach surely would emerge the victor, but their paths

---

[1] Conducted by Paul R. Farnsworth, Professor of Psychology at Stanford University.

JOHANN SEBASTIAN BACH   GEORGE FRIDERIC HANDEL

never crossed. Bach made a trip to Halle hoping to meet Handel, but Handel had already left for England. Artistically, too, these giants of the late baroque pursued divergent courses. Their temperaments ordained it. Bach was essentially a provincial burgher who never traveled far from his birthplace, a devoted family man who produced 20 children in two happy marriages, a man whose personal tranquillity was ruffled by bickering with local church, town, and school authorities. Handel, by contrast, was a true cosmopolitan who traveled widely and lived and worked in Germany, Italy, and England. He was a gregarious extrovert who fraternized with artists and persons of rank. His difficulties were with his patrons, the divas who sang his music, and with other composers who vied with him for royal favor. As would be expected, Bach's music is predominantly introspective and contemplative; Handel's is mostly dramatic and theatrical.

Overcoming strenuous parental objections, Handel obtained a broad and thorough musical training including studies in counterpoint, canon and fugue, and lessons on the harpsichord, organ, violin, and oboe. He became in turn a church organist and a violinist in an opera orchestra. While in the latter position he composed his first operas. Before he turned permanently to other forms, he wrote 46 operas in the Italian language and style in addition to four early ones in German. After 1712 Handel lived permanently in England which placed him in the curious position of being a German composer writing Italian operas for the English. His fortunes fluctuated drastically with the taste and favor of the times. The complete disenchantment of the English with the artificialities of Italian opera brought Handel to bankruptcy. Though a crushing blow at the time, it was a blessing in disguise. With the failure of his operatic ventures, Handel turned to the form which was to assure his immortality—oratorio.

As a young composer in Italy he had essayed the form. In the full maturity of his fifties he returned to it, and though the form was no longer new, his treatment of it was unprecedented. The epic proportions of his scores, the sheer mass of his performing groups, the vigor of his music, and the eloquence of his Biblical heroes combined to overwhelm audiences. The success of his oratorios surpassed by far that of his operas, reestablished his reputation, and recouped his financial position. The greater part of his creative career was devoted to operas, but the vagaries of time and taste have consigned them to the limbo of forgotten music. If he had written nothing but the English oratorios, his place in music history would be secure, but in addition he composed an enormous quantity of chamber music and a large number of concertos which exalt his position. His productivity surpasses even that of Bach. The collected edition of his works with index runs to one hundred ten large volumes.

Handel's masterpiece unquestionably is his oratorio *The Messiah* (see page 212). One operatic excerpt retains its popularity in many arrangements and adaptations: the aria *Ombra mai fu* from the opera *Serse* (1738), which is the famous *Largo* in instrumental transcriptions. Next to *The Messiah*, one of Handel's most familiar and most often performed works and certainly one of the most ingratiating is his *Water Music*.

G. F. HANDEL: *Water Music* (1717)

(1685–1759)	1. Allegro	2:25
	2. Air	4:25
	3. Bourrée	:45
	4. Horn pipe	:50
	5. Andante	2:40
	6. Allegro deciso	2:45

A fanciful tale persists about the origin of the *Water Music* to the effect that Handel composed it in an attempt to regain the good graces of the King. Handel was granted a limited leave by his employer, the Elector of Hanover, for the purpose of visiting England, so the story goes. Handel overstayed his leave (as a matter of fact stayed in England permanently) and was still in England when his former employer mounted the throne of England in 1714 as George I, placing Handel in an extremely embarrassing position. The truth seems to be that Handel composed some 20 odd pieces of "water music" over a period of years for various entertainments held on barges floating down the Thames. Several suites have been made from this music, the best known of which consists of the six movements listed arranged for modern orchestra by Sir Hamilton Harty.

The similarities and the differences between the styles of Bach and Handel are apparent when the *Brandenburg Concertos* and cantatas of the former are compared with the *Water Music* and oratorios of the latter. These were the styles of instrumental and vocal music at the end of the baroque period.

References

Manfred F. Bukofzer, *Music in the Baroque Era* (New York: W. W. Norton, 1947).

Denis Arnold, *Monteverdi* (New York: Farrar, Straus & Giroux, 1963).

Karl Geiringer, *The Bach Family: Seven Generations of Creative Genius* (New York: Oxford University Press, 1954).

Archibald T. Davison, *Bach and Handel: The Consummation of the Baroque in Music* (Cambridge: Harvard University Press, 1951).

Otto Erich Deutsch, *Handel: A Documentary Biography* (New York: W. W. Norton, 1954).

EDVARD GRIEG

ANTONIO VIVALDI

JOHANN STRAUSS

Chronology

1683		Rameau		1764		
	1719		L. Mozart		1787	
		1732		Haydn		1809
		1735		J. C. Bach	1782	
			1756	W. A. Mozart	1791	
			1770	Beethoven		1827
			1782	Paganini		1840
			1786	Weber	1826	
			1792	Rossini		1868
			1797	Schubert	1828	

CHAPTER **19**

the viennese classic period 1750-1825

Three great names dominate the music of the Viennese classic period: Haydn, Mozart, and Beethoven. Their art did not spring full-blown from the ashes of the waning baroque. Portents of the new style were stirring at least a quarter of a century earlier. Even then, in a transitory period generally designated as rococo, the majesty and pomposity of the baroque were being replaced on occasion by aristocratic elegance. Specifically in music the advent of rococo is signaled by the gallant style or, in French, *le style galant* of which Jean Philippe Rameau (1683–1764) was a leading exponent (see page 92). At about the same time a different reaction to austere polyphony was leading to musical expressions of moving simplicity and direct appeal to the common man. The best elements of these movements took root in another of the periodic returns to classic ideals.

Classicism is defined as conformity to classic principles of lucidity, simplicity, dignity, symmetry, restraint, refinement, and objectivity. In music these objectives were achieved by: (1) clarification of formal structures with emphasis on sectional homophonic forms, sonata form pre-eminent, (2) preference for compact, vocally inspired melodies possessing the quality of direct simplicity typical of folk songs, (3) elevation of homophonic texture to a position of dominance with extensive use of patterned harmonic motivation in broken-chord accompaniment figures, (4) employing imitative counterpoint essentially as a developmental device, abandoning contrapuntal forms, (5) giving harmonic clarity and simplicity precedence over complexity and ingenuity, and (6) consistently casting ideas in well-defined, regular phrases of four and eight measures.

Not all contributions of the Viennese classic period were directly inspired by classic ideals. Greater standardization of mediums also was accom-

CHAPTER **19**

the viennese classic period 1750-1825

Three great names dominate the music of the Viennese classic period: Haydn, Mozart, and Beethoven. Their art did not spring full-blown from the ashes of the waning baroque. Portents of the new style were stirring at least a quarter of a century earlier. Even then, in a transitory period generally designated as rococo, the majesty and pomposity of the baroque were being replaced on occasion by aristocratic elegance. Specifically in music the advent of rococo is signaled by the gallant style or, in French, *le style galant* of which Jean Philippe Rameau (1683–1764) was a leading exponent (see page 92). At about the same time a different reaction to austere polyphony was leading to musical expressions of moving simplicity and direct appeal to the common man. The best elements of these movements took root in another of the periodic returns to classic ideals.

Classicism is defined as conformity to classic principles of lucidity, simplicity, dignity, symmetry, restraint, refinement, and objectivity. In music these objectives were achieved by: (1) clarification of formal structures with emphasis on sectional homophonic forms, sonata form pre-eminent, (2) preference for compact, vocally inspired melodies possessing the quality of direct simplicity typical of folk songs, (3) elevation of homophonic texture to a position of dominance with extensive use of patterned harmonic motivation in broken-chord accompaniment figures, (4) employing imitative counterpoint essentially as a developmental device, abandoning contrapuntal forms, (5) giving harmonic clarity and simplicity precedence over complexity and ingenuity, and (6) consistently casting ideas in well-defined, regular phrases of four and eight measures.

Not all contributions of the Viennese classic period were directly inspired by classic ideals. Greater standardization of mediums also was accom-

237

plished during this time. The prior practice of scoring for available players in a particular court or church gave way to artistic conviction regarding suitable instrumental combinations. Toward the middle of the 18th century fairly uniform orchestras consisting of first and second violins, violas, cellos, basses, flutes, oboes, bassoons, trumpets, horns, and timpani began to take shape. By the end of the century orchestras with approximately these constituents provided composers with a perfected and widely available medium of musical expression. The art of orchestration became an essential adjunct of composition. Basso continuo was discarded, and all of the parts in a composition were written out completely. At the same time the string quartet of two violins, viola, and cello was established as the predominant chamber music medium.

Dynamic shading became an essential feature of musical expression during this time. The terraced dynamics of the baroque typified by the alternating loud and soft passages of the concerto grosso were augmented by gradual changes from soft to loud *(crescendo)* and loud to soft *(decrescendo)*, by sudden outbursts, and by moments of silence. These features first were cultivated by a series of composers attached to the court in Mannheim who wrote in the gallant style. In many ways—general style, choice and use of mediums, exploitation of dynamic effects, and employment of novel instrumental procedures—the Mannheimers were direct forerunners of the Viennese classic masters.

The names (FRANZ) JOSEPH HAYDN (1732–1809) and WOLFGANG AMADEUS MOZART (1756–1791) are frequently uttered in the same breath and with the same degree of reverence. The tragic brevity of Mozart's life is illuminated by the fact that Haydn, born 24 years earlier, survived him 18 years. Influence between them was strong and mutual. Young Mozart learned much from Haydn's music, and the older Haydn learned much from Mozart. Each acknowledged his indebtedness to the other, Mozart by dedicating six string quartets to Haydn. Their personal fortunes were very different. Haydn, starting in more humble circumstances, came along early enough to benefit from the vanishing custom of a court appointment. Mozart, though intermittently attached to a church or court, never enjoyed the security of a suitable permanent appointment. Neither did he profit much from publication or performances of his works, avenues of remuneration newly opened to composers.

Haydn's parents were amateur musicians in menial circumstances. There was music in the home, and at an early age his aptitude drew attention. From the age of 5 he had elementary instruction and soon was furthering his musical training while singing as a boy soprano in a church choir. When a teacher was negligent in his duty to provide instruction in theory and composition, Haydn purchased text books and pursued the study on his own

(FRANZ) JOSEPH HAYDN   WOLFGANG AMADEUS MOZART

initiative. He was dismissed from the choir when his voice changed. For the next ten years he eked out a meager subsistence playing accompaniments and giving music lessons, all the while working assiduously to perfect his own playing and composing. He was already in his late twenties when he obtained his first appointment. A short time later he joined the entourage of the Hungarian Esterhazy Princes. His status was essentially that of a servant, but the position provided security and not only the incentive but the necessity for composing. His initial success was not sensational, but he never ceased growing as a composer. Gradually his fame spread throughout Europe. By the time his last patron, Prince Nikolaus, died and his orchestra was dissolved in 1790, Haydn had a pension from the estate and an international reputation. That same year he accepted an urgent invitation from the impresario Johann Salomon to perform in London. He remained there until 1792 and returned in 1794–95, scoring spectacular successes both times. The age of the public concert featuring celebrities to attract paying audiences had arrived, but Mozart had not lived to see it. Haydn returned to Vienna where he lived in affluence the rest of his days. Recognized as the grand master of chamber and symphonic music, he turned after hearing the Handel festivals in England to the composition of choral music, producing six great masses and two oratorios. Though lesser known, the operas he composed while in the employ of the Esterhazys round out a career that embraced every sphere of musical activity and spanned an entire epoch. The *Surprise Symphony* is one of the 12 symphonies Haydn composed for the Salomon concerts in London.

JOSEPH HADYN: *Symphony No. 94 in G, "Surprise"* (1792)
(1732–1809)   1.   Adagio cantabile—Vivace assai   7:30
                       2.   Andante   5:40

3. Menuetto: Allegro molto   4:50
4. Allegro di molto   3:45

As was customary with Haydn, the otherwise brisk first movement
in sonata form begins with a slow introduction. The second movement, a set of variations, contains the "surprise"—a sudden loud
chord in a soft passage—about which Haydn is reputed to have
said, "That will make the ladies jump." Wit and good humor are
characteristics of his music. The menuetto is more rustic than
courtly. Few conductors play it as fast as Haydn's marking would
indicate. Literal interpretation of this tempo marking would result
in a pace and mood approaching that of a scherzo. The fourth
movement, in rondo form, displays the verve and sparkle expected
of a Haydn finale.

W. A. Mozart certainly ranks as the most precocious musical prodigy of
all time. His father, Leopold (1719–1787), was a violinist, author of a
method for violin, and a recognized composer. He started the musical training
of his son at the age of four in response to eager and intelligent interest. By
the time he was six, young Wolfgang had composed little minuets and had
appeared in his first public concert playing the harpsichord. When he was
seven he made the first of his many foreign journeys, this one to Paris. His
appearances now included giving exhibitions of improvisation in addition to
playing concertos on the harpsichord and the violin. His first published compositions, four sonatas for harpsichord with violin ad libitum, were issued
in Paris in 1764 when he was eight. That same year the Mozarts were
cordially received in England where Wolfgang's first symphonies were written
and repeatedly performed. He astounded the King with his ability to read at
sight the music of contemporary composers such as Johann Christian Bach
(1735–1782), son of J. S. Bach, who was then a leading musician in London.
Mozart visited the music capitals of Europe in rapid succession, met most of
the prominent musicians of the day, absorbed the latest styles and techniques
like a sponge, turned out an uninterrupted torrent of compositions, and all
the while dazzled audiences with his performing feats. During a brief respite
in Salzburg Mozart devoted himself to serious study and to the composition
of his first oratorio. In 1768 he was on the road again, visiting Vienna where
he wrote his first opera and conducted a performance of his *Solemn Mass*
before a large audience. After brief service to the Archbishop of Salzburg,
he took leave to visit Italy. The Italian tour was undertaken primarily for the
purpose of broadening his musical experience, but it turned out to be an
unbroken succession of triumphs. His concerts were jammed, his compositions praised, his genius applauded, and honors were bestowed on him. In
Rome Mozart wrote from memory the entire score of the nine-part *Miserere*

by Gregorio Allegri (1582–1652) after hearing it only twice. At the age of 15 his meteoric career was at its zenith.

The next year the Archbishop of Salzburg, his friendly protector, died. The Archbishop's successor was unsympathetic to the young composer and subjected him to totally unwarranted indignities. Mozart obtained a leave of absence to seek another appointment. His efforts were unsuccessful, and he returned to his unhappy position at Salzburg. The situation became unbearable, and in 1781 he resigned and settled permanently in Vienna. The wife whom he married shortly after arriving in Vienna was as improvident as he. The scanty returns from the unending stream of masterpieces that flowed from his pen and a pitifully inadequate stipend tardily granted by the emperor were squandered. Production of some of the greatest music in the entire literature, operas and symphonies which have been played untold thousands of times on programs all over the Western world from that day to this, never succeeded in raising their creator above the level of pecuniary anxiety. At thirty-five he was buried in a pauper's grave without an inkling of the untold fortunes that would be made and spent on his efforts. His genius knew no limits. He is the one composer whose operas, symphonies, chamber music, and solo works are of equal monumental significance. His concertos for violin and for piano served to crystalize the form. Typical examples of his work could be as easily selected from one category as another, but the *Symphony No. 40* epitomizes his mature style.

W. A. MOZART: *Symphony No. 40 in G minor, K.550* (1788)

(1756–1791)	1.	Allegro molto	7:15
	2.	Andante	7:50
	3.	Menuetto	4:20
	4.	Allegro assai	4:45

This is the second of three equally great symphonies composed between June 26 and August 10, 1788. That three such masterpieces could have been conceived within a period of six weeks seems almost incredible. Even more amazing is the fact that each has a distinct and separate personality. They stand as incontrovertible evidence of the depth and strength of Mozart's genius and mark a high point in the Viennese classic period.

LUDWIG VAN BEETHOVEN (1770–1827), towering giant of music and third in the triumvirate of Viennese classic composers, probably is regarded as *the* greatest composer of all time by the majority of people, both musicians and nonmusicians. This is partially because of the transcendental power of his musical achievement, the unquestioned authenticity of his genius, and partially because he exemplifies as no other composer before him or since the qualities commonly associated with the creative artist.

Beethoven, son and grandson of Flemish musicians of modest abilities who had settled in Bonn on the Rhine, began his musical training at an early age under the strict and stern tutelage of his father, who had pretensions of producing another wonderchild of the Mozartean cast. He displayed remarkable talent but nothing to rival the phenomenal abilities of Mozart. In his early teens he was assistant organist in the church, harpsichordist in the court orchestra, and violist in the theatre orchestra. He attended the public schools in Bonn and continued his studies with the local musicians. He met and elicited praise from Mozart during a short visit to Vienna in 1787. Haydn, on his way back to Vienna in 1792 after his first engagement in England, stopped over in Bonn and warmly praised a cantata by Beethoven. With this encouragement and a letter from the Elector, he left his provincial birthplace and moved to Vienna, capitol of the musical world. Beethoven studied with Haydn for a time, but, being dissatisfied with him as a teacher, switched to others. At this stage of development, Beethoven evidently was not a tractable student, and the teachers were not impressed with his scholarship. He was, however, welcomed in the palaces of music-loving aristocrats of Vienna and fraternized as an equal with the social elite of the city. His genius and nobility of character were appreciated and his uncouth appearance and occasional ill manners were tolerated if not forgiven.

Beyond his youth Beethoven never held any of the positions which till then had supported composers and had elicited from them routine quotas of music for immediate consumption. His income was from sales of his works and allowances granted him by the wealthy without exacting tribute. This left him free to compose what, when, and how he pleased and if need be to wait for inspiration, an option he often elected if one were to judge by comparing his output with that of Mozart and Haydn.

But there is more to it than that. His whole manner of working was different. Whereas with Mozart whole symphonies seem to have been conceived in a flash and dashed off at blinding speed, Beethoven started with germ motives in the rough which he inscribed in a series of sketch books. Motives and themes often were transformed, polished, perfected and left to season before they found their way into finished works. His monuments were hewn from granite, not molded in clay. Each work is a distinct and separate entity which by compelling inner logic forges its own peculiar shape. Beethoven for the most part takes cognizance of conventional forms but strives for a higher degree of integration than his predecessors. Beethoven's form is progressive. There is little literal repetition beyond that accomplished by signs in the traditional places. Otherwise each return of a theme is projected against a different background or exposed to new and more penetrating illumination. Transitions are not perfunctory passages which merely accomplish a change of key or mood. They are occasions for additional development of thematic ideas, opportunities for unexpected modulations and harmonic experimentation. Creative imagination is ever at work in Beethoven's music. Nothing is superfluous. The musical drama unfolds in every measure. He wrote few potboilers. One has the feeling that every time he took his pen in hand it was in a deliberate attempt to create a masterpiece. With a goal so high, his percentage of successes is astounding.

All of his nine numbered symphonies remain in the repertory as do his two independent overtures and various overtures for his one opera. Opera was admittedly not his forte, but his single attempt in the form still is given in spite of an absurd libretto. All of his piano music has been recorded and much of it, which includes five concertos and thirty-two sonatas, is programmed regularly. All violinists and cellists play his sonatas for these instruments. His one violin concerto is an enduring favorite. His sixteen string quartets are paragons of the form. Considering the quality, it is a respectable list. It is strongly slanted, as was his talent, toward instrumental music. In this realm he has never been equalled. His nine symphonies have been a decisive force in shaping all subsequent development of the form. No composer since Beethoven has been able or would want to escape his pervading influence. After Beethoven had composed all of his symphonies except the last, the *Eroica* was still his favorite.

L. VAN BEETHOVEN: *Symphony No. 3 in E-flat, Op. 55 "Eroica"* (1804)
(1770–1827)   1. Allegro con brio   15:15
     2. Marcia funebre: Adagio assai   15:45
     3. Scherzo: Allegro vivace   5:55
     4. Finale: Allegro molto   11:45

In more ways than the inscription on the score, this is an "heroic" symphony. It is heroic in proportions, content, and realization. Paul Henry Lang ranks it as ". . . one of the incomprehensible deeds in arts and letters, the greatest single step made by an individual composer in the history of the symphony and in the history of music in general." One has only to compare it with Mozart's *Symphony No. 40* or Haydn's *Symphony No. 94* previously cited to grasp the magnitude of Beethoven's accomplishment and to perceive the transformation of the form within a span of 16 years. This symphony is intensely dramatic, personal, powerful, monumental; terms that would scarcely be applied in the same context to any prior symphony. The music bursts the classic restraints and overflows the traditional forms. Portents of rising romanticism are evident everywhere, even in the somewhat programmatic inspiration for the work. The symphony originally was dedicated to Napoleon Bonaparte, but Beethoven tore up the title page when Napoleon proclaimed himself Emperor, betraying the ideals of equality and liberty that Beethoven held so dear. It was now a tribute "to the memory of a great man," not an individual but an immortal hero. Napoleon was not forgotten, however. When he died 17 years later, Beethoven is supposed to have said, with reference to the second movement *Funeral March*, "I have already composed the proper music for the occasion."

Beethoven was, in a very real sense, the end of the Viennese classic period and also the beginning of the romantic age.

References

Reinhard G. Pauly, *Music in the Classic Period* (Englewood Cliffs: Prentice-Hall, 1965).

Karl Geiringer, *Haydn, A Creative Life in Music* (Berkeley and Los Angeles: University of California Press, 1967).

Otto Erich Deutsch, *Mozart* (Palo Alto: Stanford University Press, 1965).

Alexander W. Thayer, *The Life of Beethoven*, edited by Elliot Forbes (Princeton: Princeton University Press, 1964).

LUDWIG VAN BEETHOVEN

Chronology

1797	Schubert	1828
1803	Berlioz	1869
1809	Mendelssohn	1847
1810	Chopin	1849
1810	Schumann	1856
1811	Liszt	1886
1813	Wagner	1883
1813	Verdi	1901
1815	Franz	1892
1822	Franck	1890
1823	Lalo	1892
1824	Bruckner	1896
1825	J. Strauss	1899
1833	Brahms	1897
1835	Saint-Saens	1921
1836	Delibes	1891
1838	Bizet	1875
1838	Bruch	1920
1840	Tchaikovsky	1893
1841	Dvorak	1904
1843	Grieg	1907
1844	Rimsky-Korsakov	1908
1845	Fauré	1924
1854	Sousa	1932
1858	Leoncavallo	1919
1858	Puccini	1924
1859	Herbert	1924
1860	Wolf	1903
1860	Mahler	1911
1863	Mascagni	1945
1864	R. Strauss	1949
1865	Dukas	1935
1865	Glazounov	1936
1865	Sibelius	1957
1873	Rachmaninoff	1943

CHAPTER 20

the romantic age
1825-1900

The romantic movement in the arts is concerned with the assertion of imagination and sentiment as opposed to logic, emphasis on the personal as opposed to the universal, stress of the subjective as opposed to the objective, and preeminence of spontaneous freedom over deliberate formality. The romantic movement in music trailed a similar movement in literature but eventually surpassed it in opulence. Music is an ideal medium for romantic utterances, and it has been referred to as *the* romantic art. In spirit, romanticism is the opposite of classicism. The pendulum swings back and forth between the two, with first one and then the other in ascendency. Music, however, is never completely lacking in either. It is simply a question of emphasis.

Romantic composers continued to use the forms and mediums perfected in the classic era, but in a freer and more personal manner. To these they made contributions of their own. The tone or symphonic poem, the character piece, and the art song are innovations of the romantic period molded to conform to its precepts. Music drama is a romantic version of opera.

There are no clear-cut dividing lines between periods in music. The transition from classic to romantic is no exception. Romantic elements are detected readily in works of Beethoven. Carl Maria von Weber (1786–1826) who died a year before him and Franz Schubert (1797–1828) who died a year after, generally are considered to be the first champions of the new movement. Full realization of the romantic impulse probably was delayed by their untimely deaths. Even so, their contributions to the romantic movement were substantial.

WEBER anticipated many romantic developments. He was among the first to write a large programmatic work *(Konzertstuck in F minor, Op. 79)*, a concert waltz *(Invitation to the Dance, Op. 65)*, patriotic songs, and occa-

C. M. von Weber

Franz Schubert

Hector Berloiz

sional pieces for the piano. He broke with the classic Italian opera traditions exemplified by Rossini (1792–1868) and founded German romantic opera, strongly influencing the ensuing music dramas of Wagner (1813–1883). *Oberon*, Weber's last opera, is replete with romantic elements, many of which are evident in the overture.

C. M. von Weber: *Oberon* (1826)
   (1786–1826)   Overture   9:30

> On the basis of previous triumphs, Weber was commissioned to provide music for an opera to be premiered at Covent Garden in London. *Oberon*, a fairy opera in 21 spectacular scenes, was the result. Weber supervised the rehearsals and conducted the first 12 performances before his death. The opera played 19 more times that season and then slipped into virtual oblivion except for the overture and an aria or two.

Schubert's symphonies and chamber music are perhaps no more romantic than Beethoven's, but his art songs (cited elsewhere) and his character pieces for piano are truly romantic expressions. It was a time of extremes—of gigantic works and miniatures. The "Great" *Symphony No. 9 in C* by Schubert is one of the former, and his little *Moments Musicaux* are examples of the latter.

Franz Schubert: *Moments Musicaux, Op. 94* (1827)
   (1797–1828)   No. 3 in F minor   2:00

> *Musical Moment* was one of the designations Schubert used for short piano pieces of a lyrical or improvisatory nature. The third is the most familiar of the six comprising the group.

The decade between 1803 and 1813 saw the birth of the first generation of full-fledged romantic composers: Hector Berlioz, Felix Mendelssohn, Robert Schumann, Frederic Chopin, Franz Liszt, Richard Wagner, and Giuseppi Verdi.

Hector Berlioz (1803–1869) had a stormy career befitting his romantic nature. He defied convention and tradition. He was ever an experimenter and innovator, so much so that most of his works were slow to win favor. His personal life was as hectic as his artistic life. He fell madly in love with an English actress and in the romantic tradition was equally unhappy at first when she rejected him and later when she finally accepted him and they were married. Though Berlioz played only the guitar and the flageolet (a flute-type instrument but never a standard orchestral instrument), he was a master of orchestration. His treatise on instrumentation is the earliest orchestration text still in print. His considerable literary talent was put to use in his position as music critic for a Paris newspaper. When he toured Germany and Italy, he reported his activities in two volumes of *Musical Travels*, and he penned the texts for his dramatic works. If he was a less complete musician than the masters of the previous periods, his interests ranged further afield. Two of his most famous works have already been discussed, the *Symphony Fantastique* (page 177) and the *Requiem* (page 69). To these should be added the *Roman Carnival Overture*.

HECTOR BERLIOZ: *Le Carnaval Romain, Op. 9* (1838)   8:40
(1803–1869)

> This music originally was the prelude to the second act of the opera *Benvenuto Cellini*. Berlioz adapted it for independent concert performance several years after the first performance of the opera. The concert version is usually classified as an overture.

FELIX MENDELSSOHN (1809–1847) was born into a wealthy and influential family. The proverbial picture of a struggling artist does not apply in his case. He was afforded every advantage and grew up in a stimulating intellectual environment. His remarkable talents were evident at an early age. His compositions never surpassed the quality of his *Midsummer Night's Dream Overture* which he wrote at the age of seventeen. He was a brilliant pianist, organist, and conductor. He toured extensively and occupied several important posts. One of Mendelssohn's greatest contributions to music was initiating and fostering the Bach revival which has been gaining momentum ever since. It was he who instigated the first performance of Bach's *St. Matthew Passion* subsequent to the composer's death, and it is a tribute to his perception to have recognized the value of this neglected masterpiece. His compositions include oratorios on the order of Handel, concertos for violin and for piano, symphonies, and a quantity of piano and chamber music. His *Songs Without Words* are not his greatest works, but they are among his best known. Unlike some of his compositions, which are rather akin to those of the baroque and classic composers, these character pieces clearly reflect the romantic spirit of his times.

FELIX MENDELSSOHN: *Songs Without Words, Op. 67* (1844)
(1809–1847)   4. Spinning Song   1:55

> Mendelssohn created a new genre of piano composition with these slight, lyric piano pieces. He wrote eight volumes of them between

FELIX MENDELSSOHN   ROBERT SCHUMANN

1830 and 1845 of which Opus 67 is the sixth. These sketches are drawn with a sure hand and with infinite charm, grace, and sensitivity.

ROBERT SCHUMANN (1810–1856) is another romanticist whose talents were both literary and musical. His career as a pianist ended abruptly when a device he was using to develop finger independence permanently injured his hand. Thenceforth he concentrated on composition and literary activities. He was a founder of the music periodical *Neue Zeitschrift für Musik* and was its editor from 1835 to 1844. The publication ardently championed liberal and progressive tendencies. Chopin and Brahms, among many others, benefited from Schumann's perceptive and knowledgeable essays and criticisms. His writings were potent, beneficial forces in music and laudable examples of music journalism. The first 23 published compositions of Schumann are for piano. Only later did he turn to songs, chamber music, and works for orchestra. Though all four of his symphonies and several of his large works remain in the repertory, he seems to have been most at home writing in the smaller forms and for piano and voice.

Because of his literary inclination, it was only natural that Schumann should be attracted to the great lyric poets and the art song. An awareness of his personal plight provides added insight to the romantic outpouring of his songs. Schumann and Clara Wieck carried on a tempestuous courtship for several years against the strenuous objections of her father. Their love prevailed against every insidious strategy, but their marriage was delayed. The consummation of their romance opened the floodgates of his inspiration. He turned from the composition of piano music to songs and wrote about 140 within the year to inaugurate his most productive period. The 16 songs of the *Dichterliebe* cycle are included in that total.

FREDERIC CHOPIN   FRANZ LISZT

ROBERT SCHUMANN: *Dichterliebe* (Poet's Love), *Op. 48* (1840)
(1810–1856)   7. Ich grolle nicht (I'll not complain)   1:50
This is the most familiar song of the cycle, but *Im wunderschönen
Monat Mai* (No. 1) follows as a close second.

FREDERIC CHOPIN (1810–1849) was the most highly specialized of
the first-rank composers. He wrote almost exclusively in small forms for
piano, but in this limited area he is supreme. His relationship to the piano
character piece is similar to that of Handel to the oratorio, Mozart to the
concerto, Beethoven to the symphony, and Schubert to the art song. Each
made a definitive contribution to the particular medium. Chopin's brief character pieces exploit a mode of expression and an instrument which came into
vogue with the romantics. Both Mozart and Beethoven played and wrote for
the piano, but for the most part in a manner also suited to the harpsichord. A
truly distinctive style of writing for the piano utilizing its full capabilities was
born with Chopin.

Chopin's fame as a composer rests on a variety of small piano pieces
of types designated with fanciful titles: ballades, etudes, mazurkas, polonaises,
waltzes, preludes, and nocturnes. The ballades, of which there are four, bor-
row their name and to an extent their spirit from the poetic form. Chopin
published two books of twelve *Etudes* (studies) each, plus a collection of
three. They are studies in the sense that they include all the pianistic difficulties and harmonic effects of a revolutionary piano style, but they never
degenerate into mere pedantic exercises. On the contrary, they include some
of Chopin's most inspired passages. Chopin left his native Poland permanently at the age of twenty, but his Slavic origin and his romantic patriotism
inspired a quantity of music. His fifty-six *Mazurkas* and twelve *Polonaises*

use Polish dance rhythms. He used waltz rhythm for fourteen famous pieces. Perhaps his most popular creations are included in the cameo-like *24 Preludes*. The very name *nocturne* (night piece) is fraught with romantic suggestions, and Chopin's poetic musical language gave eloquent voice to these suggestions in nineteen pieces with that title. The *Nocturne Op. 9 No. 2* is a celebrated gem from this collection.

FREDERIC CHOPIN: *Nocturnes, Op. 9* (1831)
   (1810–1849)   No. 2 in E-flat   4:20

     FRANZ LISZT (1811-1886) was without a doubt one of the most influential figures of his time. His career was as long and varied as it was spectacular. It began in his native Hungary when he was only nine with a public performance of a difficult piano concerto and extended to his death 66 years later in Bayreuth. His triumphs as a pianist were rivaled by his achievements as a composer, conductor, and teacher. His tours as the greatest piano virtuoso of the 19th century took him to the music capitols of Europe where he circulated in the highest circles with the famous, rich, and titled. Aspiring young musicians flocked to him, and deserving ones could count on him for instruction and assistance. During his 11 year tenure as court conductor at Weimar. it became a center for the new romantic music to which Liszt contributed prolifically as a composer. Only a few of his numerous works are still programmed, and his popular reputation is secured by the relatively trivial *Liebestraum*. He deserves a better fate, for he has a long list of worthy compositions to his credit. His piano music is brilliant, though sometimes bombastic. His 19 *Hungarian Rhapsodies* for piano, some of which he transcribed for orchestra, popularized rhapsody as a designation for musical works (see page 170). The 12 symphonic (tone) poems inaugurated a new form (see page 176). In these extended works for orchestra the form and content, liberated from classic restraints, are dictated in large measure by the literary programs which inspired them. The third and best known of the symphonic poems, *Les Preludes,* is Liszt's musical interpretation of philosophical concepts expressed in one of Lamartine's *New Poetic Meditations*.

FRANZ LISZT: *Les Preludes, Symphonic Poem No. 3* (1854)   16:00
   (1811–1886)
     The following quotation from Lamartine is printed in the score:
        What is our life but a series of preludes to that unknown song,
        the first solemn note of which is sounded by death? Love
        forms the enchanted daybreak of every life; but what is the
        destiny where the first delights of happiness are not interrupted
        by some storm, whose fatal breath dissipates its fair illusions,

whose fell lightning consumes its altar? And what wounded spirit, when one of its tempests is over, does not seek to rest its memories in the sweet calm of country life? Yet man does not resign himself long to enjoy the beneficent tepidity which first charmed him on nature's bosom; when the trumpet's loud clangor has called him to arms, he rushes to the post of danger, whatever may be the war that calls him to the ranks, to find in battle the full consciousness of himself and the complete possession of his strength.

Richard Wagner and Giuseppi Verdi complete the list of first generation romantic composers. Their contributions were primarily in the field of opera where their contributions are more properly discussed (see Chapter 14). Following Wagner and Verdi, Georges Bizet (1838–1875) and Giacomo Puccini (1858–1924) are the big names in romantic opera.

CESAR FRANCK (1822–1890) was temperamentally more of an ascetic and mystic than a romantic, but he adopted and expanded the musical materials and procedures of his immediate predecessors. In spite of early promise as a concert artist on the piano and organ, he elected to follow an unspectacular career as a church organist, teacher, and composer. He lived and died in comparative obscurity, yet he exerted a powerful influence on French music. Young composers at the Paris conservatory who objected to the dominance of opera in French music turned to Franck, who was professor of organ, for their training rather than to the regular composition classes. Many of the big names in French instrumental music received guidance from Franck, and they in turn perpetuated his ideas. Of his compositions only a small number, mostly written when he was in his sixties, are well known. His cyclic *Symphony in D minor* is one of the most played symphonies in the entire literature. His lone sonata for violin, also cyclic in form, occupies a similar position in that literature. The exquisite *Symphonic Variations* for solo piano and orchestra amply demonstrate his extraordinary mastery of musical organization and the eloquence of his highly personal harmonic idiom.

CESAR FRANCK: *Symphonic Variations* (1885)   13:50
(1822–1890)

This unique work contains brilliant and gratifying music for both the solo piano and the orchestra. The solo and accompaniment are beautifully balanced and integrated. It is one of the earliest and most successful concerto-like pieces in variation form. The treatment of variation form, however, is by no means traditional. It is played without pauses, and it lacks a well-defined theme. Instead it has three distinctive ideas which are amalgamated, fused, transformed, and developed in the continuous unfolding of the variations.

JOHANNES BRAHMS (1833–1897) is sometimes referred to as the classic romanticist. His temperament was romantic to the roots, but he opposed in principle and practice the unbridled fervor and the uncritical sentimentality of the ultraromantics. His romanticism was always restrained and disciplined. His musical utterances, no matter how impassioned, are confined to classic patterns. Brahms was the antipode of the extravagant Liszt-Wagner type of romanticism, and as such was championed by and champion of a rabid anti-Wagner clique. Brahms, to his credit, took no part in this and openly admired works of Wagner, particularly the opera *Die Meistersinger*. It was quite against his will that he found himself in the center of the Wagner controversy, and he was neither deterred by his adversaries nor deflected by his advocates. More than most composers, Brahms was free to compose according to his own dictates. He toured as a pianist and accompanist and did some conducting, but most of his life was devoted to composition without sponsorship and consequently without restriction. He eschewed program and dramatic music but wrote magnificently in all the absolute forms for voices, piano, various chamber groups, and orchestra. The quality of his music is of such uniform excellence that it is virtually impossible to choose between works except on the basis of personal preference. He wrote quantities of vocal music, both solo and ensemble, and a *German Requiem* in seven large sections using passages from the German Bible for the text. He is one of the few composers of the romantic period seriously and consistently concerned with chamber music. He wrote numerous sets of variations continuing and elaborating on the traditions of Haydn, Mozart, and Beethoven. His works involving orchestra, generally conceded to be his best, include two overtures, two piano concertos, a violin concerto, a double concerto for violin and cello, and four symphonies. In the realm of the symphony, Brahms inherited the mantle of Beethoven.

JOHANNES BRAHMS: *Symphony No. 4 in E minor, Op. 98* (1885)
(1833–1897)
1. Allegro non troppo   10:45
2. Andante moderato   10:15
3. Allegro giocoso   6:00
4. Allegro energico e passionato   9:00

The epic grandeur of Brahms' symphonies requires no explanation for those who have assimilated the symphonies of Beethoven. They continue the same traditions but clothe them in the raiment of the 19th century. It seems inconceivable now that this profoundly emotional music ever could have been considered austere as it was by early auditors. Adjectives like sombre, meditative, elegiac, now seem more appropriate for the first two movements. Their songfulness,

JOHANNES BRAHMS

tinged with a dark, melancholy romanticism, is anything but austere.
The third movement finds the staid Brahms in an unusually boister-
ous mood. It contains a remarkable example of invertible counterpoint. As the movement progresses, what was the melody in the
opening becomes the bass, and the previous bass line becomes the
melody. The finale is a set of 31 variations on the theme announced
in the first eight measures.

If any composer of symphonic music requires no introduction to the
general listener, it is PETER ILICH TCHAIKOVSKY (1840–1893). It is inconceivable that anyone has not heard some of his music, if not in the original at
least in a popular version. Biographers have bared intimate details of his
personal life. Tchaikovsky began the study of music very early, but none of his
teachers detected signs of genius in their charge. He was trained in law and
for a time worked as a clerk in the Ministry of Justice in St. Petersburg,
meanwhile continuing his musical studies. He resigned his post to devote
himself to music. He taught private lessons to augment his meager financial
resources until he was appointed professor of harmony in the Moscow Conservatory. He traveled throughout Europe while still on the staff at the
conservatory but nevertheless found the position irksome. A curious arrangement with a wealthy widow, Nadejada von Meck, eventually enabled him to
resign it. She settled on him a generous annuity, but by mutual consent they
never met (except once by accident). Their communication was by cor-
respondence exclusively. The Czar granted Tchaikovsky a pension which,
added to his annuity, left him free to travel and compose. He spent much time
abroad and in 1891 came to America where he conducted concerts in New
York, Philadelphia, and Baltimore.

Tchaikovsky is the most cosmopolitan of the 19th-century Russian composers and, with the possible exception of Rimsky-Korsakov, the most polished technically. The emotion of Tchaikovsky's music is more intense than profound. Consequently its appeal is more immediate than enduring. It must be that two new listeners arise to take the place of every one satiated with his music, for its popularity shows no signs of diminishing. Tchaikovsky's music was not sufficiently "Russian" for him to be grouped with the nationalistic composers of his time, but it abounds in Russian characteristics—folk songs and folk-like melodies, traditional rhythms, violent and sudden contrasts of mood. He composed for all mediums, but orchestra was his forte. He was a brilliant orchestrator and fecund melodist. These virtues overbalance a rather mechanical application of structural formulas. He wrote operas, ballets, tone poems, concertos, and six symphonies of which the last three are performed profusely. Like most of the late romantic composers, he was inclined toward the classic forms. The overture-fantasy *Romeo and Juliet* is an interesting blend of classic form and romantic content.

P. I. TCHAIKOVSKY: *Romeo and Juliet* (1870)   19:45
(1840–1893)

> This overture-fantasy has a regular sonata form with introduction, exposition, development, recapitulation, and coda. The themes and sections of the sonata form can be related to the characters and situations of the Shakespeare drama from which the work takes its name. The chorale-like introduction is descriptive of Friar Lawrence. The fiery principal theme portrays the feud between the houses of Montague and Capulet, and the subordinate theme is tender love music.
>
> *Romeo and Juliet* is the earliest work of Tchaikovsky to find a permanent place in the orchestral literature. He revised it twice, and the final version is heard invariably.

Several composers who were born in the 19th century but lived well into the 20th century continued to write in an essentially romantic style to the end of their creative lives. Two of these were RICHARD STRAUSS (1864–1949) and SERGEI RACHMANINOFF (1873–1943). Rachmaninoff was perhaps better known during his lifetime as a concert pianist than as a composer. He composed for orchestra and for voices, but the works which secure his position in the ranks of composers are the ones involving piano (see page 52). Strauss, born into a musical family, scored spectacular successes with a series of tone poems written while he was still in his twenties. Then he turned his talent for dramatic music to opera, for which it was equally adept. His later

PETER ILICH TCHAIKOVSKY   RICHARD STRAUSS

years (after 1910) were less productive, and he never again matched his
early triumphs. *Till Eulenspiegel* was composed while his creative powers
were at their peak.

RICHARD STRAUSS: *Till Eulenspiegel, Op. 28* (1895)   13:45
   (1864–1949)

> The complete title of this tone poem is *Till Eulenspiegel's Merry
> Pranks*, to which Strauss added the annotation, "After the old-
> fashioned roguish manner—in rondo form." Till is a puckish char-
> acter in German folklore. The composer did not provide a detailed
> account of the adventures portrayed in the music, but others have.
> Wilhelm Mauke describes it this way:
>
> > Once upon a time there was a prankish rogue, ever up to new
> > tricks, named Till Eulenspiegel. Now he jumps on his horse
> > and gallops into the midst of a crowd of market women,
> > overturning their wares with a prodigious clatter. Now he
> > lights out with seven-league boots; now conceals himself in a
> > mousehole. Disguised as a priest, he 'drips with unction and
> > morals,' yet out of his toe peeps the scamp. As a cavalier he
> > makes love, at first in jest, but soon in earnest, and is rebuffed.
> > He is furious, and swears vengeance on all mankind, but,
> > meeting some 'philistines' he forgets his wrath and mocks
> > them. At length his hoaxes fail. He is tried in a Court of Jus-
> > tice and is condemned to hang for his misdeeds; but he still
> > whistles defiantly as he ascends the ladder. Even on the scaf-
> > fold he jests. Now he swings; now he gasps for air; a last con-
> > vulsion. Till is dead.
>
> The "once upon a time" music with which the piece begins, serves
> as a coda and brings it to a close. The rondo form is far from
> typical.

In the works of Anton Bruckner (1824–1896) and Gustav Mahler (1860–1911) romanticism was already a little overripe. Reverting to classic forms was not enough to stem the tide against it. Widespread nationalism was to revitalize romanticism for a while, but the movement which began so lustily ran its course and expended its energy like the classic period before it in the span of a lifetime.

The composers of the period could point to solid achievements. Romantic music accounts for a large part of the current repertory, its popularity unchallenged. Its composers invented new forms, modified old ones, enlarged the orchestra, enriched the harmonic resources, and expanded the emotional range of music. Audiences increased in size. Composers were freed from bondage and obtained if not a more secure at least a more honored position in society. The romantic period was, in its own way, another golden age of music.

References

Alfred Einstein, *Music in the Romantic Era* (New York: W. W. Norton, 1947).

Jacques Barzun, *Berlioz and the Romantic Century* (Boston: Little, Brown, 1950).

Chronology

1804	Glinka	1857		
1811	Liszt	1886		
1824	Smetana	1884		
1833	Borodin	1887		
1835	Cui	1918		
1837	Balakirev	1910		
1839	Mussorgsky	1881		
1840	Tchaikovsky	1893		
1841	Chabrier	1894		
1841	Dvorak	1904		
1843	Grieg	1907		
1844	Rimsky-Korsakov	1908		
1844	Sarasate	1908		
1860	Albeniz	1909		
1861	MacDowell	1908		
1862	Debussy	1918		
1862	Delius	1934		
1865	Sibelius	1957		
1867	Granados	1916		
1875	Ravel	1937		
1876	Falla	1946		
1880	Bloch	1959		
1881	Bartok	1945		
1881	Enesco	1955		
1882	Kodaly	1967		
1884	Griffes	1920		
1887	Villa-Lobos	1959		
1896	Weinberger	1967		
1898	Harris			
1899	Chavez			
1900	Copland			

nationalism and impressionism

Nationalism and impressionism are musical styles which bridge the 19th and 20th centuries. Both began in the 19th century and lasted into the 20th. Nationalism is one aspect of romanticism, but a rather distinct aspect. Impressionism represents a break with romantic notions and foreshadows the more radical changes in music that were to follow.

Nationalism

Rebounding from Napoleon's grandiose schemes of subjugation and domination, a wave of nationalism swept over the various ethnic groups of Europe. Small groups struggling for identification and independence and large ones responding to the surge of expansion were equally enveloped. Nationalism is a sort of group romanticism. Composers were quick to seize the banner of the new movement, active in extolling the virtues of their particular patriotism. A certain amount of geographic and political influence in the arts is almost inevitable, but the conscious cultivation of nationalistic elements was a feature of the romantic and postromantic periods.

Nationalism in music took manifold forms. It was expressed by deliberately incorporating in the musical fabric melodic and rhythmic peculiarities of a particular region. These features usually are established by and derived from the folk songs and dances of the people. The borrowing sometimes was direct, with complete folk melodies appearing intact in composed works. The process had the effect of bringing art music closer to the common man, another facet of the romantic movement.

National heroes, folk characters, legends, epics, and myths—all were grist in the mill of patriotism. They were glorified in songs and symphonic poems. Operas were based on them. Some composers achieved enviable reputations solely on the basis of works with nationalistic pretentions. Even those not identified with the movement were not immune to its influences.

Nationalism fared better in music than in the other arts. Expressions which in prose or poetry would be blatant propaganda were interestingly exotic in music. Music dedicated to opposing ideologies was not explicit enough to be offensive. The fervent emotions of a piece like Sibelius' *Finlandia*, which might be banned in a subjugated country for inciting the people to revolt, could be appreciated by persons not partisans in the conflict. Strongly nationalistic music, far more than literature and painting, transcends geographic, political, and ethnic borders. The widespread acceptance of pieces written with avowed patriotic intent attests to this. So does the adoption of foreign dialects for specific works as in the Spanish and Italian caprices of the Russian composers Rimsky-Korsakov and Tchaikovsky respectively.

A significant effect of nationalism in music was to neutralize the worldwide domination of music by German musicians and to hasten the demise of Germanic romanticism. In this way nationalism paved the way for impressionism and the modern era, both of which contain residual traces of nationalism.

The list of composers associated with the nationalistic movement contains many familiar names. It will be observed that most of them are from smaller countries and racial groups or from countries previously lacking a thriving indigenous musical tradition, not from Germany, Italy, France, or England.

One of the first countries to turn consciously to nationalism was Russia. Michael Glinka's opera *A Life for the Czar* (1836) was an early example. Around 1875 a group of Russian composers, subsequently known as *The Five*, banded together in a united effort to build a national musical tradition. Alexander Borodin (1833–1887), Cesar Cui (1835–1918), Modest Mussorgsky (1839–1881), Mily Balakirev (1837–1910), and Nikolai Rimsky-Korsakov (1844–1908) were members of the group. Borodin is best known for his opera *Prince Igor* which contains the famous *Polovtsian Dances* and is the source of the Broadway musical show *Kismet*. Cui and Balakirev are rarely played now. Mussorgsky's masterpiece is the opera *Boris Godounov*, but his *Pictures at an Exhibition* (page 175), his symphonic poem *Night on Bald Mountain*, and some of his songs are more familiar. Rimsky-Korsakov was the least nationalistic, the most highly trained, and the most successful of the group, with a number of concert favorites to his credit including the colorful *Capriccio Espagnol* (page 103). Tchaikovsky was excluded from the group, because his music was not sufficiently "Russian," though it was permeated with Russian qualities.

Bedrich Smetana (1824–1884), the great Czech nationalist, is remembered for his comic opera *The Bartered Bride* and for his manifestly nationalistic cycle of six symphonic poems *My Fatherland* (*Ma Vlast*) of which *The Moldau* depicting the route of that river through Bohemia is most famous. Antonin Dvorak (1841–1904) is also a Czech nationalist, but two of his most popular works, the *New World Symphony* (page 159) and the *American Quartet*, are impregnated with American influences occasioned by his three-year stay in this country.

Hungarian elements lend an authentic ring to the Hungarian Rhapsodies of Franz Liszt (1811–1886) and more recently to the works of Bela Bartok (1881–1945) and Zoltan Kodaly (1882–1967).

Spanish dance rhythms are particularly infectious, and they figure prominently in the music of Spanish composers Isaac Albeniz (1860–1909), Enrique Granados (1867–1916), and Manuel de Falla (1876–1946). Iberian rhythms have also attracted non-Spanish composers Emmanuel Chabrier (1841–1894), Rimsky-Korsakov, Debussy, and Ravel. Composers Heitor Villa-Lobos (1887–1959) of Brazil and Carlos Chavez (1899–   ) of Mexico are exponents of Latin-American nationalism.

The stirrings of nationalism reached into the Scandinavian countries, and several composers of local importance imparted the flavor of the northland to their music. Edvard Grieg (1843–1907) is the name invariably associated with Scandinavian nationalism. The music of another northerner, Jean Sibelius (1865–1957), *is* the music of Finland as far as the outside world is concerned. Supposedly he did not use actual folk material, but his music is saturated with the moods and sounds regarded as typical of Finland, though it is he alone who made them so.

Confusion exists as to just what America's indigenous music is and just what constitutes "Americanism" in music. As soon as our musical traditions were sufficiently mature to resent the yoke of European influence, composers' interest in native resources roused. Negro music, Indian music, folk music (especially Western), and jazz were explored. Elements of all four have found their way into worthy compositions, but none has seemed to be ideally suited to a continuing tradition. Obvious folk and traditional elements have been included in serious American music only sporadically. Nationalism has been a peripheral rather than a central aspect of music in the United States, but American composers of late have declared their independence from Europe. It is no longer considered essential, as it was a couple of generations ago, for an American composer to complete his training abroad. It isn't even the fashion. With increasing numbers of American musicians being trained on their native soil, an autogenous musical tradition is emerging. Music is being composed which has an American sound. The American sound is still too elusive to be defined precisely, but it is heard and recognized increasingly in the music of this country. American music is achieving identity without obvious devices, and this perhaps is the best kind of nationalism. Edward MacDowell (1861–1908) used Indian themes but never outgrew his Germanic training. Though Roy Harris (1898–   ) and Aaron Copland (1900–   ) both studied in France, they are regarded as two of the more "American" composers of their generation. The young, domestically-trained composers are not as a rule consciously nationalistic in orientation.

The distinctive characteristics of each nation's music are most apparent when selections from various geographic regions are heard in succession. The suggested examples provide a panoramic view of nationalism in music.

ALEXANDER BORODIN: *Prince Igor* (1890)
(1833–1887)   Polovtsian Dances   11:35

> Borodin worked on his opera for many years but never completed it. It was finished by Rimsky-Korsakov and Glazunov and given its first performance three years after the composer's death. Borodin said, "*Prince Igor* is essentially a national opera which can be of interest only to us Russians who like to refresh ourselves at the fountainhead of our history, and to see the origins of our nationality revived upon the stage." The setting of the opera is in Central Asia during the 12th century. The Polovtsi, a Tartar race, have captured Prince Igor in the second act, and the Polovtsian maidens dance in his honor. The music for this most famous scene of the opera compounds savagery, passion, and power in music which belies Borodin's modest estimate of its worth. There are voice parts in the original, but the dances are often played in concerts with instruments taking the vocal lines.

BEDRICH SMETANA: *The Bartered Bride* (1866)
(1824–1884)   Overture   6:05

> Bohemia, an area of modern Czechoslovakia, gained a measure of political independence from Austria in 1860. Two years later a National Theater dedicated to the performance of Bohemian opera was founded by public subscription. Smetana began immediately to compose operas imbued with the nationalistic spirit and in the Bohemian language for performance there. After the enthusiastic reception of *The Bartered Bride*, the second of his eight operas, Smetana was appointed first conductor of the Opera. Excerpts from *The Bartered Bride*, and the opera itself in translation, have become international favorites. The mood of the overture and the opera is that of a festive Bohemian village.

RIMSKY-KORSAKOV   JEAN SIBELIUS

MANUEL DE FALLA: *El Amor Brujo (Love, the Sorcerer)* (1915)   15:50
(1876–1946)   Introduction
                               Dance of Terror
                               The Magic Circle
                               Ritual Fire Dance
                               Pantomime
                               Finale

When Falla returned to Spain at the beginning of World War I after
seven years in Paris, his countrymen suspected him of having diluted
his Spanish blood with French wine. After a brief period drenching
himself in the songs and dances of his native land, he silenced their
doubts by composing the thoroughly Spanish ballet *El Amor Brujo*
for the Andalusian gypsy dancer Pastora Impero.

The story of the ballet concerns a gypsy girl who is haunted by her
dead lover. His appearance whenever she is about to kiss her new
lover is frustrating the romance. The dead man, unable to resist a
pretty face in life or death, is distracted during a rendezvous by a
girl friend of his ex-sweetheart. The new lovers kiss; the spell is
broken; the spectre disappears; and all ends happily.

The *Ritual Fire Dance* from this work is one of Falla's most popular
creations. Two additional numbers with a part for contralto voice
are included in the ballet. These additional sections are included in
concert and recorded performances when a singer is used.

JEAN SIBELIUS: *Finlandia, Op. 26 No. 7* (1899)   8:45
(1865–1957)

This work was written while Finland was oppressed by the iron
rule of Imperial Russia. Its effect on the Finns was so inflammatory
that its performance was banned throughout the country. When

eventually they gained concessions and finally independence, *Finlandia* became a symbol of triumphant struggle and freedom.

AARON COPLAND: *Billy the Kid* (1938)   20:00
   (1900–   )   The Open Prairie
                          Street in Frontier Town
                          Card Game at Night
                          Gun Battle
                          Celebration after Billy's Capture
                          The Open Prairie Again

The sections listed are included in an orchestral suite taken from the ballet commissioned by Lincoln Kirstein, director of the Ballet Caravan. It is as American as apple pie. Not only is the ballet set in the old West with a legendary figure as its central character, but cowboy tunes are dextrously woven into the musical fabric. Among those included are: *Get Along Little Dogies, The Old Chisholm Trail, Old Paint,* and *The Dying Cowboy.*

Impressionism

Impressionism began as an art movement. Edouard Manet was using impressionist techniques as early as 1863, but the term was first used in a derisive commentary on a painting by Claude Monet. A group of painters which included Renoir and Degas adopted the term officially for their exhibitions starting in 1877. The impressionists, reacting negatively to the prevailing style of painting classical and sentimental subjects, used primary colors in juxtaposition to achieve greater brilliance and luminosity than was possible with the customary blended pigments. Their representation of the effects of natural sunlight blurred outlines. Minor details tended to disappear, and forms were suggested rather than defined. Spontaneous impressions were captured on canvas, not studied renderings.

The symbolist poets Stéphane Mallarmé and Paul Verlaine were kindred spirits with the impressionist painters, and like the impressionist painters they preceded and set the stage for the corresponding style in music.

Impressionism in music and the name CLAUDE DEBUSSY (1862–1918) are inseparable. He was the first impressionist composer and almost the only one whose works are regarded as exclusively and purely impressionistic, but perhaps this is because his music sets the standards by which impressionism in music is measured. Debussy drew inspiration from the impressionist painters and the symbolist poets. His music, like their pictures and poems, is subtle and suggestive rather than bold and exhuberant. It is sensuous but not passionate, picturesque but not graphic. Color and mood take precedence over line and structure. He was not prolific, but every page of his music is finely wrought. It includes two books of *Preludes* and numerous small works

CLAUDE DEBUSSY   MAURICE RAVEL

for piano, an opera *Pelleas and Melisande*, song cycles and cantatas, a small quantity of chamber music, and a few exquisitely colored orchestral works. The quintessence of impressionism is embodied in his *Clouds*.

CLAUDE DEBUSSY: *Nocturnes* (1899)
   (1862–1918)   1. Nuages (Clouds)   7:20

> *Nuages* is the first of three *Nocturnes* for which Debussy provided the following program notes:
>
>> The title *Nocturnes* is intended to have here a more general and, above all, a more decorative meaning. We, then, are not concerned with the form of the Nocturne, but with everything that this word includes in the way of diversified impression and special lights.
>>
>> Clouds: The unchangeable appearance of the sky, with the slow and solemn march of clouds dissolving in a gray agony tinted with white.

Debussy was not a nationalist in the usual sense, but he did regard impressionism as a French reaction to German romanticism. A clue to his thinking is provided by the way he signed his name: "Claude Debussy, French musician."

MAURICE RAVEL (1875–1937) is invariably linked with Debussy as an impressionist composer. He was influenced by Debussy and impressionism, but he was no slavish imitator. His music is less fragmentary than that of Debussy, more lyric and dynamic. Precision and clarity are characteristics of his art, as it is of the French language and literature. He wrote brilliant music for piano and made equally brilliant transcriptions of some of it for orchestra, in addition to his original orchestral compositions. Among his best known works are: *Alborada del gracioso*, *Bolero*, two piano concertos, a string quartet, the ballet suites *Daphnis and Chloe* and *Mother Goose, La Valse*, and the unforgettable *Pavane.*

MAURICE RAVEL: *Pavane pour une infante défunte* (1899)   5:20
    (1875–1937)

> This is one of Ravel's compositions which exists in versions for both piano and orchestra. Annotators disagree as to whether this is a "Pavane for a Dead Princess" or a "Pavane for a Dead Infant." Whichever, the pavane which started out as a stately dance in 16th-century Spain became a tender elegy in late 19th-century France. The style is not really typical of impressionism, but it is typical of Ravel.

Impressionism was almost, but not quite, a French monopoly. The Germans were not receptive to the new style, as would be expected since it was a reaction to their romanticism, but impressionist influences can be detected in many English, Italian, Spanish, and American works written during the first third of the century. Though several non-French composers were influenced by impressionism, about the only ones classified as impressionists, and these not consistently, are Frederick Delius (1862–1934) and Charles Tomlinson Griffes (1884–1920). Delius lived in France after the age of 26, so he scarcely qualified as non-French, though he was born in England of German parentage and studied music in the United States and Germany. This leaves Griffes as the one composer without French connections who can be regarded as an impressionist. The first of his *Roman Sketches* is the best known, and the fourth makes an interesting comparison with Debussy's *Nocturne* of the same title.

CHARLES GRIFFES: *Roman Sketches, Op. 7* (1917)
    (1884–1920)   1. The White Peacock   5:20
                        4. Clouds   4:20

> The four *Roman Sketches* originally were for piano. Griffes scored the first and last for orchestra before his untimely death. A quotation from the mystic poet William Sharp prefaces each of the sketches. The one preceding *The White Peacock* begins:
>
>> Here where the sunlight
>> Floodeth the garden,
>> Where the pomegranate
>> Reareth its glory
>> Where the oleanders
>> Dream through the noontides;
>
> and ends:
>
>> Pale, pale as the breath of blue
>>   smoke in far woodlands,

> Here, as the breath, as the soul of this beauty,
> Moves the White Peacock.

The lines quoted in the score of *Clouds* are:

> Mountainous glories,
> They move superbly;
> Crumbling so slowly,
> That none perceives when
> The golden domes
> Are sunk in the valleys
> Of fathomless snows.

References

Edward Lockspeiser, *Debussy, His Life and Times* (New York: The Macmillan Company, 1965).

Norman Demuth, *Ravel* (New York: Farrar, Straus, 1949).

Chronology

Born	Composer	Died
1872	Vaughan Williams	1958
1874	Schoenberg	1951
1874	Ives	1954
1879	Respighi	1936
1880	Bloch	1959
1881	Bartok	1945
1882	Kodaly	1967
1882	Stravinsky	
1883	Webern	1945
1885	Berg	1935
1885	Varese	1965
1887	Villa-Lobos	1959
1890	Martinu	1959
1890	Ibert	1962
1891	Prokofiev	1953
1892	Honegger	1955
1892	Milhaud	
1893	Haba	
1895	Hindemith	1963
1896	Hanson	
1896	Sessions	
1896	Weinberger	1967
1898	Gershwin	1937
1898	Claflin	
1898	Harris	
1899	Chavez	
1899	Thompson	
1900	Weill	1950
1900	Berezowsky	1953
1900	Copland	
1901	Partch	
1902	Walton	
1902	Rodgers	
1903	Khachaturian	
1904	Loewe	
1906	Shostakovich	
1907	Phillips	
1910	Barber	
1911	Hovhaness	
1911	Menotti	
1912	Barlow	
1912	Cage	
1913	Britten	
1913	Kennan	
1914	Kleinsinger	
1915	Persichetti	
1917	Ward	
1918	Bernstein	
1922	Foss	
1925	Boulez	
1925	Schuller	
1928	Leigh	
1928	Stockhausen	

modern music

It is a curious state of affairs when the music of our time requires special explanation, even justification. That this is so is perhaps understandable if indefensible. A more natural situation would be for the people of any age to be most receptive to the arts and crafts of their own time, which is essentially the case in literature, drama, and architecture. There is little chance that a Dickens' novel will turn up as a book-of-the-month selection, that Shakespeare will force Edward Albee off Broadway, or that Gothic-style architecture will be revived. Unhappily, the parallel does not extend to serious music. Reasons for the neglect of contemporary music are worthy of investigation.

Conductors are inclined to place the blame on audiences, who presumably demand familiar music, without conceding that the familiarity of old music is the result of its having been programmed to the exclusion of the new. With the masterpieces of the past being played because they are familiar and being familiar because they are played, contemporary works have little chance of breaking into the charmed circle. Established patterns are slow to change, and in music practical considerations retard the process.

Modern music on the whole is difficult to play. It is technically demanding and unfamiliar to the players. Readying a new work for performance requires more rehearsal time than the quick review needed for the standard repertory, and rehearsal time at union scale is expensive. Performance fees for copyrighted works are small, but there are no performance fees for works in public domain. All of the composers of the past, including Bach, Beethoven, and Mozart, are competition for living composers. These aggravating details are but a prelude to the main problem—the basic lack of understanding of the musical idioms of our time.

Performers and listeners conditioned to sweet concords, singable melodies, and symmetric rhythmic patterns are bewildered by the complexities and irregularities of contemporary music. Often their first impression is that new music has forsaken tradition and that radical innovation has replaced reason. Actually, the development of musical materials has always proceeded in a logical and orderly fashion, but the pace has accelerated tremendously in the past 50 years. The rapidity with which musical resources have expanded in recent times has made it difficult for performers and listeners alike to keep abreast of the latest styles. Though the disparity between the old and the new is more apparent than real, musical taste lags farther and farther behind the conceptions of *avant-garde* composers, and the gulf between them and the listening public continues to widen. It was not always thus!

Before 1800 most composers were attached to a court or a church which provided a ready market for their latest creations. Auspicious occasions of church and state were commemorated with special compositions. As a result of their institutional connections, composers had both the time and the incentive to produce voluminous amounts of music and in the process to become masters of their craft. That some of their works are enduring masterpieces is a purely gratuitous circumstance. A natural corollary of placing a premium on new works is that old ones are short-lived. The repetition of familiar favorites season after season was unknown in this period. Many compositions since revived were discarded in their own time after a few performances. *The Art of Fugue* by Bach, now universally regarded as a monument of musical art, sold only 30 copies in the 18th century, and the plates for it were melted for their metal by Bach's sons, themselves reputable composers.

How different the situation is now. The geniuses of the past are regarded with reverence. Even their inferior works are programmed as a sort of holy obligation while contemporary composers are denied the opportunities which made possible the achievements of their predecessors. Music students are indoctrinated so thoroughly in the musical language of the past that they adopt an archaic dialect as their own. Music listeners are subjected to the same influences. It is small wonder under these conditions that we speak most fluently and understand most readily a musical language which dates from the time of the American revolution.

It would be folly to suggest the elimination of the old, but bringing the performance of the new into balance with it is not only a desirable but a necessary objective if music is to remain a vital cultural force. Not all contemporary music measures up to the quality of masterpieces sifted from the prodigious production of past ages, but currency and freshness compensate. Besides, the expressions of qualified artists deserve hearings, and in no other way can new masterpieces be created and discovered.

Persons steeped in the musical traditions of the past sometimes are prejudiced against innovation. One who regards the style of Mozart and Beethoven an irrevocable norm is apt to consider askance that of Schoenberg and Stravinsky. It is strange and unfortunate that 18th- and 19th-century music provides the common background of listening experience, but this is a fact. Relating current practice to that of the past two centuries is one way of bridging the gap between them, but in the final analysis listening to the music of our time is the best way to become attuned to it.

At the present time, as always, each composer has a distinctive musical personality, but beneath the surface a common heritage provides a bond between them and with the musical traditions of the past. There is not a 20th-century style, but there are characteristics which distinguish the music of this century. Many features of 20th-century music which appear to be new are merely the most recent manifestations of practices rooted in tradition. Viewed in this light they are immediately more intelligible.

The melodies of primitive music were intended for untrained voices or crude instruments. They contained a limited number of pitches in a narrow range, and the motion was mostly conjunct. The first evolutionary step was to extend the range and add more notes. This was possible still within the limitations of the human voice. The development of scale patterns, tonality, and harmonic accompaniments subjected melodic invention to additional tyrannies. It is against these arbitrary limitations and not against melody itself that modern composers stand in revolt. Greatly expanded melodic resources are used in modern music, but melody is not refuted. The concept of vocal melody oriented to conventional scale and chord patterns is still valid but not exclusive. The perfection of instruments has made feasible extended ranges and angular, disjunct contours. These possibilities, latent until recent times, are now utilized fully. Melodies unshackled from vocal limitations and conventional scales and harmonies now draw materials freely from exotic scales and dissonant, widely spaced chords or progress without regard for scale or chord implications. The composer's melodic imagination while unfettered is obliged to produce logical sequences of tones. Imprudent exercise of freedom at times conceals the logic of contemporary melodies. The accusation that new music is tuneless is justified only if old-fashioned definitions of melody are applied. The listener no longer should demand tunes he can sing, but he may expect to find in modern music logically organized pitches and rhythms and themes that he can recognize. Most composers comply with this more liberal mandate.

The evolution of harmony can be traced more systematically. Music began with a single line. Probably more by instinct than design, at least in the early stages, notes were combined harmonically in order of the complexity of their vibrating ratios. The process of addition moved slowly for hun-

dreds of years. Up to the end of the 19th century the most complex sound
assimilated in the harmonic vocabulary consisted of four alternate scale tones.
The ratios of their vibrations were relatively simple, and they blended
into thoroughly agreeable sounds. Then the evolutionary process exploded.
Within 25 years harmonic materials were expanded to include chords of
seven and more tones and the most complex relationships possible between
the twelve available notes. The suddenness of the expansion eliminated the
possibility of gradual adjustment. Before the first of these new dissonant
chords had been assimilated, newer and more strident ones were introduced.
Traditional concepts of consonance and dissonance were upended. Though
the dissonant harmonies of the 20th century are the logical culmination of
evolutionary processes set in motion when two tones were first sounded together, most listeners were unprepared for the burst of speed at the finish.
Much antagonism toward new music stems from a reluctance to accept the
more complex tonal relationships as legitimate sonorities. If consonance is
equated with beauty and dissonance with ugliness, then certainly modern
music is not very pretty. However, if consonance is equated with repose and
dissonance with tension, which is more valid, the high-powered music of this
century makes that of the past seem tranquil to the point of immobility. There
is no reluctance on the part of contemporary composers to use any conceivable combination of tones, but most of them can be analyzed in terms of their
relationship to conventional arrangements. Some are conventional chord
structures with notes omitted or with foreign tones added. Some combine
two conventional structures, and some build chords from intervals other than
those found in conventional harmonies. Infinite harmonic structures are available to contemporary composers compared with a mere handful in use less
than a hundred years ago. The composer's art has become more involved and
the listener's art more exciting with the harmonic innovations of this century.

In the matter of harmonic progression, too, recent composers have explored new possibilities. They eschew the stereotyped harmonic formulas
which abound in conventional music. Freedom of chord relationship as well
as structure is constantly exploited.

Contemporary concepts of melody, harmonic structure, and progression
inevitably have weakened the bonds of tonality. Whereas traditional music
gravitates to a well defined tonal center, the tonality of modern music is often
vague, occasionally nonexistent. When tonality vanishes, a primary orienting
device for the listener is sacrificed. For this reason many contemporary composers choose to retain some semblance of tonality in their music.

Outside of harmony, the most obvious departures from convention
occur in contemporary rhythm. Regularity and symmetry have given way to
irregularity and asymmetry. The commonplace and the anticipated have
been replaced by the unusual and the unexpected. Syncopation, displaced

accents, measures and phrases in odd sizes are all patent aspects of present-day rhythm.

Counterpoint, most venerable of the musical disciplines, has been renovated, but the results are not so startling. The melodies used in contrapuntal associations may display all the characteristics of independent melodies, so a contemporary flavor is assured. The prior contrapuntal ideal of fitting melodies together in a happy blend is replaced by a concept in which melodies pursue conflicting paths with obstinate independence. Since the ear is conditioned to follow the lines of contrapuntal music, momentary clashes between them do not attract much attention.

Most phases of contemporary music have been the center of controversy at one time or another. The one aspect of modern music that has received unanimous acclaim has been reserved for last. The severest critics of contemporary music are lavish in their praise of 20th-century orchestration. The exploitation of instrumental color in the present century is unprecedented. Modern instruments and orchestras have reached a pinnacle of perfection, and composers are taking full advantage of newly discovered and developed instrumental resources. In this respect at least, the composers of our time have never been excelled.

New music is as complex and unpredictable as the times in which we live. If all kinds of complexities occurred in the same passage of music, it is doubtful that anyone could comprehend it or would consider it worthwhile to try. Such a passage is hypothetical and unlikely to be encountered in an actual composition. Usually complexities are limited to one or two musical elements at a time. For example, complicated rhythms and harmonies are often associated with elemental melodies and an absence of counterpoint. Emphasis on melodic lines and counterpoint diverts attention from harmony and from rhythm except as it figures in the lines. In other words, the composer may tax and challenge a listener's ability, but a practical composer never intentionally swamps his audience. The composer's art exists only for the listener, and it is a myth that composers deliberately write for posterity.

Creative artists sublimate the impulses of their time and place. Their creative efforts, therefore, should receive the most sympathetic reception from their contemporaries and countrymen. Evidence to the contrary can only be ascribed to unnatural conditioning. We may admire the masterpieces of the past and find escape in the rustic simplicity of a Haydn, for certainly great art is timeless and universal, but the ultimate emotional responses should be evoked by artistic creations intimately reflecting the moods of our own frantic age.

Summarizing the trends and listing the outstanding figures of this century is complicated by the lack of perspective. It is difficult to write history

ARNOLD SCHOENBERG   SERGE PROKOFIEV

while it is still being made and before the winnowing of the significant and
enduring from the trivial and transient has taken place. One conclusion, however, is inescapable. The United States has become a world center of music.
Whereas the history of music prior to 1900 could have been written with
barely a mention of this country, a large percentage of the important musicians of more recent times have lived, worked, or visited here. This premise
is supported by the composers selected to illustrate the styles of music since
the 1920's.

ARNOLD SCHOENBERG was born in Vienna in 1874. After a distinguished if controversial musical career in Europe, he came to this country in
1933. He taught briefly at the University of Southern California and then at
the University of California in Los Angeles, where he died in 1951. To
Schoenberg must be attributed one of the most profound innovations in the
annals of music. He devised a system of "composition with 12 tones related
only to one another" in which conventional principles of harmony and counterpoint are abandoned and new precepts of tonal organization promulgated.
Schoenberg's method is based on a *series* of 12 different notes in a prescribed
order which establish a pattern of intervals. This series and its resulting sequence of intervals is the total basis for a strict *serial* composition. Within the
limits imposed by the series in its various guises, the composer is free to dis-
tribute the pitches and to regulate the rhythm, texture, instrumentation, and
form according to his musical instincts. The freedom is disciplined, however,
for every note from beginning to end appears only in relation to its assigned
position in the original series. This approach seems like a radical departure
from conventional practices, but Schoenberg claimed historical precedents
for it and staunchly defended it as a logical and necessary forward step in the

evolution of music. In composing his *String Quartet No. 4* (see page 100) Schoenberg stringently observed his own principles of serial organization.

Serial music, being difficult to play and to comprehend, has never attracted a wide audience, but a host of disciples have been converted to serial composition. ALBAN BERG (1885–1935) was one of the first and most distinguished composers to come under Schoenberg's influence. His mature works are atonal, but he did not follow serial procedures as consistently or rigidly as Schoenberg. An irrepressible lyricism and romanticism broaden the appeal of his music. The opera *Wozzeck* and the *Violin Concerto* commissioned and premiered by the American violinist Louis Krasner are recognized masterpieces.

ALBAN BERG: *Violin Concerto* (1935)
(1885–1935)   1. Andante—Allegretto   10:20
               2. Allegro—Adagio   13:20

> Berg agreed to write a violin concerto early in 1935 but did not begin work on it until a beautiful young girl to whom he was deeply attached died unexpectedly. His reaction to the tragic event was to compose this monument "to the memory of an angel" in three months of feverish creativity. It was a requiem for her and for him. He did not live to hear the first performance the following year.
>
> After an introduction of approximately one minute's duration, the solo violin clearly announces the 12 notes of the series in their original order starting on the lowest pitch and ascending in an unbroken line to the last note of the series in a very high register. The flavor of the series permeates the work and provides an effective if subconscious unifying element. It is not necessary or even desirable to search for evidence of the series when listening to serial music for pleasure.

Expressionism is the name for the style of Schoenberg and his school. The term, like impressionism, was borrowed from painting and as in painting, the two styles are antithetical. Where the impressionists used ultra-refined techniques in naturalistic portrayals of the external world as perceived by the senses, the expressionists (Picasso, Kandinsky, Klee) expressed the subconscious, inner self in grotesque abstractions with utter disregard for reality and the traditional principles of beauty and design. Expressionism in music is characterized by fragmentation of thematic material, disjunct lines, discordant harmony, and a high degree of abstract organization.

ANTON WEBERN (1883–1945), a composer closely associated with Schoenberg and Berg in the early development of twelve-tone composition, was the ultimate expressionist. His music is not as accessible as that of Berg, but it has a greater direct influence on the younger generation of serialists. Composers like Pierre Boulez (1925–   ) and Karlheinz Stockhausen (1928–   ), who have extended serial procedures to parameters of music other than pitch (such as rhythm, dynamics, and tone color), pay particular homage to Webern. Webern's contact with Americans was brief and tragic. His son was killed in a World War II air raid, and he was shot fatally when he violated a curfew imposed by U.S. occupation troops. The University of Washington in Seattle acquired his manuscripts which are the object of much scholarly study. The 10 minute *Symphony, Op. 21* is probably the best example of Webern's mature style, but the *Three Songs, Op. 18* provide a more ingratiating introduction to his music.

ANTON WEBERN: *Three Songs, Op. 18* (1925)
   (1883–1945)   1. Schatzerl klein (Sweetheart, Dear)   :50
                          2. Erlösung (Redemption)   1:00
                          3. Ave, Regina   1:20

> These songs demonstrate Webern's penchant for brevity and economy of means. His music gives the impression of having been distilled to the point where only the essence remains. His texture is sparse and transparent. No masses of sound or multiplicity of lines compete with each other for attention. The problem is to perceive the thread of continuity which forges the disjointed fragments into a unified whole. When Webern conceived these songs, the principles of twelve-tone composition were newly formulated. In this, his second opus using the method, he already handles it with assurance and imagination.

If the expressionist movement emanating from Vienna exemplifies the break with musical traditions, the prevailing style of Russian music represents its continuation. SERGE PROKOFIEV (1891–1953) probably qualifies as the leading Soviet composer to date, though some would rank DMITRI SHOSTAKOVICH (1906–   ) not far behind. Two visits by Shostakovich to this country have had no visible effect on his music or ours. Many of his compositions are too closely tied to communist ideology to sustain interest abroad. He has quickly repudiated his sporadic ventures into "decadent modernism" and has done penance with the production of works strictly in accordance with the dogma of "socialist realism." Prokofiev, though highly regarded and much imitated in the Soviet Union, was more progressive and cosmopolitan. From 1918 until he established Soviet citizenship in 1933, he lived principally in the United States and France. His reputation was spread by international tours as a pianist, frequently playing his own compositions. His stature as a composer is predicated at least partially upon the

DMITRI SHOSTAKOVICH   PAUL HINDEMITH

breadth of his endeavors. He wrote in all of the conventional forms—symphonies, suites, concertos, ballets, operas, symphonic poems, piano music, and chamber music, and in addition he composed film scores and music for children. One of his most famous works, if not his greatest, is in the latter category.

SERGE PROKOFIEV: *Peter and the Wolf, Op. 67* (1936)   22:15
   (1891–1953)

> Though intended for children, Prokofiev's basic compositional techniques, somewhat simplified, are embodied in this delightful fable for narrator and orchestra. Its appeal is not limited to children. Like youth, it is almost a shame to waste it on them.

PAUL HINDEMITH (1895–1963) was a complete and practical musician. He played several instruments—the violin, viola, and piano professionally. He was a composer, conductor, teacher, theorist, and author. His impact on 20th-century music through his students, his writings, and his personal appearances has been enormous. As a composer he would be classified by contemporary standards as a traditionalist, but his music is not old-fashioned by any stretch of the imagination. His youthful works were regarded as radical, as are the works of most young composers, but he is known as the champion of *Gebrauchsmusik* (music for practical use) and *Hausmusik* (music to be played at home). The practicality of his approach can be gathered from the fact that more than 50 of his compositions are listed in the current *Schwann Long Playing Record Catalog*. He regarded composition as a craft, and he was a master craftsman. He was against atonality and serialism but not against dissonance or complexity. Critics detect in his music classic, romantic, baroque, archaic, and modern influences, which is to say that he wrote in the style that suited his purpose at the moment. His friendship with Jewish musicians brought him into conflict with the Nazi regime, and he left his native Germany the year after *Mathis der Maler* was composed. He concertized in this country during the late 1930's and settled here in 1940, teaching at Yale and Harvard before moving to Zurich in 1953.

PAUL HINDEMITH: *Mathis der Maler (Matthias the Painter)* (1934)
(1895–1963) 1. Angelic Concert 8:00
       2. Entombment 4:05
       3. The Temptation of Saint Anthony 13:30

  The symphony *Mathis der Maler* is taken from the semihistorical opera of the same name. The opera depicts episodes in the life of painter Mathis Gothart Nithart, known as Mathis Grünewald, and the symphony relates specifically to three facets of the Isenheim altarpiece which he painted. The title of each movement of the symphony is taken from the subject shown in one panel of the painting.

  BELA BARTOK (1881–1945), one of the titans of 20th-century music, developed a dynamic, personal style which is not easily categorized. He is connected with no "ism" unless it be that of modernism. He did extensive research and publication in the field of folk music but except for a few articles did not write about art music. He taught piano but not composition. His works until near the end of his career were problematical. These factors contributed to the delay in recognizing the magnitude of his genius. He first toured the United States in 1927 as a concert pianist. In 1940 he came to New York where he lived in relative poverty and obscurity until his death. Though not unknown during his lifetime, fame and remuneration commensurate with the worth of his music came posthumously. Bartok's output, just short of 100 works, includes many arrangements of folk songs and dances, and folk influences of his native Hungary abound in the other works. Practically all forms and mediums were included in his production, with piano music and chamber music especially abundant. The one form that he never attempted was a symphony, but his *Concerto for Orchestra* is very close to a symphony in concept.

BELA BARTOK: *Concerto for Orchestra* (1943)
(1881–1945) 1. Introduction: Andante non troppo—Allegro
         vivace 9:48
       2. Game of Pairs: Allegretto scherzando 6:17
       3. Elegy: Andante, non troppo 7:11

4. Interrupted Intermezzo: Allegretto   4:08
5. Finale: Presto   8:52

This work was written for the Koussevitzky Music Foundation in
memory of Mrs. Natalie Koussevitzky, wife of the then conductor
of the Boston Symphony Orchestra. It is not a problematic or experimental composition but a solid artistic achievement in the eloquent
musical language of our time. Bartok provided the following program notes for the first performance:

> The general mood of the work represents, apart from the
> jesting second movement, a gradual transition from the
> sternness of the first movement and the lugubrious death-song
> of the third, to the life-assertion of the last one . . . The title of
> this symphony-like orchestral work is explained by its ten-
> dency to treat the single orchestral instruments in a *concertant*
> or soloistic manner. The 'virtuoso' treatment appears, for in-
> stance, in the fugato sections of the development of the first
> movement (brass instruments), or in the *perpetuum mobile*-
> like passage of the principal theme in the last movement
> (strings), and especially in the second movement, in which
> pairs of instruments consecutively appear with brilliant pas-
> sages . . .

The "interruption" in the *Interrupted Intermezzo* is a parody of an
insipid theme from the Shostakovich *Seventh Symphony*. Written in
Leningrad while that city was under siege by the Nazis during World
War II, the symphony enjoyed a spectacular if short-lived success.

IGOR STRAVINSKY (1882–   ) made his first big splash in the musical
world with his ballet *The Firebird* in 1910 when impressionism was still a
controversial style. *The Firebird* (see page 189) shows definite traces of
impressionist influence, but within three years Stravinsky was blazing new
trails. The style of *The Rite of Spring* (see page 94) is anything but impressionistic. The usual label is *primitivism* or *barbarism*. The elemental force
of *The Rite's* throbbing rhythms and strident harmonies, not to mention its
sensual choreography, shocked the staid audience at the premiere and pro-
voked a near riot. Not content to capitalize on the sensation he had created,
Stravinsky turned immediately to new modes of expression exploring unusual
small instrumental combinations. These pioneering efforts paved the way for
another 20th-century style, *neoclassicism*. Where other composers of his
generation have been caught in the wake of changing styles, he has been at
the forefront spearheading the changes. His creativity did not diminish or
stagnate with advancing years. At the age of 70 he turned to a new (for him)
style of composition employing serial procedures in a distinctly personal way.
During an incredibly active and varied musical career spanning more than
six decades he composed for virtually every conventional medium and invented new ones. There is no doubt that his influence on 20th-century music

BELA BARTOK   IGOR STRAVINSKY

has been greater than that of any other composer to date. Each of his many styles has attracted a legion of imitators. Like a prophet, he has been without honor only in his own country, Russia, which he left in 1911. His many extended trips took him around the world, but he resided principally in France until 1939 when he moved to Hollywood. No single work by Stravinsky can be regarded as typical or representative, but the *Octet* is a perennial favorite and, after the ballets, one of his most influential works.

IGOR STRAVINSKY: *Octet for Wind Instruments* (1923, revised 1952) 16:00
 (1882–)   1. Sinfonia
         2. Theme with variations
         3. Finale

  The *Octet* for flute, clarinet, 2 bassoons, 2 trumpets, and 2 trombones illustrates Stravinsky's preoccupation with unusual instrumental combinations. The original version in 1923 was one of the first works in this century to revert to classic ideals, a philosophy which subsequently was embraced by many composers. Stravinsky provided the following program notes for a 1952 performance:

    Composition, structure, form, here all are in the line of the 18th-century masters. Sonority has not been my first concern, and indeed, must be considered only as a result. The introduction is comparable—has an importance in the whole scheme—to the introductions in late Haydn symphonies. The *Allegro* (1) is a typical two-theme *sonata-allegro* (form) in the key of E-flat. The second movement is a theme with variations, a form which has occupied me in many works from *Pulcinella* and the *Concerto for Two Pianos, Jeu de Cartes,* to *Danses Concertantes* and the two-piano *Sonata.* In the *Octet,* however, it is the first variation which recurs rather than the theme in its original state. The final variation is a *fugato* (with added—nonstrictly *fugato*—notes) with, as subject, the intervals of the theme inverted. A measured flute cadenza modulates to the finale in C major, a kind of rondo with coda.

Unlike the composers discussed in this chapter who were *in* but not *of* the United States, CHARLES IVES (1874–1954) was a 24-carat American. He traced his lineage back to Captain William Ives who came to Boston on the "Truelove" in 1635. His father, after service in the Civil War as a Union Army bandmaster, became the leading musician in Danbury, Connecticut where Charles was born. Young Ives learned to play the drums, cornet, piano, violin, and organ and became a member of his father's band. He listened with interest as his father had the band play with sections stationed in various locations around the town and as he dabbled with experimental tunings of a many-stringed contrivance. These effects and the sounds of rural New England were absorbed and reflected in his music. "Virtually every work he wrote," according to Nicolas Slonimsky, "bears relation to American life, not only by literary association, but through actual quotation of American music sources, from church anthems to popular dances and marches." Most of the innovations of 20th-century music—atonality, polytonality, polymeters, microtones, and tone clusters—were anticipated in his music early in the century when Schoenberg and Stravinsky were just severing their ties with romanticism. One can only imagine what his influence would have been if his music had become known as soon as it was written instead of suffering tragic neglect. His music was too far ahead of its time from the beginning, and he was too isolated from the mainstreams of musical activity to promote it. Between 1896 and 1920 he produced a profusion of works, few of which were performed until years later. He was not, however, a starving musician. After graduating from Yale in 1898 he went into business and became a partner in a prosperous insurance agency which gave him freedom to compose without concern for financial returns. He published his *Concord Sonata* for piano and 114 songs at his own expense and distributed copies gratis. His manuscript scores are now in the Yale library where they are attracting the attention they should have had 50 years ago. The first work of his to be issued by a commercial publisher was *Three Places in New England* in 1935, 21 years after it was completed and 15 years after he had virtually stopped composing.

CHARLES IVES: *Three Places in New England* (1903–1914)

(1874–1954)	1.	The "St. Gaudens" in Boston Common	8:55
	2.	Putnam's Camp, Redding, Connecticut	5:35
	3.	The Housatonic at Stockbridge	3:45

Each of the movements is vividly descriptive of the place in New England specified in the title. The first movement, subtitled *Col. Shaw and his Colored Regiment*, is prefaced by a poem (probably by Ives) which contains the lines, "Moving—Marching—Faces of Souls! . . . Slowly, restlessly—swaying us on with you Towards other Freedom!" As fragments of Civil War melodies are projected against a hauntingly dissonant background, one can easily visualize a spectral procession marching to the beat of the drum.

The second movement is a musical fantasy depicting a child's Fourth of July outing at the Revolutionary Memorial located at the site of General Israel Putnam's winter quarters. Snatches of familiar tunes are heard as two bands playing different marches approach from opposite directions, pass each other, and depart.

The summer after they were married, Ives and his wife took a walk through the meadows along the Housatonic river near Stockbridge. This walk and a poem by Robert Underwood Johnson which begins, "Contented river! in the dreamy realm . . . ." inspired the third movement of this "New England Symphony."

Ives' music is not suave or sophisticated. He had no opportunity, and perhaps no inclination, to polish and perfect his technique through repeated hearings of his own works and those of his European contemporaries. Music for him was a primordial means of expression. The approach is always simple and direct, even when the means are extremely complex. Like the New England countryside, his music has a peculiar rough-hewn beauty which is sometimes sentimental, sometimes crude, but always filled with vitality.

Concluding this chapter with works already established in the concert repertory and with composers most of whom are dead does not imply that the mantle of genius is vacant. It takes a quantity of music and many performances to establish a reputation, and it takes time to confirm greatness. The composers discussed in this chapter are giants of the first half of the century whose creative careers are behind them and whose works are already major influences in 20th-century music. A host of younger composers are well on their way toward greatness. The number of competent and gifted composers is far greater today than ever before in the history of music. Almost without exception their compositions, brilliantly conceived and skillfully executed, are as exciting as today's headlines. Care has been exercised to assure that such works are amply represented in previous chapters. The composers' names are in the chronological listing at the beginning of this chapter. The compositions being written right now represent the legacy our generation will pass on to posterity. From among them will emerge the individual masterpieces of this era. Perhaps some composer now struggling for recognition will eventually merit a place beside Bach, Mozart, and Beethoven. Only time will tell.

One thing is certain—the styles of music will continue to change as each generation assimilates some and discards other innovations of the past. Composers will continue their quest for new methods and materials, and each succeeding period will have its "new music." The more adventuresome present-day composers are exploring revolutionary pitch relationships, sound sources, and principles of organization which will surely influence the music of the future if, indeed, they do not become the music of the future.

What will the music of the future be like? No one knows, of course, but recent developments provide clues. Some theorists are advocating and some composers are using *microtones,* that is, intervals smaller than the smallest conventional interval. Microtonal intervals which would divide the octave into 19, 24, 31, 43, and 100 different pitches, compared with the conventional 12, have been proposed. Microtones provide a whole new range of pitch relationships—and create a whole new set of notation and performance problems! *Electronic music* is another recent development. The term is applied to sounds which are generated electronically and also to natural sounds which are recorded and then modified by electronic means. Electronic music rarely uses conventional pitch relationships, so it is also, in a sense, microtonal. A more advanced electronic procedure is to program a computer to produce music. Computers have been programmed to select tones and rhythms (i.e., compose) and to generate electronic sounds with specified characteristics. In the matter of musical organization, two divergent trends can be detected in recent music. One is moving toward the systematic control and total organization of musical elements according to preconceived rational procedures. The other invokes the vagaries of chance, random selection, and improvisation in the spontaneous creation of music. These contrasting approaches to musical organization are sometimes linked together as *system and chance music.* Further discussion of avant-garde music is beyond the scope of this book, but the suggested Additional Examples will provide an introduction to the new music of our time.

Additional Examples

Microtonal Music

> ALOIS HABA: *Fantasy for Violin Solo in Quarter-Tones, Op. 9a*
> HARRY PARTCH: *The Bewitched*
> *The Sound Phenomenon of Quarter-Tone Music* (Mesurgia A–8)

Electronic Music

> KARLHEINZ STOCKHAUSEN: *Gesang der Jünglinge*
> EDGARD VARESE: *Poème Électronique*

System and Chance Music

   Pierre Boulez: *Le Marteau sans Maître*

   John Cage: *Indeterminacy*

   Lukas Foss: *Time Cycle*

   Ernest Krenek: *Sestina*

Miscellaneous

   Sounds of New Music (Folkways FX–6160)

References

William Austin, *Music in the Twentieth Century* (New York: W. W. Norton, 1966).

Leon Dallin, *Techniques of Twentieth Century Composition*, second edition (Dubuque: Wm. C. Brown Company Publishers, 1964).

folk music

Folk music is the expression of a group of kindred people bound together by ties of race, language, religion, or custom. It has existed since the first spontaneous stamping of rhythm and chanting of melody. It includes all the songs and dances originated or used among the common people. The words of the songs generally are artless poems dealing with mundane phases of everyday life, but texts of genuine charm, wit, and pathos are not foreign to the genre. The mores and folkways of the people are reflected in the lines. Tales of romantic and tragic love, patriotism, moral lessons, legendary figures, bits of philosophy and history, all are suitable subjects. Any thought or emotion which touches the lives and fancies of an ethnic group may find expression in song and dance.

The songs, requiring only the voice for performance, greatly exceed the number of dance tunes. The latter are inconsequential by comparison but make a fascinating study, partially because of their association with distinctive instruments such as bagpipes, zithers, guitars, and fiddles and with distinctive manners of playing. The folk instruments and playing styles are also used in accompaniments for singing.

A traditional view that folk songs develop anonymously as the result of concerted action and that folk dance music springs from unpremeditated accompaniments for rustic entertainments is valid only for aboriginal peoples in primitive societies. The folk music of Europe and the Americas is too sophisticated to have originated in deliberate joint ventures. The initial spark in folk music, as in art music, must come from an individual intellect. The will of the people is manifest in the selection and modification of its folk art. Acceptance is a more cogent reason for the classification than origin. Applying this criterion, the songs of Stephen Foster (1826–1864) and Irving

Berlin's *White Christmas* (1942) are as much a part of our folk heritage as the songs of anonymous origin handed down through generations. Anonymity of authorship, often cited as a characteristic of folk music, is increasingly rare in these days of copyrights and publication. Most of the songs whose composers are unknown date from earlier times.

Few folk songs, if any, however, date back to ancient times. If any do, they have been so transformed through the years it has been impossible to trace them. Of course it is difficult to verify the lineage of a song which has been sung for generations in innumerable variations before it assumed definitive, written form. Modifications occur even after a song is notated and published. Community sings always turn up slightly discrepant versions of familiar songs. Tracing a folk song back to its origin is complicated by the fact that the text is as prone to change as the music. Not only do folk melodies exist in several versions (a traditional song learned by word of mouth is almost never sung in exactly the same way by two singers), but each locale may have a different set of words. The earliest authenticated secular folk songs date from the 13th century. Several are preserved from the 15th and 16th centuries, but living folk songs are mostly of more recent origin, predominantly from the 18th and 19th centuries.

Everyone agrees that folk music possesses certain national traits, but objective descriptions of these traits are not easily formulated. Short notes occurring on the beat (*Scotch snaps*) sometimes are pointed out as characteristics of Scotch music. Certain cadence formulas (approaching the tonic note from a third above or below) are mentioned as characteristics of American music. While it is true that these features appear in the literatures indicated, they also appear elsewhere. Obvious similarities are observable in the folk music of widely separated cultures. A person attuned to the dialects of folk music can identify the sources of tunes and styles with which he is acquainted even though he may have difficulty describing them. It can only be deduced that the composite sound somehow reflects the national personality. The locality from which a folk song comes can be pinpointed more accurately by its text and the manner of performance than by its musical traits.

Folk melodies have a proven ability to attract and to communicate with listeners. In the folk song literature composers have a tested treasury of thematic material. As early as the 15th century they started taking advantage of it. A French folk song *L'homme armé* was used in at least thirty polyphonic masses between the 15th and 17th centuries. The practice of using thematic elements of folk origin in art music continues unabated to the present time. It was and is particularly prevalent in the music of nationalistic composers.

Borrowing between folk music and art music is not a one-way street. Individually composed and published songs are assimilated directly into the folk song literature. A whole body of songs by Stephen Foster have assumed the status of folk songs during the last century. In addition to the outright adoption of complete songs, the folk song literature of anonymous origin shows evidence of art music's rational procedures in its forms and melodic contours. Continuous interaction between folk and art music is an established custom.

The United States has one of the largest and most varied folk song literatures. Immigrants from all over the world brought with them the songs and dances of their native lands. To this imported folk music was added music of essentially indigenous origin: American Indian and Negro music, our own patriotic songs, cowboy songs, revivalist hymns, spirituals, blues, and jazz. An incomparable treasury of recorded folk music is deposited in the Library of Congress.

The ethnic groups that have poured into the United States melting pot have tended to lose their identity, with some exceptions. In the process of Americanization their native tongues and customs have been forgotten and their musical traditions transformed and assimilated. Each has made a contribution to the total body of American folk music and then adopted it as its own.

For a long time the music of the people in urban America was jazz and popular music. This is less true now than formerly. Authentic folk music and newly composed songs in folk style are sweeping the country. Some of the most popular and prosperous singing stars and groups sing folk and folk-like music. If national television seems a strange place to practice folk art, it is only one part of the picture. Intimate coffee houses that are much in vogue feature folk entertainment almost exclusively. The most exciting aspect of the new folk movement, however, is that America is again becoming a singing nation. Teen-agers and college students particularly are active participants, not just observers, in the folk music revival which is still gaining momentum.

Folk music is not something to read about, and most of the fun is missed when it is heard from commercial recordings and broadcasts. (Authentic specimens are always recorded in the field.) To really experience the joy of folk music, get together with a few friends, a collection of folk songs if necessary, and a guitar. It will not be difficult to find a friend with a guitar. Guitars are selling at the rate of one and a half million per year, which gives some measure of the current boom in folk music.

Folk Song Collections

Leon and Lynn Dallin, *Folk Songster* (Dubuque: Wm. C. Brown Company Publishers, 1967).

—————. *Heritage Songster* (Dubuque: Wm. C. Brown Company Publishers, 1966).

Burl Ives, *Song Book* (New York: Ballantine Books, Inc., 1953).

John A. and Alan Lomax, *Folk Song: U. S. A.* (New York: Duell, Sloan & Pearce, 1947).

jazz and popular music

There are no adequate designations for broad musical types. *Classical* and *longhair* on the one hand and *popular* and *jazz* on the other are used so loosely as to be almost meaningless. Devotees are inclined to develop precise terminology for music in their particular sphere of interest and to lump together that which is excluded under one all-inclusive, disparaging title. In jazz circles the music (except folk) considered up to this point is classical or "longhair." The subject of this chapter is the other kind of music, jazz and popular.

The terms *jazz* and *popular* are sometimes used indiscriminately for a wide variety of musical styles. At other times and in certain contexts the two terms have definite and distinct meanings. In the *Schwann Long Playing Record Catalog*, for example, popular and jazz are separate categories. Popular music includes the singing and playing of most radio, television, and motion picture stars, country and western music, barbershop ballads, Hawaiian music, the Beatles, Tijuana Brass, and all kinds of dance music. Under the jazz heading are found Dixieland, small combos, jam sessions, blues, swing, hot and cool improvisation, and just plain jazz.

Music which is already "popular" clearly requires no study. The types of music classified as popular in the Schwann catalog do not stand up well under scrutiny or through repeated hearings. The superficiality of popular tunes accounts for their transitory existence. Hits catch on and fads come and go with no apparent rhyme or reason. The catalog of pop tunes is so unstable that it is impractical to suggest examples for listening. Music of this type is pleasant enough in situations where it is not the center of attention. It does not distract auditors who wish to concentrate on something else, so they find it pleasing. In other words, its appeal is primarily to uncritical and unperceptive listeners.

True jazz, as opposed to the popular music with which it is sometimes grouped, attracts a following fully as informed and dedicated as any symphony or string quartet audience. Critical reviews of performances and recordings appear in general interest periodicals. Without becoming totally disassociated from dance elements, jazz is becoming increasingly a pure listening experience independent of overt physical responses. It is assuming the status of an abstract art form.

Jazz and popular music cannot be divorced completely. The distinction between them is by no means as clear-cut as the catalog headings would make them seem. The same pieces in different versions appear on both sides of the fence, and popular music inherits many characteristics from primitive jazz. The differences which separate jazz proper from popular music are in the manner of performance and not in the original conception of the tune. Old antagonisms between advocates of various styles are disappearing, and performers are becoming more versatile. Some of the best are adept in all styles, including that of the classics.

Still, jazz is regarded by some as an upstart whose sudden appearance on the musical scene will be matched by an equally sudden demise, and the sooner the better. Others regard the classics as remnants of the past outliving their usefulness but refusing to die. If history continues to repeat itself, both views are wrong. Different modes of musical expression are as old as the history of music itself, dating back at least to the ancient Greeks. Jazz and classics are merely current versions of these differences. The history of jazz begins around the turn of the century in the Storyville section of New Orleans.

There is no general agreement on the exact moment when jazz emerged as a distinct musical style or on its precise ingredients. Rags, hymns, spirituals, blues, work songs, quadrilles, marches, waltzes, minstrels, Spanish and French music, all have been pointed to as ancestors of jazz. Whatever its forebears, the miracle that is jazz was synthesized from diverse elements by a people in a new environment without any ready-made, adequate and appropriate means of musical expression. From its beginning jazz was Negroid and American, native to both of them, and relatively free of European influences.

Some obvious features of earlier music, such as syncopation and the pentatonic (five-tone) scale which exist in primitive African music and several other traditions, were appropriated by jazz for its own use. Outright borrowing of tunes from other styles, a practice which continues today, started at once. Early rag pieces like *High Society* and *I Wish I Could Shimmy Like My Sister Kate* were being played in quite different versions by the brass bands of the town. The still popular *Tiger Rag* was based on the quadrille

Get Out of Here. In spite of this borrowing, jazz was essentially something new, something more than the sum of its components.

Though its genesis may be earlier, the documented story of jazz commences with the piano rags played in New Orleans during the final decade of the last century. Ragtime piano playing was mostly improvisatory in a percussive style with little use of pedal. The absence of a text was conducive to nonlyric, instrumental melodies. Harmony was basically the primary chords of conventional music. Rhythm, the most distinctive feature of ragtime, was characterized by elaborate syncopations, sometimes created by short notes in accented portions of the measure (and conversely, longer notes in unaccented portions) and sometimes by cross rhythms between melodic groupings of three and six notes in conjunction with underlying beat patterns of two and four. Other rhythmic devices included placing accents just before and after the normal pulse and using rests where accents normally fall. These rhythmic characteristics are the common denominators of jazz.

A few rags were written down, and as early as 1895 one, *Harlem Rag*, was published. Two years later Ben Harney's *Ragtime Instructor*, a piano method, appeared. Harney was a white pianist playing in New York. At this early date jazz already had crossed the color line and the boundaries of New Orleans, but it was to remain for some time essentially but not exclusively a product of the southern Negro culture.

Concurrently with ragtime piano playing, small miscellaneous groups of instrumentalists, many of whom could not read music, collectively improvised for popular entertainments, parades, and dances. The results could not have been other than wildly contrapuntal and shockingly dissonant. Free improvisation, however, was to become a continuing feature of the infant art.

The publication in 1912 and 1914 respectively of the *Memphis Blues* and the *St. Louis Blues* by the Negro cornettist W. C. Handy (1873–1958) ushered in the next jazz epoch. The blues, stemming more or less directly from Negro spirituals and work songs, introduced several characteristics of subsequent jazz. They were different from rags in several respects. As songs, their melodies are vocal in style rather than instrumental. The texts, usually lamenting the absence or loss of a lover, typically are sung in a declamatory manner over a steady pulsating accompaniment. The tempo generally is slow, though faster blues are not unknown. Whereas ragtime harmonies are mostly triads, blues traditionally are based on a standard chord progression which includes seventh chords. Like most popular music, blues are predominantly major, but notes approximating the third and seventh scale degrees of natural minor are featured melodically, sometimes while the corresponding major note is in the accompaniment. These *blue notes* take their name from the style. Blues singers often slide into blue notes, and others at their discretion, hovering in the vicinity but not exactly on the notated pitch. Brief improvised solos by one instrument, called *breaks*, occur in blues and have been incorporated in other styles of jazz. Twelve-measure strains are a unique feature of blues, contrasting with the typical eight-measure units in other types of music. The blues as a form and as a performance style have persisted from the early 1900's to the present time.

The styles of ragtime and the blues coalesced in jazz, a term of unsavory origin which did not appear in print before the second decade of the century. By this time jazz bands had migrated from New Orleans and were appearing regularly in Chicago, New York, and San Francisco. Chicago was the new mecca.

With the entrance into the field of white and trained musicians, a refining, and in a sense, a corrupting process began. The crude virility of primitive jazz was mellowed by the intrusion of European elements—sentimental melodies of the ballad and Viennese operetta type and impressionist harmonies. The lusty blues singers were largely replaced by crooners. The bands grew to sizes which made improvisation impractical, and written arrangements became the rule. With the addition of the strings the bands became so large and the arrangements so pretentious that the anomalous name *symphonic jazz* was coined for the style. What must have appeared to Paul Whiteman, his admirers and imitators as a great elevation of jazz style and a popularization of classic values, in restrospect seems to have been a rather unfortunate compromise for both. Before the roaring twenties were over, there were three distinct branches of jazz: *symphonic, sweet*, and *hot*. Symphonic and sweet popular music retained some of the superficial aspects of jazz and were appropriate for dancing all the varied steps of the fox trot, but only hot was true to the original traditions.

Small groups, mainly Negro and including such illustrious characters as Louis Armstrong, continued to play hot jazz all through this period, not only preserving the tradition but enhancing it. *Scat* singing, that is, interpolating nonsense syllables, and other peculiar vocal effects associated with hot singing are contributions of these groups.

In the thirties the spotlight fell on big bands of astounding power and precision, and *swing* was born. Swing was much closer to the spirit of early jazz than the sweet and commercial music which was still played. Improvisation was not possible in the big bands of the swing era. Except for breaks and hot choruses, they punctiliously executed written arrangements. The arrangements, however, incorporated many features of jazz rhythm and made provision on occasion for individual improvisation in breaks and over subdued backgrounds. In addition, the tradition of improvising was kept alive within the swing bands by featured smaller combinations drawn from the large group.

Many of the musicians in the swing bands were real jazz enthusiasts, and often after engagements with the band they congregated in small clubs for impromptu *jam sessions*. The jam sessions were completely unwritten, unrehearsed, and unstandardized. Any number could play. Patrons oftentimes found inspired, uninhibited improvisation more appealing than the studied perfection of formal performances and listening more enjoyable than dancing. Staged jam sessions became a regular form of entertainment.

Boogie-woogie and *Kansas City* are other styles of the thirties. Boogie is a type of freely improvised blues over a constantly reiterated rhythmic bass figure. The most significant contribution of Kansas City style was the *riff* technique in which one instrument improvised over a background of short, repeated melodic figures. Kansas City style featured a heavy, four-beat rhythm in contrast with the two-beat rhythm of New Orleans style.

With the end of World War II the curtain rang down on the era of swing. The power and discipline of its full-throated sections were muffled and the very foundations of jazz were assailed by a disturbing upheaval known as *bebop* or merely *bop*. Bop shunned time-honored formulas to experiment with exciting new rhythmic, melodic, and harmonic materials. As is often the case with experimenters, their music was sometimes pointlessly eccentric and sometimes merely misunderstood. The men of swing and Dixie were united in their resistance to the inroads of bop. Its frenzied repetition of trivial melodic tidbits was a threat to the traditions for which they stood. This iconoclastic parvenu succeeded in splitting jazz men into warring factions and alienated them from their fans, but from the rubble of the battle arose a rejuvenated art which is contemporary jazz. The older styles survive in modified forms, and new ones have been added.

The commercial varieties of popular music are reaping unparalleled financial rewards for their purveyors. Every season sees a new crop of singers come and go on television while a few perennial favorites retain their ratings. Most of the offerings on television are slightly warmed-over sweet jazz with plenty of seasoning from the light classics. Broadway shows and movies contribute a fair share of material to this pot, and the musical highlights of all three mediums—TV, movies, and musical shows—find a ready radio and record market. This is the kind of music featured by disc jockeys, and it accounted for a large part of the $830 million the American public spent on records in 1966.

Farfetched fads in popular music come and go with such monotonous regularity that even their names are forgotten in a few years. Most of them vanish without a trace and have no more influence on the course of music than a ripple on a pond.

Dixieland is a style which very nearly spans the history of jazz, sufficient proof that it is no mere fad. The first white jazz band, one instrumental in introducing the new style of music north of the Mason-Dixon line, was the Original Dixieland Jazz Band. The traditional Dixieland style is still coarse and undisciplined, as it was half a century ago. Studied perfection is foreign to its nature, though a certain refinement is evident in the performances of some present-day Dixieland groups (for example, The Dukes of Dixieland). Vigor and abandon are its trademarks. Dirty tone and crude technique are part of the bargain. Dixieland may very well be the purest form of jazz, and after a series of recessions it is again riding a crest of public favor. Dixieland groups, both old and new, are still heard in the French Quarter of New Orleans and throughout the land.

The swing style and big band concept which were mainstream jazz in the thirties and forties are kept alive and essentially intact in the "stage bands" which now flourish in high schools and colleges. Among the pro's, *progressive jazz* with Stan Kenton (1912–   ) as its leading exponent was the successor to symphonic jazz and swing. Kenton used to play for dances, but his ideas are more dramatically embodied in recordings and concert performances which are quite undanceable. He often abandons rigid, conventional rhythmic patterns, prime requisites of dance music, in favor of fluid pulses and asymmetric meters. The instrumentation is large and lavish, including on occasion strings and such unlikely jazz instruments as flutes, oboes, and French horns. Symphonic materials and techniques are borrowed freely—not insipid romantic melodies but the heady harmonies and dissonant counterpoint of the 20th century. The term "neophonic" is now used by Kenton for his performing groups and the music they play. The neophonic sound is a further development of progressive jazz. It, like swing, is being introduced in certain educational institutions. Whether or not it is really jazz depends upon the point of view, but there is no denying that it is a style with logical antecedents pursued with conviction by dedicated musicians.

Modern jazz, to which the West Coast School has contributed many luminaries, descends directly from the improvisations of small groups in previous periods and especially the jam sessions of the thirties and forties. The combos are small and the instrumentation is completely flexible. Along with all the usual instruments of jazz, some of recent vintage such as vibes (vibraphone) and electric guitars are included. The players of modern jazz are younger men. Most are thoroughly knowledgeable musicians with solid academic training and virtuoso techniques. Versed in both the classics and jazz, they achieve a highly polished style even in spontaneous performances. In their hands the traditional elements of jazz become suave and sophisticated. Modern jazz is not so much something new as it is a new perfection of old methods. It is the type of jazz most generally admired by nonjazz musicians and the type which seems to proffer the greatest potential for future development.

The latest kind of music to acquire a name is *third stream,* an expression first used around 1960 by Gunther Schuller (1925–   ) to denote music which is a synthesis of jazz and the most recent "classical" elements. Creators of third stream music must, of course, be well grounded in jazz and the other contemporary techniques. The synthesis is accomplished in several ways. For example, two performing mediums may be combined as they are in Schuller's *Conversation* for jazz quartet and string quartet and his *Concertino* for jazz quartet and orchestra, or a twelve-tone row may be used as the basis for jazz improvisation as in *Improvisational Suite No. 1* by Don Ellis (1934–   ). The Modern Jazz Quartet (John Lewis, musical director and pianist) frequently performs third stream music and has been an active force in its development. The same impulses which led to symphonic jazz almost half a century ago are now finding expression in the third stream.

Jazz since its inception has demonstrated a pronounced tendency to restyle itself almost every decade, but a thread of continuity runs through the history of jazz. Consistent elements link the changing styles and preserve its identity.

Jazz structures are rudimentary and relatively stereotyped. Eight-measure ideas in an A A B A pattern are the rule except in blues. "B" is the *bridge* in popular terminology. It connects (and separates) repetitions of "A," which invariably contains the more pungent ideas. The brevity and simplicity of popular lyrics and suitability for dancing dictate small, regular forms. Dimensions are extended by repeating the entire pattern. Arrangements typically change key for the second chorus. Except for isolated examples in progressive and third stream jazz, the developmental procedures and extended forms of concert music have not been used.

Harmonically, jazz started with and periodically reverts to the most elemental materials. In between it has borrowed heavily from other styles, particularly impressionism. Certain chord structures and progressions which have become jazz clichés originated elsewhere. Jazz is more imitative than creative in this respect. Real innovation is rare. Sonorities attributed to jazz composers usually were only popularized by them, but in this they are rendering a service to serious music. Listeners conditioned to the sounds of Kenton and Schuller are not easily shocked by Stravinsky or Schoenberg. The fact that the *St. Louis Blues* and *The Rite of Spring* are contemporaneous should dispel the rather prevalent notion that symphonists appropriate harmonic materials from jazz. The best claim jazz can make to harmonic innovation may be the blue notes which are more properly a melodic phenomenon. Even these appeared early in other mediums (*Bartok String Quartet No. 2, Op. 17,* 1915–1917). Influence either way is improbable since it is unlikely that Bartok or early blues singers ever heard of each other.

Melodic contour in jazz can lay little claim to distinction. The predominantly vocal orientation of popular music and the demand to conceive melodies the man in the street can whistle places severe limitations on composers. The limitations do not apply to the instrumentalist who uses these melodies as a point of departure for free improvisation. The simplicity of the original conceptions and the intricacy of the elaborations based on them are two fundamental characteristics of jazz. Ornamenting familiar tunes beyond recognition is the stock in trade of modern jazz and the delight of its growing public. Improvisation itself is one of the most persistent features of jazz.

Rhythm is the realm of undisputed jazz originality. The rhythmic devices of ragtime have endured without interruption through all the changing styles and locales from early New Orleans to the present. Rhythm more than any other element makes jazz stand apart as a distinctive, homogeneous, body of music. Cataloging its obvious features—syncopation, displaced accents, and conflicting melodic-accompaniment grouping—does little to explain its vitality or originality. All of these devices occur in other music, but the effect is not the same. One reason is that the subtle effects of jazz rhythm defy precise notation. They must be felt.

Jazz rhythms, in spite of their attractiveness, have exerted comparatively little influence on other musical styles due to one peculiarity. They are completely meaningful only in terms of a rigid underlying beat. The beat is supplied by a rhythm section, a section not to be confused with the percussion of a symphony. The rhythm section of a dance band is fully as important and almost as large, not to mention as loud, as the other sections. Piano, string bass, guitar, and drums commonly are included. The drums are not a single instrument but a whole set of traps played by one player using both hands and both feet. When necessary for balance the guitar and bass are amplified electronically. Together they provide a foil for the syncopation and shifted accents of the reeds, brasses, and the vocalists. Without the ryhthm section, a dancer never would know when to put his foot down! When the medium is reduced to piano, the left hand plays a steady beat while the right exercises characteristic freedom. Lacking the equivalent of a jazz beat, the other elements of jazz rhythm are of little use in classic idioms.

Interaction between popular and classic music has been and probably will continue to be limited. The absence of techniques in either immediately accessible to the other precludes the danger of assimilation. It also assures the healthy preservation of two distinct aspects of music.

Though jazz is a newcomer in the field of the arts, it is the logical inheritor of honorable traditions. Some of the most venerable musical practices are preserved only in popular music. Playing keyboard instruments from symbols other than notation was an indispensable accomplishment for musicians of the baroque period. This practice, a lost art as far as other musicians are concerned, flourishes with the players of jazz and popular music. The symbols have changed from numbers to letters-plus-numbers, but the principles are the same. Improvisation, another lost art for academic musicians, is revived in jazz. Bach, whose prowess in playing from symbols and in improvising was legendary, would probably be disenchanted with colleagues less ably endowed and delighted with the fresh new turn these ancient arts have taken in the hands of jazz musicians.

Jazz and popular music, though in a state of flux during their entire existence, still represent a continuous and more important a growing tradition. Juke boxes have created a prosperous new industry, and record sales are soaring. Radio and television are devoting more time to music and are attracting ever larger audiences. Popular music might engulf the other styles if they were not capturing a fair share of the expanded listening public, but they are. While the classics and the more progressive styles of jazz may not be keeping pace with the commercial varieties of popular music, at least they are moving in the same direction. The net result is that more people are hearing more music than ever before. There is no real competition between the various styles of music, because the objectives are different.

The composers and players of the standard literature are searching for enduring values worthy to pass on to posterity, while jazz musicians deal in styles with immediate but transient appeal. Universality is unlikely in music grooved precisely to a particular time and taste, and it is axiomatic that a piece which can be comprehended immediately is unlikely to survive indefinitely. In jazz this transciency takes two forms. The commercial variety with its stereotyped lyric and melody rockets to the top of the hit parade and in a few short weeks declines to a well deserved oblivion. The improvised jazz is born in the heads and fingers of the players and dies as the tone fades into silence unless it is preserved by the miracle of recording. Jazz catches the spirit and reflects the kaleidoscopic changes of current taste the way a newspaper reports the events of the day. A newspaper is not a novel, and a jazz performance is not a symphony, but jazz and all the other idioms of organized pitches and rhythms including the ultramodern electronic and computer creations and the experiments with chance music and total organization are essential to the universe of musical sound. Each makes its own special contribution to the glorious art of music.

Records

THE STORY OF JAZZ, Folkways 7312
JAZZ, Folkways 2801–11
JAZZ ODYSSEY, Columbia C3L–30, 32, 33
JAZZ STORY, Capitol WEO–2109

References

Paul O. W. Tanner and Maurice Gerow, *A Study of Jazz* (Dubuque: Wm. C. Brown Company Publishers, 1964).

Marshall Stearns, *The Story of Jazz* (New York: Oxford University Press, 1956). Also available as a paperback Mentor Book.

Nat Hentoff and Albert J. McCarthy, *Jazz* (New York: Holt, Rinehart and Winston, 1959).

General References

Schwann Long Playing Record Catalog. Issued monthly. Available at record dealers.

Bakers Biographical Dictionary of Musicians, 5th edition, revision and 1965 supplement by Nicolas Slonimsky. (New York: G. Schirmer).

Willi Apel, *Harvard Dictionary of Music* (Cambridge: Harvard University Press, 1944).

Grove's Dictionary of Music and Musicians, 5th edition edited by Eric Blom with 1961 supplement by Denis Stevens, 10 vols. (New York: St. Martin's Press).

Percy A. Scholes, *The Oxford Companion to Music*, 9th edition (New York: Oxford University Press, 1955).

Donald J. Grout, *A History of Western Music* (New York: W. W. Norton & Company, Inc., 1960).

Paul Henry Lang, *Music in Western Civilization* (New York: W. W. Norton & Company, 1941).

appendix of
musical examples

BARBER: *Symphony No. 1* (p. 68)*, Large orchestra

*Page of text where the example is cited.

SCHUBERT: *Who Is Sylvia* (p. 85 & p. 86), Melodic contour

1. Who   is   Syl - via,   what   is   she,   that   all   our swains com -
1. Was   ist   Syl - via,   sa -   get   an, __ dass   sie   die wei - te

mend   her?   Ho - ly   fair __   and __ wise   is   she; __   the
Flur   preist? Schön und zart __   seh' __ ich   sie   nah'n; __   auf

heav'ns such grace did lend __ her,   That   a - dor - ed   she   might __
Him-mels Gunst und Spur __ weis't,   Dass   ihr __ al - les   un - ter -

be, __   that   a - dor - ed   she   might __ be.
than, __   dass   ihr   al - les   un - ter - than.

GREGORIAN CHANT: *Alleluia, Vidimus stellam* (p. 105), Monophonic texture

(Solo)   (Chorus)
Al -le-lu __ ia __   * Al - le - lu __ ia __

(Solo)
__   ✗ Vi __ di __ mus __ stel __ lam e -

__ jus   in   O - ri - en __

__ te __ et ve __ ni __ mus __

cum __ mu - ne __   ri - bus

(Chorus)
ad __ o - ra - re __ * Do __ mi - num __

(Solo)   (Chorus)
Al - le - lu __ ia __   (a) __

Source: *Liber Usualis*, Copyright 1934 by Desclee & Cie., Tournai, Belgium. Reprinted from *Masterpieces of Music Before 1750*, An Anthology of Musical Examples Compiled and Edited by Carl Parrish and John F. Ohl. Copyright 1951 by W. W. Norton & Company, Inc., and used with the permission of the publishers.

BACH: *Two-Part Invention No. 3* (p. 108), Polyphonic texture

MENDELSSOHN: *Elijah, No. 15* (p. 114), Homophonic texture

BEETHOVEN: *Symphony No. 5* (p. 120), Motive

BACH: *French Suite No. 4* (p. 125), Binary form

SCHUMANN: *Scenes from Childhood, No. 13* (p. 126), Ternary form

CHOPIN: *Nocturne No. 4* (p. 126), Ternary form

*Identifying letters and numbers above the theme correspond with the form diagram in the text.

SCHUMANN: *Scenes from Childhood, No. 7* (p. 127), Ternary form

SCHUMANN: *Scenes from Childhood, No. 1* (p. 128), Ternary form

TCHAIKOVSKY: *Nutcracker Suite* (p. 129), Ternary form

HINDEMITH: *Mathis der Maler* (p. 129), Ternary form

SOUSA: *Hands Across the Sea* (p. 130), Compound binary form

BEETHOVEN: *Piano Sonata No. 11* (p. 131), Compound ternary form

BEETHOVEN: *Violin Sonata No. 5* (p. 132), Compound ternary form

HANDEL: *The Messiah* (p. 133), Compound ternary form

BACH: *Partita No. 3 for Violin* (p. 135), Old rondo form

MOZART: *Serenade "Eine Kleine Nachtmusik"* (p. 136), Rondo form, five-part

BEETHOVEN: *Piano Sonata No. 2* (p. 138), Rondo form, seven-part

BEETHOVEN: *Piano Sonata No. 8* (p. 140), Sonata form

BACH: *Musical Offering* (p. 146), Canon

BACH: *Well-Tempered Clavier Vol. I, No. 16* (pp. 148,149), Fugue

HAYDN: *String Quartet, "Emperor"* (p. 151), Theme and variations

BEETHOVEN: *Piano Sonata No. 12* (p. 151), Theme and variations

BRAHMS: *Variations on a Theme of Haydn* (152), Theme and variations

Haydn theme

RACHMANINOFF: *Rhapsody on a Theme of Paganini* (p. 153), Theme and variations

Paganini theme

PURCELL: *Dido and Aeneas* (p. 154), Continuous variations

Ground

BACH: *Passacaglia and Fugue* (p. 155), Continuous variations

Theme

DVORAK: *Symphony No. 5* (p. 159), Cyclic form

Motto theme

Vivaldi: *Violin Concerto in A minor* (p. 166), Ritornello form

Ritornello theme

Bach: *Schübler Chorale Prelude No. 1* (p. 169), Chorale prelude

Chorale melody

Mussorgsky: *Pictures at an Exhibition* (p. 175), Program music

Promenade theme

BERLIOZ: *Symphonie Fantastique* (p. 177), Program symphony

Idée fixe

BACH: *Wie schön leuchtet der Morgenstern* (p. 211), Cantata

Chorale melody

glossary and index
of terms

Absolute music—Abstract music with no extramusical associations.
A cappella—In the church style, that is, without accompaniment.
Adagio—Comfortable, easy. A slow tempo.
Ad libitum (ad. lib.)—At will.
Affettuoso—With feeling.
Agitato—Agitated.
Agnus Dei—Lamb of God. The fifth and final composed item of the Mass.
Air—A simple melody.
Alborada—Morning song.
Allegretto—Somewhat slower than allegro.
Allegro—Cheerful. A lively, brisk tempo.
Allemande—160
Alto—Low female voice. The second highest part in four-part music.
Andante—Going along, walking. The median tempo indication.
Andantino—Somewhat faster or slower than andante. 81
Animato—Animated.
Anthem—208
Antiphonal—Singing or playing by two groups alternately.
Appassionato—With passion.
Arch form—142
Aria—A lyric song with instrumental accompaniment.
Art song—An independent song for solo voice and piano.
Assai—Very
Atonal, atonality—Without tonality. Not in a key.
Augmentation—Increased rhythmic values, usually doubled.
Augmented interval—An interval a semitone larger than the corresponding
    major or perfect interval.
Avant-garde—At the forefront. In the newest style.

Bagatelle—A trifle. A piece of modest pretensions.
Ballade—A word of varied meanings now usually applied to lyric or dramatic
    pieces.

Chords—91
Choreography—The composition and arrangement of dance movements, as for a ballet.
Chromatic—Denoting a note or chord foreign to the tonality.
Clarinets—30
Clavier—Keyboard.
Coda—A concluding section added to a musical form.
Codetta—A small coda added to a principal part within a form.
Coloratura—Colorful, florid. Applied to highly ornamented passages in vocal music and to the voices that sing them.
Combo—A small jazz ensemble.
Con—With.
Concertmaster—The leader of the first violins in an orchestra.
Concertino—A small concerto. The solo group in a concerto grosso.
Concerto—A composition for a solo instrument with orchestra.
Concerto grosso—167
Continuo—The figured bass part or its realization. 228
Contrabass—24
Contrabassoon—35
Contralto—Alto voice.
Contrapuntal—Employing counterpoint. Polyphonic.
Cornet—37
Counterpoint—The art of combining melodies and the melodies thus combined.
Countersubject—A thematic counterpoint, especially to the subject of a fugue.
Courante—160
Credo—I believe. The third composed item of the Mass.
Crescendo—Progressively louder.
Cyclic Form—158
Cymbals—43

Da capo (D.C.)—Repeat "from the beginning."
Da capo aria—133
Damper—A mechanism that stops the vibration of a sound source, such as a piano string.
Decibel—The smallest unit of perceived loudness.
Deciso—With decision.
Decrescendo—Progressively softer.
Development—A section, particularly in a sonata form, in which the themes are worked out.
Di—Of.
Dies irae—Day of wrath. A section of the Requiem Mass and the plainsong melody associated with it.
Diminution—Decreased rhythmic values, usually halved.
Divertimento—A multimovement instrumental form. 162
Dixieland—291, 295
Dominant—The fifth degree of the scale and the chord and key associated with it.
Double bass—24
Doux—Sweet.
Drums—43
Duet, duo—A composition for two performers.

Half-step—A minor second.
Harmonium—48
Harmony—The sounding together of different tones, especially in chord progressions.
Harp—44
Harpsichord—48
Hausmusik—Music to be played at home.
Heterophony—106
Hydraulis—220

Imitation—Repetition in another part after a short time lapse.
Impresario—An agent, manager, or producer.
Impressionism—266
Impromptu—A casual character piece, usually for piano.
Incidental music—191
Instrumentation—The writing of music for particular instruments or the instruments written for.
Intensity—The physical characteristic of sound that produces loudness.
Intermezzo—A digression interposed between parts of a more profound work.
Interval—The difference in pitch between two tones.
Intervals—89
Introduction—A passage or section preceding the main body of a form.
Invention—A term used by Bach for two-part contrapuntal compositions.
Inversion—Contrary motion, ascending intervals becoming equivalent descending intervals and vice versa, or the reversal of the above-below relationship between two melodic lines.

Jam session—A spontaneous jazz performance.
Jazz—291
   Kansas City style—295
   modern—296
   neophonic—296
   progressive—296
   symphonic—294
   third stream—297

K., Koechel catalog—Source of the identifying numbers for Mozart works.
Kettledrums—42
Key—The tonal center of a work or passage identified by a letter name.
Keynote—The central note of the key. The first degree of the scale in tonal music. The tonic note.
Key relationships—100
Konzertstuck—Concert piece.
Kyrie—Lord have mercy. The first composed item of the Mass.

L., Longo edition—Source of the identifying numbers for Domenico Scarlatti works.
Larghetto—Not quite as slow as largo.
Largo—Broad, large. A very slow tempo.
Leitmotiv—182

Lent, lento—Slow.
Libretto—The story and words of a dramatic musical work.
Lied—Song.
Lieder—Plural of lied.
Linear—Pertaining to lines, emphasizing the horizontal (contrapuntal) aspect of music as opposed to the vertical (harmonic).
Lyric—Song-like, expressing intimate rather than epic or heroic ideas.

Ma—But.
Madrigal—57, 209
Maestoso—Majestically.
Magnificat—The canticle of the Virgin Mary.
Major—A term denoting a quality of interval, scale, chord, key, tonality, or mode.
Manual—One of the keyboards of an organ or harpsichord.
Marcato—Marked.
March form—129
Marcia, marciale—March, march-like.
Mass—The solemn rite of the Roman Catholic Church commemorating the sacrifice of Christ. 205.
Measure—A metric unit in music consisting of a specific number and pattern of beats.
Mediant—The third degree of the scale and the chord and key associated with it. The relative major of a minor key.
Medley—A hodgepodge of loosely connected tunes.
Menuet, menuetto—Minuet.
Meter—The number and pattern of beats in a measure of music.
Meter signature—79
Metronome—A mechanical device for measuring units of time.
Mezzo-soprano—The female voice range between soprano and alto.
Microtone—An interval smaller than the smallest conventional interval.
Mikrokosmos—Microcosm.
Minnesingers—221
Minor—A term denoting a quality of interval, scale, chord, key, tonality, or mode.
Minuet—A French dance of rustic origin but courtly style in a moderately fast triple meter.
Miserere—Vulgate Psalm 50.
M.M., Maelzel Metronome—Numbers following the abbreviation indicate the number of beats per minute.
Mode—Pertaining to major or minor or to one of the scale patterns of early church music.
Moderato, modéré—Moderate.
Modulation—Change of key. 100
Molto—Very, much.
Monophony—Music consisting of a single, unaccompanied line.
Mosso—Motion.
Motet—208
Motive—The smallest recognizable structural unit of music. 120
Moto—Motion.
Motto theme—A theme of special significance in a multimovement or programmatic work.

Movement—A complete and relatively independent division of an extended work.
Musica Transalpina—210
Music drama—A special type of opera written by Wagner. 182
Musicologist—One devoted to the scientific study of music, particularly its history and literature.
Mute—A device used to soften and modify the tone of instruments.

Nationalism—261
Nocturne—A night piece.
Non—Not.
Nonet—A composition for nine performers.
Non troppo—Not too much.
Nuove Musiche—227

O—Or.
Oboe—31
Octave—A very consonant interval formed by two closely related tones which span eight scale degrees.
Octet—A composition for eight performers.
One-part form—123
Opera—180
Operetta, light opera—187
Opus (op.)—Work. Opus numbers ordinarily are assigned to the compositions of a composer in chronological order of publication.
Oratorio—212
Orchestration—The art of writing and arranging music for orchestra.
Ordinary—The unchanging parts of the Mass.
Organs—47
Orgelbüchlein—Little organ book (Bach).
Overtones—9
Overture—164

Partita—A group of dance movements, like a suite. 162
Parallel keys—The major key and the minor key with the same keynote.
Passacaglia—154
Passionato—Impassioned.
Pasticcio—An operatic work pieced together from various sources.
Pastorale—A simple piece in an idyllic or rustic mood.
Pathetique—Pathetic.
Pavane—268
Pedalboard—The keyboard of an organ played with the feet.
Percussion instruments—41
Period—121
Perpetuum mobile—Perpetual motion.
Phrase—120
Piano—47
Piccolo—28
Piu—More.
Piu tosto—Rather.
Pizzicato—Plucked.

Plainchant, plainsong—See Gregorian chant.
Poco—Little.
Polka—A dance of Bohemian origin.
Polonaise—A dance of Polish origin.
Polyphony—Music conceived as a combination of two or more melodies.
Polytonality—The presence of two or more tonalities (keys) at the same time. 98
Popular music—291
Potpourri—A medley of tunes from another source.
Prelude—167
Premiere—First performance.
Prestissimo—Faster than presto. The fastest tempo marking.
Presto—Very fast, rapid.
Program music—Music with literary or pictorial associations.

Quadrille—A dance of 19th-century French origin.
Quartet—A composition for four performers.
Quintet—A composition for five performers.

Rags, ragtime—293
Recapitulation—The section of a sonata form in which the thematic material of
    the exposition returns.
Recitative—A passage in declamatory style for solo voice with a simple harmonic
    accompaniment.
Reed—The vibrating member of woodwind instruments. 25
Register—A portion of the pitch range of an instrument or voice.
Relative keys—The major key and the minor key that have all seven notes in
    common. See also Mediant and Submediant.
Religioso—Religiously.
Repertoire, repertory—A treasury, collection, or list of works ready or available
    for performance.
Requiem—A Mass for the dead. 206
Repeat signs—128
Rest—A symbol representing silence in music or such a period of silence.
Retrograde—Reversed end for end, backwards.
Retrograde inversion—A combination of retrograde and inversion.
Rhapsody—170
Riff—295
Ritornello form—166
Rococo—237
Rondeau—Rondo.
Rondo—A piece or movement in rondo form.
Rondo form—135
Rondo-sonata form—137
Rota—A round canon.
Round, round canon—A canon in which the end leads back to the beginning.
Rubato—A term suggesting freedom in rhythm and tempo.

S., Schmieder catalog—Source of the identifying numbers of Bach works.
Sanctus—Holy. Fourth composed item of the Mass.
Sarabande—160
Saxophones—30

Scale—A stepwise arrangement of the tones of a given key and/or mode.
Scherzando—Playful, sportive.
Scherzo—Joke, jest. A piece or movement characterized by vivacious rhythm or humor.
Score—A composite of all the parts of a composition.
Seguidilla—A Spanish dance.
Semitone—A minor second, the smallest conventional interval.
Sentence—121
Sempre—Always.
Septet—A composition for seven performers.
Sequence—The immediate repetition at a different pitch level of a musical segment.
Serenade—Evening music, particularly a lover's song or a multimovement instrumental composition.
Serial music—99, 276
Sextet—A composition for six performers.
Sinfonia—An instrumental composition, often with an introductory function.
Solo—Alone. A piece or passage for one instrument or voice, alone or predominant.
Sonata—A multimovement composition for one or two instruments.
Sonata form—139
Sonata-rondo form—137
Song cycle—199
Song without words—A song-like instrumental piece.
Sonority—Sound. Used as a more inclusive term than chord.
Soprano—High female or unchanged voice. The highest part.
Sostenuto—Sustained.
Sousaphone—41
Spiccato—Separated.
Spirito, spiritoso—Spirited.
Stabat mater—A 13th-century addition to the feast of the Seven Dolours.
Stopped notes—Notes produced on a horn with the hand tightly inserted in the bell.
Stradivarius—One of the extremely valuable string instruments made by Antonio Stradivari (1644-1737).
Stretto—In a fugue, overlapping statements of the subject. Elsewhere, a faster tempo.
String bass—24
String instruments—20
Strophic form—196
Subdominant—The fourth degree of the scale and the chord and key associated with it.
Subject—The main theme of a fugue.
Submediant—The sixth degree of the scale and the chord and key associated with it. The relative minor of a major key.
Subtonic (leading tone)—The seventh degree of the scale and the chord and key associated with it.
Suite—160
Supertonic—The second degree of the scale and the chord and key associated with it.
Swing—294

index of composers and works